Entrepreneurship Trajectories

Entrepreneurship Trajectories

Entrepreneurial Opportunities, Business Models, and Firm Performance

Diego Matricano
Università degli Studi della Campania "L. Vanvitelli"
Capua (CE), Italy

G. Giappichelli Editore

ACADEMIC PRESS

An imprint of Elsevier

Academic Press is an imprint of Elsevier
125 London Wall, London EC2Y 5AS, United Kingdom
525 B Street, Suite 1650, San Diego, CA 92101, United States
50 Hampshire Street, 5th Floor, Cambridge, MA 02139, United States
The Boulevard, Langford Lane, Kidlington, Oxford OX5 1GB, United Kingdom

Notices
Knowledge and best practice in this field are constantly changing. As new research and experience broaden our
understanding, changes in research methods, professional practices, or medical treatment may become
necessary.

Practitioners and researchers must always rely on their own experience and knowledge in evaluating and using
any information, methods, compounds, or experiments described herein. In using such information or
methods they should be mindful of their own safety and the safety of others, including parties for whom they
have a professional responsibility.

To the fullest extent of the law, neither the Publisher nor the authors, contributors, or editors, assume any
liability for any injury and/or damage to persons or property as a matter of products liability, negligence or
otherwise, or from any use or operation of any methods, products, instructions, or ideas contained in the
material herein.

British Library Cataloguing-in-Publication Data
A catalogue record for this book is available from the British Library

Library of Congress Cataloging-in-Publication Data
A catalog record for this book is available from the Library of Congress

ISBN: 978-0-12-818650-3

For Information on all Academic Press publications
visit our website at https://www.elsevier.com/books-and-journals

Publisher: Candice Janco
Acquisition Editor: Candice Janco
Editorial Project Manager: Ruby Smith
Production Project Manager: Paul Prasad Chandramohan
Cover Designer: Christian J. Bilbow

Typeset by MPS Limited, Chennai, India

Working together
to grow libraries in
developing countries

www.elsevier.com • www.bookaid.org

Dedication

To Matteo,
my beloved nephew,
who gave a new and positive
meaning to all my life

Contents

Acknowledgments

The writing of this volume was possible due to the contribution and support of many people.

A special thanks goes to Prof. Mario Sorrentino with whom I have had the honor of collaborating for several years. For me, the daily comparison with him was a reason for scientific growth and human enrichment.

I would like to thank Prof. Francesco Izzo, Director of the Department of Management (located in Capua) of Università degli Studi della Campania "L. Vanvitelli." I would also like to thank all the professors of the department who gave me the opportunity to improve my studies and myself over the years.

An individual thanks goes to Prof. Piero Formica and to all the scholars I met during my stay at Jönköping International Business School (Jönköping, Sweden). With them I shared my first international research experience.

I would like to express my gratitude to Prof. Ian MacMillan, Director of the Snider Entrepreneurial Research Center of the Wharton School of the University of Pennsylvania (Philadelphia, United States). During my stay in the United States, I had the opportunity to explore different aspects related to the theme of entrepreneurship.

I would like to thank Prof. Louis Marino, from Culverhouse College of Business at the University of Alabama, for his availability and his continuous stimuli about the study of entrepreneurship.

A special thanks goes to all those—my parents first of all, and also all my family and my friends—who have always and unconditionally supported me. In particular, I would like to thank Daria and Simone, who unknowingly taught me to see everything from the right perspective, and Matteo, who gave a new and positive meaning to my life.

Framing the entrepreneurship phenomenon

1.1 The state-of-the-art of entrepreneurship studies

Since its origins,[1] and despite a huge number of trials, the field of entrepreneurship has never been defined in a univocal way. Over the years, in fact, many overlapping and fuzzy terms and concepts have been used in order to point out, support, criticize, modify, or deny the essence of entrepreneurship. Not surprisingly, several reviews proposed in reference to entrepreneurship (Gartner, 1990; Shane, 2000; Shane and Venkataraman, 2000; Westhead and Wright, 2000; Audretsch, 2002, 2003; Acs and Audretsch, 2003; Casson, 2003; Sciascia and De Vita, 2004; Simpeh, 2011; Audretsch et al., 2015; Matricano, 2015; Kuratko and Morris, 2018) reach the same conclusions:

- Several research paths can be used to approach the study of entrepreneurship;
- Several theoretical frameworks can be used to investigate entrepreneurship;
- Several empirical tests can be used to verify the intensity of entrepreneurship; and
- Scholars mainly do not agree on any of the achieved results and—thus—still debate about them.

In reference to the conclusions presented above, it is appropriate to recall some contributions that can help to clarify and comprehend the origins of entrepreneurial research and its evolution.

Audretsch et al. (2015, p. 703) highlight that "because entrepreneurship is multifaceted, it is studied from many different perspectives, yet, that has fostered a multitude of definitions. Even the scholarly literature is rife with disparities and even contradictions about what is and is not entrepreneurship." According to them, the

---

[1] As a practice, origins of entrepreneurship date back to 1911 when Schumpeter defined the characteristics of entrepreneurs. According to the Schumpeterian definition, entrepreneurs are individuals who can exploit market opportunity through technical and/or organizational innovation. As a matter of fact, origins of entrepreneurship should date back to 1755 when Cantillon used—for the first time ever—the word "entrepreneur" to describe an individual that buys some inputs at a fixed price, transforms inputs into outputs and sells the outputs at a not-fixed price. According to Cantillon's view, entrepreneurs bear the risk related to the prices of acquiring inputs and selling outputs. This is the main characteristic that distinguishes the entrepreneurs (who act like arbitragers) from capitalist (landowners) and wageworkers (hirelings). In 1803 Say recalls the word "entrepreneur" proposed by Cantillon but his definition is quite different. According to Say, in fact, entrepreneurs start productive processes by mixing several resources (labor, capital, and land). With no apparent reason, the sporadic definitions of entrepreneurs proposed by Cantillon (1755) and Say (1803) did not get enough interest by entrepreneurship and economics scholars. It was just in 1911, thanks to Schumpeter, that "entrepreneur" and "entrepreneurship" become very common and largely discussed topics of research.

Entrepreneurship Trajectories. DOI: https://doi.org/10.1016/B978-0-12-818650-3.00001-5

most critical aspect that can be ascribed to entrepreneurship seems to relate to the fact that some topics of research are wrongly included in the field of entrepreneurship research. Consequently, the pertinence of a topic to a research area needs to be evaluated in a very accurate way. Even if entrepreneurship scholars largely agree on the above assumption and embrace it, this error is not easy to fix. In other words, assuring that a topic of research falls within the body of entrepreneurship research is not an effortless task.[2]

Beyond evidence that shows if a topic is related to entrepreneurship studies, there is another critical aspect that might emerge. This aspect deals with the number of research topics that—over time—have been proposed and affirmed in the entrepreneurship field. In reference to this point, it is not possible to forget Shane and Venkataraman's (2000, p. 217) statement, according to which "entrepreneurship has become a broad label under which a hodgepodge of research is housed."

Scholars clearly underline that entrepreneurship encompasses several areas of research that might confuse—rather than support—any scholars who approach entrepreneurship studies. The fact that several areas of research coexist in the entrepreneurship field and that—on the other hand—the field itself is highly fragmented might cause some difficulties in properly framing entrepreneurship. In fact, if several lenses can be used to investigate the same phenomenon in practice, then it may be possible that none of them are correctly used, as each might miss some relevant aspects. Thus this point cannot be underestimated when carrying out entrepreneurial studies.

Due to the abovementioned controversial aspects of the discipline and its related uncertain results, it seems appropriate to recall some dedicated contributions at this point in order to try to capture the essence of entrepreneurship.

1.2 Overview of the main research themes in entrepreneurship studies

Needless to say, the following literature review cannot be comprehensive because of the high amount of dedicated contributions proposed over the years. It does not cover all the existing works on entrepreneurship but it does condense selected studies and research. However, this limitation does not prevent the review from being carried out. Its final aim is to reveal the major research themes in entrepreneurship studies in order to attempt to clarify what can or cannot be included in the field of entrepreneurship research and—hopefully—to outline the essence of entrepreneurship.

---

[2] For example, a very debated topic—which might or not fall in the area of research of entrepreneurs—is the one related to entrepreneurship in developing or transitional economics. In this case, macroeconomic aspects might prevail over entrepreneurial ones and thus this topic might not be considered properly entrepreneurial.

Starting with Schumpeter's contribution (1911)—according to which entrepreneurs aim to introduce innovations onto markets[3]—a conspicuous group of entrepreneurship scholars converges toward the *teleological approach* and thus investigates the aims/scopes that entrepreneurs try to achieve (Cooper and Dunkelberg, 1981; Low and MacMillan, 1988; Shane and Venkataraman, 2000; Matricano, 2015).

In contrast to Schumpeter (1911), some scholars propose the idea that entrepreneurs aim to foresee the future of markets in order to satisfy the needs of forthcoming consumers (Knight, 1921), governmental or societal requirements (Kilby, 1971), or to improve the social well-being (Baumol, 1990).

More recently, other scholars who embrace the teleological approach have recalled Schumpeter's view and have again proposed the idea that entrepreneurs aim to introduce new products/technologies into already existing markets or to seek new markets (Lumpkin and Dess, 1996; Dess et al., 1997; Zahra et al., 1999; Wiklund and Shepherd, 2003). Among the aims pursued by entrepreneurs, Klyver et al. (2011) recognize that two primary aims have attracted noticeable interest. Respectively, they are the perceiving of entrepreneurial opportunities (Kirzner, 1973, 1997; Leibenstein, 1978, 1979; Drucker, 1985; Bygrave and Hofer, 1991) and the creation of new ventures (Gartner, 1985, 1988, 1990, 2001; Katz and Gartner, 1988; Low and MacMillan, 1988; Gartner and Gatewood, 1992; Larson and Starr, 1993; Woo et al., 1994; Cooper, 1995; Ucbasaran et al., 2001).

Contemporarily with the development of the teleological approach, another group of scholars converge their attention toward the *psychological approach* and investigate the individual characteristics of entrepreneurs. Beyond the need for achievement (McClelland, 1961) and alertness[4] (Kirzner, 1973), these entrepreneurship scholars ascribe other characteristics to entrepreneurs, such as risk propensity (Timmons, 1978; Welsh and White, 1981; Churchill, 1997), tolerance for ambiguity (McGrath, 1999), self-efficacy (Boyd and Vozikis, 1994; Krueger and Brazeal, 1994; Chen et al., 1998; Hmieleski and Corbett, 2008), self-esteem (Rosenberg, 1965), and locus of control (Koh, 1996; Cromie, 2000; Mueller and Thomas, 2001; Rauch and Frese, 2007).

Another approach assumes that scholars should address their attention mainly toward the context and its impact on entrepreneurial activities (Reynolds et al., 2002, 2003; Autio, 2005). This is the *contextual approach*. Beyond the differences that can emerge at a country or regional level (Bird, 1988; Dubini, 1989; Acs et al., 1994; Audretsch and Fritsch, 1994; Davidsson et al., 1994; Garofoli, 1994; Chrisman et al., 2002; O'Gorman and Kautonen, 2004), in reference to industrial districts (Marshall, 1890; Becattini, 1989) or to incubators (Autio and Klofsten, 1998; Phan et al., 2005; Ratinho and Henriques, 2010), a very intriguing stream of research focuses its attention on the comparison between positive and hostile

---

[3] Schumpeter (1911) clearly expresses this concept when he talks about "creative destruction."

[4] Kirzner writes: "pure entrepreneur whose entire role arises out of his alertness to hitherto unnoticed opportunities" (1973, p. 39).

contexts (Covin and Slevin, 1989; Covin and Covin, 1990; Miles et al., 1993; Zahra, 1993; Ucbasaran et al., 2001; Welter, 2011).

The last approach adopted by entrepreneurship scholars is known as the *relational approach*. In this case, scholars—beginning with Granovetter's contribution (1985)—pay attention to entrepreneurial networks (Birley, 1985; Aldrich and Zimmer, 1986; Johannisson, 1986, 1988; Starr and MacMillan, 1990). In particular, attention is focused toward subjects involved in these networks (Scott, 1991; Greve, 1995; Johannisson, 1998) and toward the ties between them (Birley, 1985; Burt, 1992, 2000; Podolny and Baron, 1997; Ahuja, 2000). The main topics of research interest for each of the four approaches are summarized in Table 1.1.

These four approaches[5] (that stand for a macro level of analysis) and the variables considered in each (micro level of analysis) can give an overview of all the research paths addressed by entrepreneurship scholars, however, at the same time, they do not assist with the understanding of what can and cannot be included in the entrepreneurship research field.[6] For this reason, a different criterion on the basis of the review needs to be evoked.

In particular, a classification of the main research themes proposed in reference to entrepreneurship studies (that can stand for a meso level of analysis) seems more useful than a classification of the approaches themselves (teleological, psychological, contextual, and relational) and of the variables to be considered (a macro and a micro level of analysis, respectively).

Through a web-based survey, Landström and Harirchi (2018) investigated the dimensions of research that entrepreneurship scholars perceive as interesting. According to the descriptive statistics reported in their contribution, most of the entrepreneurship scholars (74% out of 915 respondents) perceive some topics and subjects—related mainly to entrepreneurial intentions, effectuation, or entrepreneurial finance—as interesting. Few scholars, however, perceive aspects related to methodology (12.7%), to relevance—that is, practical studies (11.8%)—and to the context (10.3%) as interesting. This confirms that a focus on the main themes of research is necessary.

In this vein, Audretsch et al. (2015, p. 704) declare that "the word entrepreneurship implies many different things: innovation, ideas, creativity, new venture development, discovery, and economic growth." According to the scholars, all these topics of research have been used to reconcile the theoretical aspects with the practical ones that emerge when studying entrepreneurship.

Similarly, Welter et al. (2017) list a set of dichotomies that can be useful for describing entrepreneurship, which they define as "a messy phenomenon" (p. 314). These dichotomies range from opportunity versus necessity entrepreneurship to formal versus informal entrepreneurship, from male versus female entrepreneurs to

---

[5] For a more in-depth review of the four approaches and of the topics of research included in each of them see Matricano (2015).

[6] The main limitation of the above review is related to the level of analysis that moves from macro (when talking about the four approaches) to micro (when listing the specific considered variables).

Table 1.1 The main topics of research interest for the four approaches to entrepreneurship.

Approach	Main topics
Teleological	• Introduction of innovations onto markets (Schumpeter, 1911) • Foreseeing the future of markets (Knight, 1921; Kilby, 1971) • Improvement of the well-being (Baumol, 1990) • Introduction of new products/technologies into already existing markets or seeking new markets (Lumpkin and Dess, 1996; Dess et al., 1997; Zahra et al., 1999; Wiklund and Shepherd, 2003) • Perceiving of entrepreneurial opportunities (Kirzner, 1973, 1997; Leibenstein, 1978, 1979; Drucker, 1985; Bygrave and Hofer, 1991) • Creating new ventures (Gartner, 1985, 1988, 1990, 2001; Katz and Gartner, 1988; Low and MacMillan, 1988; Gartner and Gatewood, 1992; Larson and Starr, 1993; Woo et al., 1994; Cooper, 1995; Ucbasaran et al., 2001)
Psychological	• Need for achievement (McClelland, 1961) • Alertness (Kirzner, 1973) • Risk propensity (Timmons, 1978; Welsh and White, 1981; Churchill, 1997) • Tolerance for ambiguity (McGrath, 1999) • Self-efficacy (Boyd and Vozikis, 1994; Krueger and Brazeal, 1994; Chen et al., 1998; Hmieleski and Corbett, 2008) • Self-esteem (Rosenberg, 1965) • Locus of control (Koh, 1996; Cromie, 2000; Mueller and Thomas, 2001; Rauch and Frese, 2007)
Contextual	• Country or regional level (Bird, 1988; Dubini, 1989; Acs et al., 1994; Audretsch and Fritsch, 1994; Davidsson et al., 1994; Garofoli, 1994; Chrisman et al., 2002; O'Gorman and Kautonen, 2004) • Industrial districts (Marshall, 1890; Becattini, 1989) • Incubators (Autio and Klofsten, 1998; Phan et al., 2005; Ratinho and Henriques, 2010) • Positive versus hostile contexts (Covin and Slevin, 1989; Covin and Covin, 1990; Miles et al., 1993; Zahra, 1993; Ucbasaran et al., 2001; Welter, 2011)
Relational	• Entrepreneurial networks (Birley, 1985; Aldrich and Zimmer, 1986; Johannisson, 1986, 1988; Starr and MacMillan, 1990) • Subjects involved in the networks (Scott, 1991; Greve, 1995; Johannisson, 1998) • Ties established in the networks (Birley, 1985; Burt, 1992, 2000; Podolny and Baron, 1997; Ahuja, 2000)

Source: Personal elaboration.

innovator versus replicator, from growth-oriented versus lifestyle to entrepreneur versus small business owner.

Even if the scholars aim to embrace entrepreneurial diversity and to include in the mainstream research trends some topics that—in practice—are underestimated, they propose another useful excursion through the field of entrepreneurship, one that, again, does not clarify what can and cannot be included in the field of entrepreneurship.

Recently, Kuckerts and Prochotta (2018) have proposed a contribution that is based on the opinions of 225 experienced scholars and that identifies the most promising areas of research in entrepreneurial studies. These topics include entrepreneurial process, entrepreneurial behavior, social entrepreneurship, psychology in entrepreneurship, entrepreneurship and innovation, entrepreneurship itself, entrepreneurial finance, economics of entrepreneurship, entrepreneurial opportunities, corporate entrepreneurship, international entrepreneurship, geography of entrepreneurship, entrepreneurship education, and family firms. This study seems to pursue the right direction (by focusing on the themes to be investigated) even if the survey has some limitations that cannot be ignored (it is based on a sample of 225 respondents only).

A contribution that seems to overcome the above limitation and to fit much better with the aim of this volume is the one authored by Kuratko and Morris (2018). These scholars[7] examine the major themes that characterize research about entrepreneurship. According to them, it is possible to list ten themes that seem to catalyze the attention of entrepreneurship scholars:

1. Opportunities and the entrepreneurial process;
2. Venture financing;
3. Entrepreneurial cognition;
4. Economic development and entrepreneurship;
5. Family business;
6. Corporate entrepreneurship;
7. Social entrepreneurship and sustainability;
8. Women and minority entrepreneurship;
9. Global entrepreneurship; and
10. Entrepreneurship research, education, and pedagogy.

The list of possible themes that characterize the research about entrepreneurship proposed by Kuratko and Morris (2018) is the one considered hereinafter. The main reason behind this choice is the fact that they do not describe the results of a survey among scholars but review the themes presented and discussed by and large. Hence, each of the above themes is briefly going to be defined and reviewed in the following subsections.

1.2.1 Opportunities and the entrepreneurial process

Entrepreneurial opportunities have always attracted eminent interest in entrepreneurship studies even if the way scholars have approached them has radically

---

[7] In 2015 Kuratko, Morris, and Schindehutte proposed another classification comprehending eight major themes characterizing entrepreneurship research. These themes were: (1) venture financing; (2) corporate entrepreneurship; (3) social entrepreneurship and sustainability; (4) entrepreneurial cognition; (5) women and minority entrepreneurs; (6) the global entrepreneurial movement; (7) family businesses; and (8) entrepreneurial education. The recent article published in 2018 by Kuratko and Morris expands the above classification by adding the themes of opportunities/entrepreneurial process and of economic development.

changed over the years (Eckhardt and Shane, 2003; Shane, 2003; Companys and McMullen, 2007). In particular, it is possible to observe the different approaches adopted by recalling two contributions, one authored by Bygrave and Hofer (1991) and the other by Shane and Venkataraman (2000).

Bygrave and Hofer (1991) make no reference to a largely shared theoretical background and argue that entrepreneurs are involved in the "perceiving of opportunities" (p. 14) even if they do not clarify what this means exactly. The act of perceiving is something subjective. It deals with the way individuals interact with innovations (revealing themselves in the shape of entrepreneurial opportunities) and so it is difficult to explain and generalize it.

Shane and Venkataraman (2000)—following the proposal and widespread use of strategic entrepreneurship framework[8]—define the ideas of entrepreneurial opportunities and the involvement of entrepreneurs in a more accurate manner in order to identify, select, and exploit them.

The idea that earning a profit can drive entrepreneurs through identifying, selecting, and exploiting entrepreneurial opportunities underlines the idea that entrepreneurship is a process (Eckhardt and Shane, 2003; Shane, 2003; Companys and McMullen, 2007; McMullen et al., 2007; Eckhardt and Ciuchta, 2008; Foss and Foss, 2008). Congruently, entrepreneurship takes place over time. Individuals analyze the context they are in and the industry they aim to enter; they need some time to create their own network and then they put into practice specific actions that can hopefully lead them to expected results. Several aspects need to be considered and evaluated in order to disclose entrepreneurial phenomena. In this vein, Johannisson (2008, 2011) proposes talking about *entrepreneuring.*[9]

Similarly to the perceptions of entrepreneurial opportunities, the entrepreneurship process cannot be totally generalized. For example, it is feasible to identify the three phases (identification, selection, and exploitation) of the process and the passage from one phase to another. However, defining the duration of each phase and of the whole process is not as straightforward. Also, in this case, it is not possible to generalize the way individuals interact with entrepreneurial opportunities that stand for innovations to be exploited.

From the studies focused on entrepreneurial opportunities and entrepreneurial processes, the individual-opportunity nexus emerges as being of great relevance (Shane, 2003). It is the innovation at the basis of each entrepreneurial opportunity that, in turn, affects the entrepreneurial process. As a result, studies about these topics suggest starting from an *ex ante* analysis, which is related to the level of innovativeness embodied in entrepreneurial opportunities, and then focusing on the actions to put into practice in order to exploit them.

---

[8] Strategic entrepreneurship is a theoretical framework aiming to reduce the distance between entrepreneurship and strategic management (Meyer and Heppard, 2000), two fields of research that are expected to nurture each other (Hitt et al., 2002). Several scholars have contributed to its proposal and its further development: McGrath and MacMillan (2000); Meyer and Heppard (2000); Ireland et al. (2001); Hitt et al. (2001, 2002); Venkataraman and Sarasvathy (2001).

[9] In his work, Johannisson (2011) recalls what Drucker (1985) said about entrepreneurship: it is neither art nor science, but practice.

1.2.2 Venture financing

The growing interest that scholars show about crowdfunding as a technique able to finance entrepreneurial activities (Bruton et al., 2015; Short et al., 2017; da Cruz, 2018; Wallmeroth et al., 2018) has confirmed the relevance of the issues related to venture financing. As already noted, these issues cannot be ignored when discussing the way in which entrepreneurial projects are going to be started. Beyond personal capital[10] that can be invested, entrepreneurs need to seek "love money," debt, and/ or equity financing in order to try to launch their ventures.

Generally speaking, "love money" stands for the financial resources provided by family, friends, and fools (Ang, 1991, 1992; Brinlee et al., 2004; Kotha and George, 2012; Frid, 2014; Bellavitis et al., 2017; Sieger and Minola, 2017; Matricano and Sorrentino, 2019). Scholars investigating this research topic strongly underline the investor–entrepreneur relationship at the basis of this exchange. As a result of the strong relationship between the partners involved—which is based on trust (Aldrich and Zimmer, 1986; Ehrlich et al., 1994; Steier and Greenwood, 1995; Sapienza and Korsgaard, 1996; Shane and Cable, 2002)—the economic evaluation of entrepreneurial projects might not be very objective. Thus the relevance of "love money" in reference to venture financing is still debated.

Debt and equity financing, instead, are assigned to entrepreneurs according to selective and objective evaluations that clearly depend on the information asymmetry between the entrepreneurs who seek capital to finance their projects and the financiers (Cole and Sokolyk, 2018). Of course, entrepreneurs aim to reduce information asymmetry (Jensen and Meckling, 1976; Leland and Pile, 1977) but the extent to which this happens is not clear.

In reference to debt financing provided by banks, distinguishing between "the debt obtained in the name of the business (business debt) versus external debt obtained in the name of the firm's owner and used to finance the start-up firm (personal debt)" appears to be of interest, because the nature of debt can affect the success of entrepreneurial firms in different ways (Cole and Sokolyk, 2018, p. 610).

With respect to equity financing, scholars have paid attention to those financiers who can put into practice different approaches (Drover et al., 2017). Venture capitalists, who raise funds from a limited set of partners, select a project to be financed in order to provide a return to the partners themselves. The support given to entrepreneurial projects is linked to the return that partners involved expect. Corporate venture capitalists (CVCs), instead, are established corporations that realize equity investments in entrepreneurial firms that operate in the same industry or in a related one. Thus beyond capital, they also provide formal and informal knowledge about their industry itself. Consequently, the impact on the entrepreneurial firms thus financed is expected to be higher. Eventually, business angels (BAs), who are former entrepreneurs, invest their own personal capital into entrepreneurial firms that act in their area of expertise. In this case, they also provide capital and, above all, knowledge and expertise about their industry. The fact that they choose

---

[10] In reference to personal capital, decisions about investments depend on entrepreneurs themselves.

and act individually—unlike the CVCs—makes the relationship between the entrepreneurs and the BAs more informal, which is expected to have a different impact on the performance of entrepreneurial ventures.

Generally speaking, the theme of venture financing focuses the scholars' attention toward the relationship (formal or informal) established between the entrepreneurs and financiers and, most importantly, on the economic performance that can be derived from it.

1.2.3   Entrepreneurial cognition

Generally speaking, entrepreneurial cognition stands for knowledge structures or mental mechanisms that entrepreneurs leverage in order to evaluate external stimuli and, in turn, make their choices (Kuratko and Morris, 2018).

The basis of this stream of research in entrepreneurial studies is rooted in cognitive sciences (Krueger, 2003). Both theoretical and empirical research related to cognitive studies suggests that cognitive mechanisms are far from rational. On the contrary, cognitive mechanisms are strongly characterized by bias and errors (Baron, 1998).

When the concept of cognitive mechanisms is applied to entrepreneurship, the resulting perceptions—that is, mental schemas that individuals use in order to evaluate external stimuli—do affect the way entrepreneurs acquire information, process it, and make decisions (Sánchez et al., 2011; Arafat and Saleem, 2017). Put simply, perceptions affect cognitive processes managed by entrepreneurs. Hence, understanding the cognitive mechanisms underlying entrepreneurial behavior is an important way to better support and nurture entrepreneurship (Shepherd and Krueger, 2002; Krueger, 2003; Feola et al., 2017).

Nowadays, the application of cognitive mechanisms to entrepreneurship is changing. Most scholars apply cognitive mechanisms to entrepreneurial processes in order to investigate the ways in which entrepreneurs acquire information, elaborate on it, and make decisions when they are acting (Baron, 2000; Gaglio, 2004; McMullen, 2010; Prandelli et al., 2016). However, as noted by Frederiks et al. (2018), cognitive mechanisms can also be used to try to foresee the quality of new venture ideas (which result from entrepreneurial processes investigated in the past).

The stream of research proposed by Frederiks et al. (2018) underlines the main aspect that is investigated when cognitive mechanisms are applied to entrepreneurship. Even if we consider one entrepreneurial opportunity, its evaluations can change—from positive to negative—because of individual perceptions. Cognition, therefore, is relevant in entrepreneurial studies because it affects the evaluation of entrepreneurial opportunities and determines the results that can be achieved.

1.2.4   Economic development and entrepreneurship

As argued by Kuratko and Morris (2018), the idea underlying the topic economic development and entrepreneurship is that entrepreneurship is a driving force that can generate employment, income, wealth, and economic growth as well as improve social quality of life at the same time. In this vein, Audretsch (2003) argues that entrepreneurship is an "engine of economic and social development throughout the world" (p. 5).

Scholars largely share the idea that entrepreneurship is an important driver of economic and social growth (Audretsch and Thurik, 2001; Audretsch, 2003; Aparicio et al., 2016; Bjørnskov and Foss, 2016; Bosma et al., 2018). Even if the debate about the true meaning of performance is ongoing (Bjørnskov and Foss, 2016; Urbano et al., 2018), it seems that the idea that the most typical measure of performance is economic growth is largely agreed upon. Audretsch (2003) remarks that, in fact, "the relationship between entrepreneurship and economic performance is remarkably robust" (p. 1).

Despite the indicators that can be used to measure achieved performances (particularly growth in the number of employees and contribution to GDP), the main question to answer deals with the way entrepreneurship induces positive performances. Innovation that lies at the basis of entrepreneurship is expected to be radical innovation that, by definition, modifies the *status quo* by destroying previous competences[11] (Tushman and Anderson, 1986) and by introducing new ways of doing things (new products, services, or processes).

Somehow, competence-destroying innovations[12] recall Baumol's distinction (1990) between unproductive and productive entrepreneurship. According to this scholar, unproductive entrepreneurship refers to all the activities started in order to capture existing wealth. Productive entrepreneurship, instead, refers to the activities started in order to create new wealth. As argued and demonstrated by other scholars —see, for example, Reynolds et al. (1999)—only productive entrepreneurship generates economic growth in a specific context (by fostering job creation, increasing local income, and making local economy grow) since it is based on the exploitation of radical innovations.

1.2.5 Family business

Family business research, both in management and in entrepreneurship studies, has grown noticeably. In reference to management studies and in line with other extensive literature reviews (De Massis et al., 2014; Sciascia et al., 2015; Feranita et al., 2017), eight subtopics that characterize studies about family business have been disclosed (Williams et al., 2018). These subtopics are: (1) family presence; (2) role of individual family members; (3) founder influence and leadership; (4) family history and culture; (5) socio-emotional wealth; (6) organizational identity; (7) succession intentions; and (8) national culture and ethnicity. All these subtopics are able to express the complexity of family business studies in the field of management in a

---

[11] The origins of this competence-destroying innovation can be rooted in the concept of "creative destruction" that Schumpeter (1911) proposes in reference to entrepreneurship. According to the scholar, in fact, entrepreneurship causes fundamental changes in technology, products, and processes.

[12] By definition, competence-destroying innovations, which are based on new skills, abilities, and knowledge (Tushman and Anderson, 1986), definitely modify the *status quo* in the market. They are opposed to competence-enhancing innovations that do not radically modify it.

clear way. For each of the above subtopics, of course, different theoretical frameworks and empirical approaches can be used, which makes the proceeding of these studies even more difficult.

Instead, in reference to entrepreneurship, family business has shown a great impact on the perceptions and initial performances of new ventures (Chrisman et al., 2002). Belonging to a family business is proven to affect an individual's entrepreneurial intentions and behavior (Altinay et al., 2012). People with a family business background are more likely to become entrepreneurs (Altinay and Altinay, 2006). In addition to the influence that family can have on entrepreneurial intentions, it is also important to consider the fact that families can be a critical source of financial resources for startups (Habbershon and Williams, 1999; Steier and Greenwood, 2000). Moreover, individuals with a family business background are more comfortable with the idea of receiving challenging results because they already know what managing a venture involves.

The abovesaid in reference to family business studies and entrepreneurship highlights that the main differences between people with or without family business experience affect their inclination toward the launching of new ventures (as well as the underlying perceiving of innovations) and the expected results. By recalling what was said in reference to entrepreneurial cognition, people with family business experience have certain perceptions than differ from those without family business experience. However, this does not necessarily imply that new ventures are launched more easily and that superior performances are really achieved.

1.2.6 Corporate entrepreneurship

Corporate entrepreneurship stands for the innovative actions that take place within large organizations in which an entrepreneurial culture is shared (Kuratko and Morris, 2018). According to the above definition, it is clear that corporate entrepreneurship takes place inside established organizations. This setting can facilitate the emergence of the entrepreneurship phenomena. Since their foundation, established organizations began innovating either in order to develop their competitive advantage (Covin and Miles, 1999; Covin et al., 2000), to increase their profitability (Zahra, 1993), or to start internationalization processes (Birkinshaw, 1997). As specified by Miles and Covin (2002), organizations leverage corporate entrepreneurship to build their innovative capabilities, to get greater value linked to organizational competences, and to obtain financial returns in a short time. Whatever the reason, it is unquestionable that established organizations have always attributed a certain relevance to corporate entrepreneurship.

Very recently, the concept of corporate entrepreneurship is evolving and, as a result, scholars share the idea that it can be considered a major strategy for all types of ventures (Kuratko et al., 2015). As noted by Zahra et al. (2013), it is very intriguing to focus on organizational mechanisms that favor the passage from informal to formal corporate entrepreneurship activities. Scholars mainly agree that innovative actions at the basis of corporate entrepreneurship begin in an informal way.

In established organizations, very often, knowledge processes at the basis of corporate entrepreneurship—including knowledge creation, sharing, absorption, conversion, and integration (Zahra et al., 2013; Matricano et al., 2019)—can be thought of and implemented in a formal way. However, they can also, and very often do, begin in a spontaneous, informal way in accordance with the emerging needs of an organization itself. In this case, since informal corporate entrepreneurship activities respond to the needs that emerge in organizations, it is necessary to formalize them so that consequent results can be even more satisfactory.

Despite the several possible research paths that entrepreneurship scholars have identified to investigate corporate entrepreneurship (and which vary from knowledge management to emerging strategies, from organizational to exploitation mechanisms), the scholars' attention has always been focused on innovation that lies at the basis of corporate entrepreneurship.

1.2.7   Social entrepreneurship and sustainability

Origins of sustainable entrepreneurship date back to 1960, when the Organization for Economic Co-operation and Development (OECD) declared that one of its aims was to promote policies designed "to achieve the highest sustainable economic growth and employment and a rising standard of living in member countries, while maintaining financial stability, and thus to contribute to the development of the world economy" (p. 2). Despite the relevance attributed to sustainability issues by the OECD, scholars have taken some time to introduce the concept into the field of economics and management (Georgescu-Roegen, 1971, 1975; Baumol, 1996) and to investigate it in a comprehensive way (Cohen, 2006; Gibbs, 2006; Cohen and Winn, 2007; Dean and McMullen, 2007; Katsikis and Kyrgidou, 2007; Hall et al., 2010; Hockerts and Wüstenhagen, 2010; Parrish, 2010; Schaltegger and Wagner, 2011; Shepherd and Patzelt, 2011; Spence et al., 2011; Muñoz and Dimov, 2015; Soto-Acosta et al., 2016; Annunziata et al., 2018).

The most important aspect that scholars suggest considering when dealing with sustainable entrepreneurship is the simultaneous focus on short-, medium-, and long-term goals (Motomura, 2006; Batra, 2012). Put simply, it is a largely shared and supported idea that a long-term impact of entrepreneurship cannot be ignored in favor of a short-term one. Of course, when talking about impact, scholars refer to a social, economic, and ecological impact[13] generated by entrepreneurial action (Shepherd and Patzelt, 2011; Fischer and Comini, 2012). In this vein, it is important to underline that sustainable entrepreneurship "can be contrasted to the concept of selfish entrepreneurship in which people seek advantages only for themselves own

---

[13] In reference to the definition of the impact, Shepherd and Patzelt argue: "sustainable entrepreneurship is focused on the preservation of nature, life support, and community in the pursuit of perceived opportunities to bring into existence future products, processes, and services for gain, where gain is broadly construed to include economic and noneconomic gains to individuals, the economy, and society" (2011, p. 142).

and often at any cost" (Motomura, 2006, p. 1). Individual values, beliefs, and behaviors, thus, totally change if one is in the field of sustainable entrepreneurship.

In sum, the theme of sustainable entrepreneurship enlarges the aims and scopes of entrepreneurship, both in terms of the time to consider (goals refer to short-, medium-, and long-term) and of the impact generated (social, economic, and ecological).

1.2.8 Women and minority entrepreneurship

On their list of the main themes that characterize entrepreneurship research, Kuratko and Morris (2018) include women and minority entrepreneurship. This choice results from the fact that these specific groups of entrepreneurs (i.e., female and ethnic entrepreneurs) face specific obstacles and difficulties that other entrepreneurs do not (of course, entrepreneurship scholars usually compare women with men and ethnic with local/native entrepreneurs).

Due to the specific obstacles that female and ethnic entrepreneurs have to face, these research themes have developed along different paths.

With respect to female entrepreneurship, several contributions can be recalled (Hisrich and Brush, 1986; Bowen and Hisrich, 1986; Birley, 1989; Brush et al., 2001; Allen et al., 2007; Minniti, 2010; Jennings and Brush, 2013; Chreim et al., 2018; Matricano and Sorrentino, 2018). In particular, Chaganti (1986) and Brush (1992) disclose that female entrepreneurs: manage their firms in a more adaptive and flexible way than male entrepreneurs do; use a style of leadership that can engage and encourage people working with them; and that they do not evaluate results only in terms of revenues (but consider personal goals to be as important as economic results). Some years later, Brush et al. (2001) discuss and criticize eight myths[14] about female entrepreneurship in order to propose a new way of approaching female entrepreneurship. However, despite the above results, the idea that female entrepreneurs have to face and overcome more difficulties than their male counterparts is still legitimate[15] (Zhang et al., 2009). In particular, the relevance of entrepreneurial network is still a huge obstacle for female entrepreneurs (Matricano and Sorrentino, 2018).

On the other hand, the obstacles and difficulties for ethnic entrepreneurs to overcome are related to the concepts of opportunity and necessity (Reynolds et al.,

---

[14] The eight myths that scholars discuss and criticize are: (1) women do not want to own high growth businesses; (2) women do not have the right educational backgrounds to build large ventures; (3) women do not have the right types of experience to build large ventures; (4) women are not in the network and lack the social contacts to build a credible venture; (5) women do not have the financial savvy or resources to start high growth businesses; (6) women do not submit business plans to equity providers; (7) women-owned ventures are in industries unattractive to venture capitalists; and (8) women are not a force in the venture capital industry.

[15] Zhang et al. (2009) demonstrate that female entrepreneurs are less inclined toward seeking for angel financing; they need to provide more guarantees for a loan; they invest less resources (both financial and human ones) in entrepreneurial activities; and they cannot easily reach potential customers outside their network.

2001, 2002). By definition, opportunity entrepreneurs decide to be involved in entrepreneurship because they perceive the context they are in as positive and, thus, they try to exploit the opportunities that can be derived from it.[16] In this case, the difficulties they have to face are similar to those of the local entrepreneurs (Uhlaner and Thurik, 2007; Verheul et al., 2010; Giacomin et al., 2011). Necessity entrepreneurs, instead, undergo unfavorable working circumstances. Generally speaking, they actually decide to start an entrepreneurial activity because they do not have any working alternative in the mainstream market (Waldinger et al., 1990; Feagin and Imani, 1994). They realize the negative context around them and so they perceive the achievement of their entrepreneurial aims as more challenging.[17]

Specific obstacles and difficulties faced by female and ethnic entrepreneurs, respectively, and the performances they achieve (both in economic and social terms) have driven entrepreneurship scholars to consider them as autonomous fields of research and to develop them along distinct research paths.

1.2.9 Global entrepreneurship

Global entrepreneurship faces the challenge of fostering entrepreneurial activity around the world (Kuratko and Morris, 2018). Obviously, the entrepreneurial phenomenon can take place all around the world. On the one hand, it is possible to hypothesize that the phenomenon could assume the same characteristics—as previously stated, individuals exploit entrepreneurial opportunities (Acs, 1992; Oviatt and McDougall, 1995; Hornsby et al., 2018; Kyvik, 2018). On the other hand, by reflecting on the idea that the phenomenon can take place in different countries, one might hypothesize that the phenomenon could be highly country-specific and, in turn, could assume specific characteristics. By following this second option, several differences can arise and—as noted by several scholars (Levie et al., 2014; Wu and Huarng, 2015)—it is worthy to underline them.

The fact that entrepreneurship can take place in different contexts[18] invites thinking about the historical changes, the role played by institutions, and the entrepreneurial mindset of each country. Briefly, political stability (or instability) can favor the entrepreneurial phenomenon and institutions can be more (or less) inclined toward policies that support entrepreneurship (investments in educational or R&D activities, in actions and tools able to support entrepreneurship programs). This can generate a positive (or a negative) context from which new entrepreneurial opportunities can come (or not). Consequently, individuals can be more (or less) interested in starting and managing new ventures.

At the same time, the fact that entrepreneurship can take place in different contexts can affect achievable results. Firms located in different countries but working

---

[16] De Freitas (1991) calls this opportunities "mobility motives."

[17] De Freitas (1991) calls this challenges "escape motives."

[18] In reference to the context, entrepreneurship scholars leverage several classifications. The most common ones refer to the comparison between developed and developing (or emerging) countries or to macro-regions (European, America, Asiatic, African countries). Of course, according to the classification criterion that is adopted, noticeable differences can emerge between countries.

in the same industry might be compelled to define and implement different strategies and/or face different competitors.

In the debate about the similarities and differences that can emerge when entrepreneurship takes place across borders, scholars focus their attention on the conditions (either country-specific or global) that can generate a positive context that can stimulate entrepreneurship or affect achievable performances.

1.2.10 Entrepreneurship research, education, and pedagogy

The last theme that Kuratko and Morris (2018) consider in reference to entrepreneurship studies is related to entrepreneurship research, education, and pedagogy. In particular, these scholars refer to all the entrepreneurship-related activities offered by business and engineering schools or even campus programs.

Rebuilding the origins of entrepreneurial training is a very challenging task. Some scholars underline the supply and demand of entrepreneurial training programs and thus address their interest toward the practical aspects of the phenomenon (Vesper and Gartner, 2001; Katz, 2003; Volkmann, 2004). Other scholars, instead, focus their attention on the theoretical aspects of the phenomenon, its usefulness, and its impact (Fayolle, 2003; Warren, 2004; Wilson, 2004; Kuratko, 2005; Leitch and Harrison, 2008; Matricano, 2014, 2017).

Beyond the practical and theoretical aspects that might have affected the origins of this theme, what matters the most is to try to provide a clear definition of entrepreneurial training. This is a very difficult task because two different concepts, namely, education and training, overlap with one another (Hynes, 1996; Henry et al., 2015).

According to Jamieson (1984) it is important to distinguish between three concepts: (1) education about enterprise; (2) education for enterprise; and (3) education in enterprise. Instead, according to Kirby (2002), it is appropriate to distinguish between "education about entrepreneurship," concerning the concept and definition of venture, and "education for entrepreneurship," concerning the activities necessary to start a new venture. In line with this, Hytti and O'Gorman (2004) propose that entrepreneurial education and training should be divided into three main categories parts dealing with "understanding about entrepreneurship," "entrepreneurial behavior," and "becoming an entrepreneur." The first, exclusively theoretical, is focused on the concept of entrepreneurship. The second and third, mainly practical, are concerned with the behavior to adopt and the processes to carry out in order to be an entrepreneur.

In order to shed some light on the differences between entrepreneurial education and training, it might be helpful to refer to two studies that have investigated these concepts separately. Alberti et al. (2004) investigated entrepreneurial education and Mullins (2010) investigated entrepreneurial training.

According to Alberti et al. (2004), entrepreneurial education refers to the theoretical concepts, capabilities, and knowledge that may be used for launching startups. According to Mullins (2010), entrepreneurial training refers to practical knowledge, skills, and attitudes necessary to act in an efficient and effective way. By embracing this difference, it is possible to include among entrepreneurial training activities what Jamieson (1984) calls "education for enterprise" and "education in enterprise," what Kirby (2002) calls "education for entrepreneurship," and what Hytti and O'Gorman (2004) call "entrepreneurial behavior" and "becoming an entrepreneur."

As a result, while entrepreneurial education is more about the preliminary involvement in entrepreneurship, entrepreneurial training is more about the practical aspects that can provide entrepreneurs with specific useful tools for managing their ventures. In reference to both entrepreneurial education and training, it is worth highlighting that the way individuals perceive educational and training stimuli— that is, the pedagogical aspects (Cardow and Smith, 2015; Klapper et al., 2015; Ismail et al., 2018)—makes a noticeable difference in terms of achieved results.

1.3 Reflections about the main research themes in entrepreneurship studies

The above reviews of the main themes that Kuratko and Morris (2018) propose in reference to entrepreneurship (summarized in Table 1.2) need to be properly evaluated and discussed in order to try to outline − if possible − the essence of entrepreneurship.

Despite achieved results, which can either be already consolidated or still in fieri, largely agreed upon or strongly debated, it is suggested herein that reflections about the research themes should be carried out as a whole.[19]

This is useful for overcoming the idea that entrepreneurship research is a vast and fragmented field and for the making the attempt to capture the essence of entrepreneurship.

What appears to be very intriguing, in fact, is not a comparison that is able to assess which are the most (or least) relevant themes in entrepreneurship. On the contrary, it is more interesting to try to catch the *leitmotiv* of entrepreneurship— that is, what underpins all the above-given research themes and bonds them.

By reflecting on the theoretical results that have emerged previously in reference to the aforementioned themes, it seems possible to identify two extremes of a *continuum*. One extreme makes it possible to find the role of innovation that, in the shape of entrepreneurial opportunities, lies at the basis of entrepreneurship and affects its rise and development. The other extreme makes it possible to find the impact of entrepreneurship (economic and/or social growth) that is measured through a comparison of achievable and achieved results.

---

[19] In reference to this, Audretsch et al. (2015) propose an eclectic view of entrepreneurship. In their view, this paradigm comprehends organizational status (which can be referred to the person, the firm or the team), behavior (which includes motivation and can be meant at an individual or organizational level), and performance (which can be read in terms of growth, innovation or social performance).

Beyond the choice of the elements at the basis of this eclectic view (organizational status, behavior, and performance), what entrepreneurship scholars are hoped to catch is the multilens approach to the study of entrepreneurship.

Table 1.2 The major themes in entrepreneurial studies and their state-of-the-art.

Theme	Emerging theoretical results
Opportunities and the entrepreneurial process	Role of innovation is embodied in entrepreneurial opportunities and affects entrepreneurial processes
Venture financing	The relationship (formal or informal) established between entrepreneurs and financiers affects the economic performance that can be derived from it
Entrepreneurial cognition	Cognition is relevant because it affects the evaluation of entrepreneurial opportunities and determines the results that can be achieved
Economic development and entrepreneurship	Entrepreneurship is the engine of economic and social development
Family business	Family business experience affects the underlying perceiving of innovations and the expected results
Corporate entrepreneurship	Innovation lies at the basis of corporate entrepreneurship
Social entrepreneurship and sustainability	Enlarges the aims and scopes of entrepreneurship, both in terms of the time to refer to and of the impact generated (social, economic, and ecological)
Women and minority entrepreneurship	Focus on obstacles/difficulties faced by female and ethnic entrepreneurs and on performances achieved (both economic and social)
Global entrepreneurship	Conditions (country-specific or global) that can generate a positive context stimulating entrepreneurship or affecting achievable performances
Entrepreneurship research, education, and pedagogy	The way in which individuals perceive educational and training stimuli (i.e., the pedagogical aspects) makes a difference in terms of achieved results

Source: Personal elaboration.

From the main research themes investigated before,[20] entrepreneurial processes, entrepreneurial cognition, and corporate entrepreneurship are mainly focused on innovation and its exploitation. Venture financing and social entrepreneurship and sustainability are mainly concerned with the impact of entrepreneurship. Other themes, such as family business, women and minority entrepreneurship, global entrepreneurship, and entrepreneurship research, education, and pedagogy, fall halfway between the two extremes (see Table 1.3).

These three theme groups, which can be found along the above-imagined *continuum*, cause two main questions to be raised. First, the theoretical results that emerge from the dedicated literature review range from entrepreneurial opportunities to an achieved performance economic development (or they take both into consideration).

---

[20] Entrepreneurial opportunities and economic development are not considered here since any comments about them would be tautological.

Table 1.3 A possible classification of the main themes of entrepreneurship research.

Themes focused on innovation and its exploitation	Themes of research falling halfway	Themes focused on the impact of entrepreneurship
• Opportunities and entrepreneurial processes • Entrepreneurial cognition • Corporate entrepreneurship	• Economic development • Family business • Women and minority entrepreneurship • Global entrepreneurship • Entrepreneurship research, education, and pedagogy	• Venture financing • Social entrepreneurship and sustainability

Source: Personal elaboration.

Thus the question—is it possible to assume them as the boundaries of entrepreneurial phenomena?—is posed.

If the response to the above question is affirmative, then how can we investigate and rebuild what really happens from the point at which entrepreneurs identify an entrepreneurial opportunity up until they achieve a certain performance?

The answers to the above questions are going to define the structure of this book.

1.4 The structure of the book

In reference to the first question—concerning the assumption that entrepreneurial opportunities and achieved performance can be considered the boundaries of entrepreneurial phenomena—the answer needs to be properly discussed. Some scholars, for example, Kuratko and Morris (2018), consider entrepreneurial opportunities and economic development to be two research themes, similar to the other ones. They do not assign a dominant role to these themes. However, the review and the analysis presented above seem to suggest that these themes are tacitly included in the other ones instead. Unconsciously—it could be said—they are taken for granted and affect the development of the other themes. This result, of course, does not reduce the relevance of the other themes but, on the contrary, it strengthens the relevance of entrepreneurial opportunities and achieved performance. With some reservation, this can drive one to answer affirmatively to the above-posed question and thus it can be assumed that the entrepreneurial opportunities and impact generated (in terms of achievable/achieved results) can stand for the boundaries of entrepreneurship.

At this stage, the second question—regarding how can we investigate and rebuild what really happens from the point at which entrepreneurs identify an entrepreneurial opportunity up until they achieve a certain result—also needs an answer. In order to do so, that part of entrepreneurial literature that considers entrepreneurship as a practice, an organizational process (Johannisson, 2008, 2011)—

from which the word *entrepreneuring* was derived—needs to be recalled. In this stream of literature (Eckhardt and Shane, 2003; Shane, 2003; Companys and McMullen, 2007; McMullen et al., 2007; Eckhardt and Ciuchta, 2008; Foss and Foss, 2008; McMullen and Dimov, 2013; Davidsson, 2016), Cha and Bae (2010, p. 31) support the idea that the entrepreneurial process "involves a journey of improvising and coping with uncertainty." Thus these scholars focus their attention on the internal driving forces (i.e., entrepreneurial intent) that interact "with and against internal and external conditions and changes" (Cha and Bae, 2010, p. 31). According to them, specific actions (put into practice to achieve established aims) and individual motivations (at the basis of those actions) are the core of the entrepreneurial journey and, hence, particular attention needs to be paid to them.

By reflexive thinking, an intriguing insight seems to emerge. The entrepreneurial process (i.e., a set of actions put into practice in order to achieve a certain aim) involves a journey (i.e., a specific intent that needs to be mixed with internal and external factors) that takes place along a roadmap or a trajectory that, at least by definition, identifies the destination to be achieved. Entrepreneurs, putting into practice a process and experiencing a journey, are thus expected to be interested in the trajectory to address. By definition, a trajectory is the result of the intertwining of unexpected events with purposeful decisions. As such, it requires a system of assumptions, choices, and changes that are related to unexpected events, which can come from the environment or result from the dynamics of the market itself, and to the purposeful decisions that entrepreneurs make when they plan a strategy to implement. In this vein, it is intriguing to investigate and rebuild what really happens from the point at which an entrepreneurial opportunity is identified up until the point when a certain performance is achieved. Accordingly, the volume aims to provide a conceptual toolkit that enables entrepreneurs to draw entrepreneurship trajectories and scholars to formalize and catalogue them.

Just like travelers, entrepreneurs are expected to start planning from their destination and to proceed in a reverse manner by defining their in-between stops. This implies that, at first, entrepreneurs need to look at the results they want to achieve. At large, it is hypothesized that firms aspire to survive or to grow. Thus it is worth questioning how entrepreneurs can make this happen.

According to a conspicuous stream of research, attention needs to be paid to the business model that, generally speaking, explains how ventures create value (Amit and Zott, 2001; Zott and Amit, 2007, 2010). Scholars investigating this topic have advanced several proposals in order to clarify the above concept (Chesbrough and Rosenbloom, 2002; Casadesus-Masanell and Ricart, 2010; Zott et al., 2011). Among them, the contribution proposed by Zott and Amit (2010) that concerns the business models of entrepreneurial firms, seems very useful. These scholars, in fact, encourage paying attention to the specific configurations[21] of content, structure, and governance of activities put into practice by firms of this type.

At this point, a couple of genuine questions arise: Why do entrepreneurs prefer a certain configuration of business model over another? What are the criteria at the

---

[21] The specific configurations Zott and Amit (2010) talk about are going to be reviewed in Chapter 3.

Table 1.4 The elements at the basis of the entrepreneurial trajectories and the structure of the book.

The performance of entrepreneurial firms Chapter 2		
⬇	Entrepreneurship trajectories Chapter 5	Selected cases Chapter 6
Business model Chapter 3		
⬇		
Entrepreneurial opportunities Chapter 4		

Source: Personal elaboration.

basis of the entrepreneurs' choices? As a matter of fact, personal factors (such as risk propensity) seem to play a narrow role and they do not seem related to the business model. Innovation at the basis of the entrepreneurial process (which reveals itself in the shape of entrepreneurial opportunities), instead, seems to play a relevant role (Zott and Amit, 2010). By employing reverse thinking (i.e., starting from the end), the elements at the basis of the entrepreneurial trajectories are identified (the entrepreneurial opportunities and the business models that drive toward a certain performance are in the toolkit) and the structure of the book is defined (Table 1.4).

Before proceeding with the analysis, a recommendation is necessary. Scholars, practitioners, and students might intend for all the topics recalled and investigated in the following chapters (achievable/achieved results, business models, and entrepreneurial opportunities) as standing alone. Each of them is, in fact, rooted in specific streams of literature and each has been widely discussed—and is actually still being discussed—by other entrepreneurship scholars. Without questioning their relevance in entrepreneurial studies, the present volume aims to read and interpret these topics as pieces of a puzzle that need to come closer together to provide, hopefully, an intriguing view of entrepreneurship trajectories.

References

Acs, Z.J., 1992. Small business economics: a global perspective. Challenge 35 (6), 38–44.
Acs, Z.J., Audretsch, D.B., 2003. Handbook of Entrepreneurship Research. An Interdisciplinary Survey and Introduction. Springer, New York.
Acs, Z.J., Audretsch, D.B., Feldman, M.P., 1994. R&D spillover and recipient firm size. Rev. Econ. Stat. 100 (1), 336–367.

Ahuja, G., 2000. Collaboration networks, structural holes, and innovation: a longitudinal study. Adm. Sci. Q. 45 (3), 425−455.

Alberti, F., Sciascia, S., Poli, A., 2004. Entrepreneurship education: notes on an ongoing debate. Paper presented at the 14th Annual IntEnt Conference, Naples, Italy.

Aldrich, H.E., Zimmer, C., 1986. Entrepreneurship through social networks. In: Aldrich, H.E. (Ed.), Population Perspective on Organizations, Acta Universitatis Upaliensis, Uppsala, Sweden.

Allen, E., Langowitz, N., Minniti, M., 2007. The 2006 Global Entrepreneurship Monitor Special Topic Research: Women in Entrepreneurship. Center for Women Leadership. Babson College, Babson Park, MA.

Altinay, L., Altinay, E., 2006. Determinants of ethnic minority entrepreneurial growth in the catering sector. Serv. Ind. J. 26 (2), 203−221.

Altinay, L., Madanoglu, M., Daniele, R., Lashley, C., 2012. The influence of family tradition and psychological traits on entrepreneurial intention. Int. J. Hosp. Manag. 31 (2), 489−499.

Amit, R., Zott, C., 2001. Value creation in e-business. Strat. Manag. J. 22 (6−7), 493−520.

Ang, J.S., 1991. Small business uniqueness and the theory of financial management. J. Small Bus. Fin. 1 (1), 1−13.

Ang, J.S., 1992. On the theory of finance for privately held firms. J Entrepr. Fin. 1 (3), 185−203.

Annunziata, E., Pucci, T., Frey, M., Zanni, L., 2018. The role of organizational capabilities in attaining corporate sustainability practices and economic performance: evidence from Italian wine industry. J. Clean. Prod. 171 (10), 1300−1311.

Aparicio, S., Urbano, D., Audretsch, D., 2016. Institutional factors, opportunity entrepreneurship and economic growth: panel data evidence. Technol. Forecast. Soc. Change 102, 45−61.

Arafat, M.Y., Saleem, I., 2017. Examining start-up intention of Indians through cognitive approach: a study using GEM data. J. Global Entrepr. Res. 7 (13), 1−11.

Audretsch, D.B., 2002. Entrepreneurship: A Survey of the Literature. Enterprise Directorate General, European Commission, EU.

Audretsch, D.B., 2003. Entrepreneurship policy and the strategic management of places. In: Hart, D.M. (Ed.), The Emergence of Entrepreneurship Policy. Cambridge University Press, Cambridge, MA.

Audretsch, D.B., Fritsch, M., 1994. The geography of firm births in Germany. Region. Stud. 28 (4), 359−365.

Audretsch, D.B., Thurik, A.R., 2001. What's new about the new economy? Sources of growth in the managed and entrepreneurial economies. Ind. Corp. Change 10 (1), 267−315.

Audretsch, D.B., Kuratko, D.F., Link, A.N., 2015. Making sense of the elusive paradigm of entrepreneurship. Small Bus. Econ. 45 (4), 703−712.

Autio, E., 2005. Global Entrepreneurship Monitor—Executive Report.

Autio, E., Klofsten, M., 1998. A comparative study of two European business incubators. J. Small Bus. Manag. 36 (1), 30−43.

Baron, R.A., 1998. Cognitive mechanisms in entrepreneurship: why and when entrepreneurs think differently than other people. J. Bus. Ventur. 13 (4), 275−294.

Baron, R.A., 2000. Psychological perspectives on entrepreneurship: cognitive and social factors in entrepreneurs' success. Curr. Dir. Psychol. Sci. 9 (1), 15−18.

Batra, M.M., 2012. The sustainability challenge and its business solution. Compet. Forum 10 (1), 182−190.

Baumol, W.J., 1990. Entrepreneurship: productive, unproductive and destructive. J. Pol. Econ. 98 (3), 893–921.

Baumol, W.J., 1996. Entrepreneurship, Management, and the Structure of Payoffs. MIT Press, Cambridge, MA.

Becattini, G., 1989. Modelli locali di sviluppo. Il Mulino, Bologna, IT.

Bellavitis, C., Filatotchev, I., Kamuriwo, D.S., Vanacker, T., 2017. Entrepreneurial finance: new frontiers of research and practice: editorial for the special issue embracing entrepreneurial funding innovations. Vent. Cap.: Int. J. Entrepr. Fin. 19 (1–2), 1–16.

Bird, B.J., 1988. Implementing entrepreneurial ideas: the case for intention. Acad. Manag. Rev. 13 (3), 442–453.

Birkinshaw, J., 1997. Entrepreneurship in multinational corporations: the characteristics of subsidiary initiatives. Strat. Manag. J. 18 (3), 207–229.

Birley, S., 1985. The role of networks in the entrepreneurial process. J. Bus. Ventur. 1 (1), 107–117.

Birley, S., 1989. Female entrepreneurs: are they really any different? J. Small Bus. Manag. 27 (5), 32–37.

Bjørnskov, C., Foss, N.J., 2016. Institutions, entrepreneurship, and economic growth: what do we know and what do we still need to know? Acad. Manag. Persp. 30 (3), 292–315.

Bosma, N., Content, J., Sanders, M., Stam, E., 2018. Institutions, entrepreneurship, and economic growth in Europe. Small Bus. Econ. 51, 483–499.

Bowen, D.D., Hisrich, R.D., 1986. The female entrepreneur: a career development perspective. Acad. Manag. Rev. 11 (2), 393–407.

Boyd, N.G., Vozikis, G.S., 1994. The influence of self-efficacy on the development of entrepreneurial intentions and actions. Entrepr.: Theory Pract. 18 (4), 63–77.

Brinlee, J.B., Franklin, G.M., Bell, J.R., Bullock, C.A., 2004. Educating entrepreneurs on angel venture capital financing options. J. Bus. Entrepr. 16 (2), 141–156.

Brush, C., 1992. Research on women business owners: past trends, a new perspective and future directions. Entrepr.: Theory Pract. 16 (4), 5–30.

Brush, C., Carter, N., Gatewood, E., Greene, P., Hart, M., 2001. The Diana project. Women business owners and equity capital: the myths dispelled, Report by Kauffman Center for Entrepreneurial Leadership. Retrieved from <http://www.entreworld.org>.

Bruton, G., Khavul, S., Siegel, D., Wright, M., 2015. New financial alternatives in seeding entrepreneurship: microfinance, crowdfunding, and peer-to-peer innovations. Entrepr.: Theory Pract. 39 (1), 9–26.

Burt, R.S., 1992. Structural Holes: The Social Structure of Competition. Harvard University Press, Cambridge, MA.

Burt, R.S., 2000. Structural holes versus network closure as social capital. In: Lin, N., Cook, C.S., Burt, R.S. (Eds.), Social Capital: Theory and Research. Aldine de Gruyter, New York.

Bygrave, W.D., Hofer, C.W., 1991. Theorizing about entrepreneurship. Entrepr.: Theory Pract. 16 (2), 13–22.

Cantillon, R., 1755. Essai sur la Nature du Commerce en Général (1964 edition), with trans. by H. Higgs (Ed.). AM Kelley, New York.

Cardow, A., Smith, R., 2015. Using innovative pedagogies in the classroom: re-storying gothic tales as entrepreneur stories. Ind. High. Educ. 29 (5), 361–374.

Casadesus-Masanell, R., Ricart, J.E., 2010. From strategy to business models and onto tactics. Long Range Plan. 43 (2–3), 195–215.

Casson, M., 2003. The Entrepreneur: An Economic Theory, second ed. (first ed. in 1982) Edward Elgar Publishing, Cheltenham, UK.

Cha, M.S., Bae, Z.T., 2010. The entrepreneurial journey: from entrepreneurial intent to opportunity realization. J. High Technol. Manag. Res. 21 (1), 31−42.

Chaganti, R., 1986. Management in women-owned enterprises. J. Small Bus. Manag. 24, 18−29.

Chen, C.C., Green, P.G., Crick, A., 1998. Does entrepreneurial self-efficacy distinguish entrepreneurs from manager? J. Bus. Ventur. 13 (4), 295−316.

Chesbrough, H., Rosenbloom, R.S., 2002. The role of the business model in capturing value from innovation: evidence from Xerox Corporation's technology spin-off companies. Ind. Corp. Change 11 (3), 529−555.

Chreim, S., Spence, M., Crick, D., Liao, X., 2018. Review of female immigrant entrepreneurship research: past findings, gaps and ways forward. Eur. Manag. J. 36 (2), 210−222.

Chrisman, J.J., Gatewood, E., Donlevy, L.B., 2002. A note on the efficiency and effectiveness of outsider assistance programs in rural versus non-rural states. Entrepr.: Theory Pract. 26 (3), 67−81.

Churchill, N.C., 1997. Breaking down the wall: scaling the ladder. In: Birley, S., Muzyka, D. (Eds.), Mastering Enterprise. Financial Times/Pitman, London, UK.

Cohen, B., 2006. Urbanization in developing countries: current trends, future projections, and key challenges for sustainability. Technol. Soc. 28 (1−2), 63−80.

Cohen, B., Winn, M.I., 2007. Market imperfections, opportunity and sustainable entrepreneurship. J. Bus. Ventur. 22 (1), 29−49.

Cole, R.A., Sokolyk, T., 2018. Debt financing, survival, and growth of start-up firms. J. Corp. Fin. 50, 609−625.

Companys, Y.E., McMullen, J.S., 2007. Strategic entrepreneurs at work: the nature, discovery, and exploitation of entrepreneurial opportunities. Small Bus. Econ. 28 (4), 301−322.

Cooper, A.C., 1995. Challenges in predicting new firm performance. In: Bull, I., Thomas, H., Willard, G. (Eds.), Entrepreneurship: Perspectives on Theory Building. Pergamon-Elsevier, Oxford−New York.

Cooper, A.C., Dunkelberg, W., 1981. A new look at business entry: experience of 1805 entrepreneurs. In: Vesper, K.H. (Ed.), Frontiers of Entrepreneurship Research. Babson College, Wellesley, MA.

Covin, J.G., Slevin, D.P., 1989. Strategic management of small firms in hostile and benign environments. Strat. Manag. J. 10 (1), 75−87.

Covin, J.G., Covin, T.J., 1990. Competitive aggressiveness, environmental context, and small firm performance. Entrepr.: Theory Pract. 14 (4), 35−50.

Covin, J.G., Miles, M.P., 1999. Corporate entrepreneurship and the pursuit of competitive advantage. Entrepr.: Theory Pract. 23 (3), 47−63.

Covin, J.G., Slevin, D.P., Heeley, M.B., 2000. Pioneers and followers: competitive tactics, environment, and firm growth. J. Bus. Ventur. 15 (2), 175−210.

Cromie, S., 2000. Assessing entrepreneurial inclinations: some approaches and empirical evidence. Eur. J. Work Org Psychol. 9 (1), 7−30.

da Cruz, J.V., 2018. Beyond financing: crowdfunding as an informational mechanism. J. Bus. Ventur. 33 (3), 371−393.

Davidsson, P., 2016. The field of entrepreneurship research: some significant developments. In: Bögenhold, D., Bonnet, J., Dejardin, M., Garcia Pérez de Lema, D. (Eds.), Contemporary Entrepreneurship. Springer, Cham, pp. 17−28.

Davidsson, P., Lindmark, L., Olofsson, C., 1994. New firm formation and regional development in Sweden. Regio. Stud. 28 (4), 395−410.

De Freitas, G., 1991. Inequality at Work: Hispanics in the U.S. Labor Force. Oxford University Press, New York.

De Massis, A., Kotlar, J., Chua, J.H., Chrisman, J.J., 2014. Ability and willingness as sufficiency conditions for family-oriented particularistic behavior: implications for theory and empirical studies. J. Small Bus. Manag. 52 (2), 344–364.

Dean, T.J., McMullen, J.S., 2007. Toward a theory of sustainable entrepreneurship: reducing environmental degradation through entrepreneurial action. J. Bus. Ventur. 22 (1), 50–76.

Dess, G.G., Lumpkin, G.T., Covin, G.J., 1997. Entrepreneurial strategy making and firm performance: test of contingency and configurational models. Strat. Manag. J. 18 (9), 677–695.

Drover, W., Busenitz, L., Matusik, S., Townsend, D., Anglin, A., Dushnitsky, G., 2017. A review and road map of entrepreneurial equity financing research: venture capital, corporate venture capital, angel investment, crowdfunding, and accelerators. J. Manag. 43 (6), 1820–1853.

Drucker, P.F., 1985. Innovation and Entrepreneurship. Harper & Row, New York.

Dubini, P., 1989. The influence of motivations and environment on business start-ups: some hints for public policies. J. Bus. Ventur. 4 (1), 11–26.

Eckhardt, J.T., Shane, S., 2003. The individual-opportunity nexus. In: Acs, Z.J., Audretsch, D.B. (Eds.), Handbook of Entrepreneurship Research: A Interdisciplinary Survey and Introduction. Kluwer Academic Publishers, UK.

Eckhardt, J.T., Ciuchta, M.P., 2008. Selected variation: the population-level implications of multistage selection in entrepreneurship. Strat. Entrepr. J. 2 (3), 209–224.

Ehrlich, S.B., De Noble, A.F., Moore, T., Weaver, R.R., 1994. After the cash arrives: a comparative study of venture capital and private investor involvement in entrepreneurial firms. J. Bus. Ventur. 9 (1), 67–82.

Fayolle, A., 2003. Using the theory of planned behaviour in assessing entrepreneurship teaching program. Paper presented at the IntEnt 2003 Conference, Grenoble, France.

Feagin, J.R., Imani, N., 1994. Racial barriers to African entrepreneurship: an exploratory study. Soc. Problems 41 (4), 562–584.

Feola, R., Vesci, M., Botti, A., Parente, R., 2017. The determinants of entrepreneurial intention of young researchers: combining the theory of planned behavior with the Triple Helix model. J. Small Bus. Manag. Available from: https://doi.org/10.1111/jsbm.12361Online Version of Record.

Feranita, F., Kotlar, J., De Massis, A., 2017. Collaborative innovation in family firms: past research, current debates and agenda for future research. J. Fam. Bus. Strat. 8 (3), 137–156.

Fischer, R.M., Comini, G., 2012. Sustainable development: from responsibility to entrepreneurship. Revista de Administração 47 (3), 363–369.

Foss, K., Foss, N.J., 2008. Understanding opportunity discovery and sustainable advantage: the role of transaction costs and property rights. Strat. Entrepr. J. 2 (3), 191–207.

Frederiks, A.J., Englis, B.G., Ehrenhard, M.L., Groen, A.J., 2018. Entrepreneurial cognition and the quality of new venture ideas: an experimental approach to comparing future-oriented cognitive processes. J. Bus. Ventur. Available from: https://doi.org/10.1016/j.jbusvent.2018.05.007. Available online.

Frid, C.J., 2014. Acquiring financial resources to form new ventures: the impact of personal characteristics on organizational emergence. J. Small Bus. Entrepr. 27 (3), 323–341.

Gaglio, C.M., 2004. The role of mental simulations and counterfactual thinking in the opportunity identification process. Entrepr.: Theory Pract. 28 (6), 533–552.

Garofoli, G., 1994. Formazione di Nuove Imprese: Un'Analisi Comparata a Livello Internazionale. Franco Angeli, Milano, IT.

Gartner, W.B., 1985. A conceptual framework for describing the phenomenon of new venture creation. Acad. Manag. Rev. 10 (4), 696–706.

Gartner, W.B., 1988. Who is an entrepreneur? Is the wrong question. Am. Small Bus. J. 12 (4), 11–31.

Gartner, W.B., 1990. What are we talking about when we talk about entrepreneurship? J. Bus. Ventur. 5 (1), 15–28.

Gartner, W.B., 2001. Is there an elephant in entrepreneurship? Blind assumptions in theory development. Entrepr.: Theory Pract. 25 (4), 27–39.

Gartner, W.B., Gatewood, E., 1992. Thus the theory of description matters most. Entrepr.: Theory Pract. 17 (1), 5–10.

Georgescu-Roegen, N., 1971. The Entropy Law and the Economic Process. Harvard University Press.

Georgescu-Roegen, N., 1975. Dynamic models and economic growth. World Devel. 3 (11–12), 765–783.

Giacomin, O., Janssen, F., Guyot, J., Lohest, O., 2011. Opportunity and/or Necessity Entrepreneurship? The Impact of the Socio-Economic Characteristics of Entrepreneurs (MPRA Paper No. 29506). University Library of Munich, Germany.

Gibbs, D., 2006. Sustainability entrepreneurs, ecopreneurs and the development of a sustainable economy. Green. Manag. Int. 55, 63–78. autumn.

Greve, A., 1995. Networks and entrepreneurship: an analysis of social relations, occupational background, and the use of contacts during the establishment process. Scand. J. Manag. 11 (1), 1–24.

Habbershon, T.G., Williams, M.L., 1999. A resource-based framework for assessing the strategic advantages of family firms. Fam. Bus. Rev. 12 (1), 1–25.

Hall, J.K., Daneke, G.A., Lenox, M.J., 2010. Sustainable development and entrepreneurship: past contributions and future directions. J. Bus. Ventur. 25 (5), 439–448.

Henry, C., Foss, L., Fayolle, A., Walker, E., Duffy, S., 2015. Entrepreneurial leadership and gender: exploring theory and practice in global contexts. J. Small Bus. Manag. 53 (3), 581–586.

Hisrich, R.D., Brush, C.G., 1986. The Woman Entrepreneur. Lexington Books, Lexington, MS.

Hitt, M.A., Ireland, R.D., Camp, S.M., Sexton, D.L., 2001. Guest editors' introduction to the special issue strategic entrepreneurship: entrepreneurial strategies for wealth creation. Strat. Manag. J. 22 (6–7), 479–491.

Hitt, M.A., Ireland, R.D., Camp, S.M., Sexton, D.L., 2002. Strategic Entrepreneurship – Creating a New Mindset. Blackwell Publishing, Oxford, UK.

Hmieleski, K.M., Corbett, A.C., 2008. The contrasting interaction effects of improvisational behavior with entrepreneurial self-efficacy on new venture performance and entrepreneur work satisfaction. J. Bus. Ventur. 23 (4), 482–496.

Hockerts, K., Wüstenhagen, R., 2010. Greening Goliaths versus emerging Davids: theorizing about the role of incumbents and new entrants in sustainable entrepreneurship. J. Bus. Ventur. 25 (5), 481–492.

Hornsby, J.S., Messersmith, J., Rutherford, M., Simmons, S., 2018. Entrepreneurship everywhere: across campus, across communities, and across borders. J. Small Bus. Manag. 56 (1), 4–10.

Hynes, B., 1996. Entrepreneurship education and training-introducing entrepreneurship into non-business disciplines. J. Eur. Ind. Train. 20 (8), 10–17.

Hytti, U., O'Gorman, C., 2004. What is "enterprise education"? An analysis of the objectives and methods of enterprise education programmes in four European countries. Educ. Train. 46 (1), 11–23.

Ireland, R.D., Hitt, M.A., Camp, S.M., Sexton, D.L., 2001. Integrating entrepreneurship and strategic management actions to create firm wealth. Acad. Manag. Exec. 15 (1), 49–63.

Ismail, A.B., Sawang, S., Zolin, R., 2018. Entrepreneurship education pedagogy: teacher-student-centred paradox. Educ. Train. 60 (2), 168–184.

Jamieson, I., 1984. Education for enterprise'. In: Watts, A.G., Moran, P. (Eds.), CRAC. Ballinger, Cambridge, MA.

Jennings, J.E., Brush, C.G., 2013. Research on women entrepreneurs: challenges to (and from) the broader entrepreneurship literature? Acad. Manag. Ann. 7 (1), 663–715.

Jensen, M.C., Meckling, W.H., 1976. Theory of the firm: managerial behavior, agency costs and ownership structure. J. Fin. Econ. 3 (4), 305–360.

Johannisson, B., 1986. Network strategies: management technology for entrepreneurship and change. Int. Small Bus. J. 5 (1), 19–30.

Johannisson, B., 1988. Business formation: a network approach. Scand. J. Manag. 4 (3/4), 83–99.

Johannisson, B., 1998. Personal networks in emerging knowledge-based firms: spatial and functional patterns. Entrepr. Region. Devel. 10 (4), 297–312.

Johannisson, B., 2008. Bengt Johannisson's prize lecture: towards a practice theory of entrepreneuring. Int. Award Entrepr. Small Bus. Res. 1–12.

Johannisson, B., 2011. Towards a practice theory of entrepreneuring. Small Bus. Econ. 36 (2), 135–150.

Katsikis, I.N., Kyrgidou, L.P., 2007. The concept of sustainable entrepreneurship: a conceptual framework and empirical analysis. Acad. Manag. Proc. 1, 1–6.

Katz, J.A., 2003. The chronology and intellectual trajectory of American entrepreneurship education: 1876–1999. J. Bus. Ventur. 18 (2), 283–300.

Katz, J.A., Gartner, W., 1988. Properties of emerging organizations. Acad. Manag. Rev. 13 (3), 429–441.

Kilby, P., 1971. Hunting the Heffalump. In: Kilby, P. (Ed.), Entrepreneurship and Economic Development. The Free Press, New York.

Kirby, D.A., 2002. Entrepreneurship education: can business school meet the challenge?'. Paper presented at the ICSB World Conference, San Juan, Puerto Rico.

Kirzner, I.M., 1973. Competition and Entrepreneurship. University of Chicago Press, Chicago, IL.

Kirzner, I.M., 1997. Entrepreneurial discovery and the competitive market process: an Austrian approach. J. Econ. Lit. 35 (1), 60–85.

Klapper, R.G., Feather, D., Refai, D., Thompson, J., Fayolle, A., 2015. Special issue: innovative pedagogy in entrepreneurship: introduction. Ind. High. Educ. 29 (5), 321–325.

Klyver, K., Evald, M.R., Hindle, K., 2011. Social networks and new venture creation: the dark side of networks. In: Hindle, K., Kliver, K. (Eds.), Handbook of Research on New Venture Creation. Edward Elgar Publishing Ltd, Cheltenham, UK.

Knight, F.H., 1921. Risk, Uncertainty and Profit. Houghton Mifflin, Boston, MA.

Koh, H.C., 1996. Testing hypotheses of entrepreneurial characteristics: a study of Hong Kong MBA students. J. Manag. Psychol. 11 (3), 12–26.

Kotha, R., George, G., 2012. Friends, family, or fools: entrepreneur experience and its implications for equity distribution and resource mobilization. J. Bus. Ventur. 27 (5), 525–543.

Krueger, N.F., 2003. The cognitive psychology of entrepreneurship. In: Acs, Z.J., Audretsch, D.B. (Eds.), Handbook of Entrepreneurship Research. International Handbook Series on Entrepreneurship, vol. 1. Springer, Boston, MA, pp. 105−140.

Krueger Jr., N.F., Brazeal, D.V., 1994. Entrepreneurial potential and potential entrepreneurs. Entrepr.: Theory Pract. 18 (3), 91−104.

Kuckertz, A., Prochotta, A., 2018. What's hot in entrepreneurship research 2018? Hohenheim Entrepr. Res. Brief 4, 1−7.

Kuratko, D.F., 2005. The emergence of entrepreneurship education: development, trends, and challenges. Entrepr.: Theory Pract. 29 (5), 577−597.

Kuratko, D.F., Morris, M.H., 2018. Examining the future trajectory of entrepreneurship. J. Small Bus. Manag. 56 (1), 11−23.

Kuratko, D.F., Morris, M.H., Schindehutte, M., 2015. Understanding the dynamics of entrepreneurship through framework approaches. Small Bus. Econ. 45 (1), 1−13.

Kyvik, O., 2018. The global mindset: a must for international innovation and entrepreneurship. Int. Entrepr. Manag. J. 14 (2), 309−327.

Landström, H., Harirchi, G., 2018. That's interesting! in entrepreneurship research. J. Small Bus. Manag. Available from: https://doi.org/10.1111/jsbm.12500Online Version of Record.

Larson, A., Starr, J.A., 1993. A network model of organization formation. Entrepr.: Theory Pract. 17 (2), 5−15.

Leibenstein, H., 1978. General X-Efficiency Theory and Economic Development. Oxford University Press, New York.

Leibenstein, H., 1979. The general X-efficiency paradigm and the role of the entrepreneur. In: Rizzo, M.J. (Ed.), Time, Uncertainty, and Disequilibrium. D.C. Health, Lexington, MA.

Leitch, C., Harrison, R.T., 2008. Entrepreneurial learning: a review and research agenda'. In: Harrison, R.T., Leitch, C. (Eds.), Entrepreneurial Learning: Conceptual Frameworks and Applications. Routledge, London, UK.

Leland, H.E., Pile, D.H., 1977. Information asymmetries, financial structure, and financial intermediation. J. Fin. 32 (2), 371−387.

Levie, J., Autio, E., Acs, Z., Hart, M., 2014. Global entrepreneurship and institutions: an introduction. Small Bus. Econ. 42 (3), 437−444.

Low, M.B., MacMillan, I.C., 1988. Entrepreneurship: past research and future challenges. J. Manag. 14 (2), 139−162.

Lumpkin, G.T., Dess, G.G., 1996. Clarifying the entrepreneurial orientation construct and linking it to performance. Acad. Manag. Rev. 12 (1), 135−172.

Marshall, A., 1890. Principles of Economics. Macmillan, London, UK.

Matricano, D., 2014. Entrepreneurial Training: a comparative study across fifteen European countries. Ind. and Higher Edu. 28 (5), 311−330.

Matricano, D., 2015. Lo studio dell'imprenditorialità. Un approccio di indagine multidimensionale. Carocci, Roma, IT.

Matricano, D., 2016. Can policy makers improve the effectiveness of entrepreneurship training programmes? Evidence from Italy. Ind. and Higher Edu. 31 (1), 51−61.

Matricano, D., Sorrentino, M., 2018. Gender equalities in entrepreneurship: how close, or far, have we come in Italy? Int. J. Bus. Manag. 13 (3), 75−87.

Matricano D., Sorrentino M., 2019. Does love money affect vocational behavior? Empirical evidence from Italian entrepreneurs. Int. J. Bus. Manag. 14 (7), 110−123.

Matricano, D., Candelo, E., Sorrentino, M., Martinez-Martinez, A., 2019. Absorbing inbound knowledge within open innovation processes: the case of Fiat Chrysler automobiles. J. Knowledge Manag. 23 (4), 786−807.

McClelland, D.C., 1961. The Achieving Society. Van Nostrand, Princeton, NJ.

McGrath, R.G., 1999. Falling forward: real options reasoning and entrepreneurial failure. Acad. Manag. Rev. 24 (1), 13–30.

McGrath, R.G., Macmillan, I., 2000. The Entrepreneurial Mindset. Harvard Business School Press, Boston, MA.

McMullen, J.S., 2010. Perspective taking and the heterogeneity of the entrepreneurial imagination. In What Is so Austrian About Austrian Economics? Emerald Group Publishing Limited, pp. 113–143.

McMullen, J.S., Dimov, D., 2013. Time and the entrepreneurial journey: the problems and promise of studying entrepreneurship as a process. J. Manag. Studies 50, 1481–1512.

McMullen, J.S., Plummer, L.A., Acs, Z.J., 2007. What is an entrepreneurial opportunity? Small Bus. Econ. 28 (4), 273–283.

Meyer, G.D., Heppard, K.A., 2000. Entrepreneurship as Strategy: Competing on the Entrepreneurial Edge. Sage Publications, Thousand Oaks, CA.

Miles, M.P., Covin, J.G., 2002. Exploring the practice of corporate venturing: some common forms and their organizational implications. Entrepr.: Theory Pract. 26 (3), 21–40.

Miles, M.P., Arnold, D.R., Thompson, D.L., 1993. The interrelationship between environmental hostility and entrepreneurial orientation. J. Appl. Bus. Res. 9 (4), 12–24.

Minniti, M., 2010. Female entrepreneurship and economic activity. Eur.J. Devel. Res. 22 (3), 294–312.

Motomura, O., 2006. Sustainable Entrepreneurship. Amana-Key Development & Education, BrazilReport available at. Available from: www.amana-key.com.br.

Mueller, S.L., Thomas, A.S., 2001. Culture and entrepreneurial potential: a nine country study of locus of control and innovativeness. J. Bus. Ventur. 16 (1), 51–75.

Mullins, L.J., 2010. Management and Organizational Behaviour. Pearson Education Ltd, London.

Muñoz, P., Dimov, D., 2015. The call of the whole in understanding the development of sustainable ventures. J. Bus. Ventur. 30 (4), 632–654.

O'Gorman, C., Kautonen, M., 2004. Policies to promote new knowledge-intensive industrial agglomerations. Entrepr. Region. Devel.: Int. J. 16 (6), 459–479.

Oviatt, B.M., McDougall, P.P., 1995. Global start-ups: entrepreneurs on a worldwide stage. Acad. Manag. Persp. 9 (2), 30–43.

Parrish, B.D., 2010. Sustainability-driven entrepreneurship: principles of organization design. J. Bus. Ventur. 25 (5), 510–523.

Phan, P.H., Siegel, D.S., Wright, M., 2005. Science parks and incubators: observations, synthesis and future research. J. Bus. Ventur. 20 (2), 165–182.

Podolny, J.M., Baron, J.M., 1997. Resources and relationships: social networks and mobility in workplace. Am. Soc. Rev. 62 (5), 673–693.

Prandelli, E., Pasquini, M., Verona, G., 2016. In user's shoes: an experimental design on the role of perspective taking in discovering entrepreneurial opportunities. J. Bus. Ventur. 31 (3), 287–301.

Ratinho, T., Henriques, E., 2010. The role of science parks and business incubators in converging countries: evidence from Portugal. Technovation 30 (4), 278–290.

Rauch, A., Frese, M., 2007. Let's put the person back into entrepreneurship research: a meta-analysis on the relationship between business owners' personality traits, business creation, and success. Eur. J. Work Org Psychol. 16 (4), 353–385.

Reynolds, P.D., Hay, M., Camp, S.M., 1999. Global Entrepreneurship Monitor—Executive Report. Babson College, London, UK.

Reynolds, P.D., Camp, S.M., Bygrave, W.D., Autio, E., Hay, M., 2001. Global Entrepreneurship Monitor: Executive Report. Babson College, London, pp. 1−59, Business School and Kauffman Foundation, London, UK.

Reynolds, P.D., Bygrave, W.D., Autio, E., Cox, L.W., Hay, M., 2002. Global Entrepreneurship Monitor: Executive Report 2002. Babson College, London, pp. 1−47, Business School and Kauffman Foundation, London, UK.

Reynolds, P.D., Bygrave, W.D., Autio, E., 2003. Global Entrepreneurship Monitor— Executive Report. Babson College, London, UK.

Rosenberg, M., 1965. Society and Adolescent Self-Image. Princeton University, Princeton, NJ.

Sánchez, J.C., Carballo, T., Gutiérrez, A., 2011. The entrepreneur from a cognitive approach. Psicothema 23 (3), 433−438.

Sapienza, H.J., Korsgaard, M.A., 1996. Procedural justice in entrepreneur-investor relations. Acad. Manag. J. 39 (3), 544−574.

Say, J.B., 1803. A Treatise on Political Economy: Or, the Production, Distribution and Consumption of Wealth, 1964 ed. Augustus M, Kelley, New York.

Schaltegger, S., Wagner, M., 2011. Sustainable entrepreneurship and sustainability innovation: categories and interactions. Bus. Strat. Environ. 20 (4), 222−237.

Schumpeter, J.A., 1911. The Theory of Economic Development: An Inquiry Into Profits, Capital, Credit, Interest and Business Cycle, 1934 ed. Harvard University Press, Cambridge, MA.

Sciascia, S., De Vita, R., 2004. The Development of Entrepreneurship Research. Liuc Papers No. 146, Serie Economia Aziendale 19, 1−37.

Sciascia, S., Nordqvist, M., Mazzola, P., De Massis, A., 2015. Family ownership and R&D intensity in small and medium sized firms. J. Product Innov. Manag. 32 (3), 349−360.

Scott, J., 1991. Social Network Analysis: A Hanbook. Sage Publications, London, UK.

Shane, S., 2000. Prior knowledge and the discovery of entrepreneurial opportunities. Org. Sci. 11 (4), 448−469.

Shane, S., 2003. A General Theory of Entrepreneurship. The Individual-Opportunity Nexus. Edward Elgar Publishing, Cheltenham, UK.

Shane, S., Cable, D., 2002. Network ties, reputation, and the financing of new ventures. Manag. Sci. 48 (3), 364−381.

Shane, S., Venkataraman, S., 2000. The promise of entrepreneurship as a field of research. Acad. Manag. Rev. 25 (1), 217−226.

Shepherd, D.A., Krueger, N.F., 2002. An intentions−based model of entrepreneurial teams' social cognition. Entrepr.: Theory Pract. 27 (2), 167−185.

Shepherd, D.A., Patzelt, H., 2011. The new field of sustainable entrepreneurship: studying entrepreneurial action linking "what is to be sustained" with "what is to be developed.". Entrepr.: Theory Pract. 35 (1), 137−163.

Short, J.C., Ketchen Jr., D.J., McKenny, A.F., Allison, T.H., Ireland, R.D., 2017. Research on crowdfunding: reviewing the (very recent) past and celebrating the present. Entrepr.: Theory Pract. 41 (2), 149−160.

Sieger, P., Minola, T., 2017. The family's financial support as a "poisoned gift": a family embeddedness perspective on entrepreneurial intentions. J. Small Bus. Manag. 55 (S1), 179−204.

Simpeh, K.N., 2011. Entrepreneurship theories and empirical research: a summary review of the literature. Eur. J. Bus. Manag. 3 (6), 1−8.

Soto-Acosta, P., Cismaru, D.M., Vătămănescu, E.M., Ciochină, R.S., 2016. Sustainable entrepreneurship in SMEs: a business performance perspective. Sustainability 8 (4), 342−353.

Spence, M., Gherib, J.B.B., Biwolé, V.O., 2011. Sustainable entrepreneurship: is entrepreneurial will enough? A north–south comparison. J. Bus. Ethics 99 (3), 335–367.

Starr, J.A., MacMillan, I.C., 1990. Resource cooptation via social contracting: resource acquisition strategies for new ventures. Strat. Manag. J. 11 (1), 79–92.

Steier, L., Greenwood, R., 1995. Venture capitalist relationships in the deal structuring and post-investment stages of new firm creation. J. Manag. Stud. 32 (3), 337–357.

Steier, L., Greenwood, R., 2000. Entrepreneurship and the evolution of angel financial networks. Org. Stud. 21 (1), 163–192.

Timmons, J.A., 1978. Characteristics and role demands of entrepreneurship. Am. J. Small Bus. 3 (1), 5–17.

Tushman, M.L., Anderson, P., 1986. Technological discontinuities and organizational environments. Adm. Sci. Q. 31 (3), 439–465.

Ucbasaran, D., Westhead, P., Wright, M., 2001. The focus of entrepreneurial research: contextual and process issues. Entrepr.: Theory Pract. 25 (4), 57–80.

Uhlaner, L.M., Thurik, A.R., 2007. Post-materialism: a cultural factor influencing total entrepreneurial activity across nations. J. Evol. Econ. 17 (2), 161–185.

Urbano, D., Aparicio, S., Audretsch, D., 2018. Twenty-five years of research on institutions, entrepreneurship, and economic growth: what has been learned? Small Bus. Econ. Available from: https://doi.org/10.1007/s11187-018-0038-0.

Venkataraman, S., Sarasvathy, S.D., 2001. Strategy and entrepreneurship: outline of an untold story. In: Hitt, M., Freeman, E., Harrison, J. (Eds.), Handbook of Strategic Management. Blackwell Publishers, Oxford.

Verheul, I., Thurik, R., Hessels, J., Van der Zwan, P., 2010. Factors Influencing the Entrepreneurial Engagement of Opportunity and Necessity Entrepreneurs (EIM Research Reports, pp. 1–24).

Vesper, K.H., Gartner, W.B., 2001. Compendium for Entrepreneur Programs, University of South California, Lloyd Greif Centre for Educational Studies, Los Angeles.

Volkmann, C., 2004. Entrepreneurial studies in higher education: entrepreneurship studies an ascending academic discipline in the twenty-first century. Higher Educ. Eur. 29 (2), 177–185.

Waldinger, R., Aldrich, H., Ward, R., 1990. Ethnic Entrepreneurs: Immigrant Business in Industrial Societies. Sage Publishing, Newbury Park, CA.

Wallmeroth, J., Wirtz, P., Groh, A.P., 2018. Venture capital, angel financing, and crowdfunding of entrepreneurial ventures: a literature review. Found. Trends Entrepr. 14 (1), 1–129.

Warren, L., 2004. A systemic approach to entrepreneurial learning: an exploration using storytelling. Syst. Res. Behav. Sci. 21 (1), 3–16.

Welsh, J.A., White, J.F., 1981. Converging on characteristics of entrepreneurs. In: Vesper, K. H. (Ed.), Frontiers of Entrepreneurship Research. Babson College, Wellesley, MA.

Welter, F., 2011. Contextualizing entrepreneurship-conceptual challenges and ways forward. Entrepr.: Theory Pract. 35 (1), 165–184.

Welter, F., Baker, T., Audretsch, D.B., Gartner, W.B., 2017. Everyday entrepreneurship: a call for entrepreneurship research to embrace entrepreneurial diversity. Entrepr.: Theory Pract. 41 (3), 311–321.

Westhead, P., Wright, M., 2000. Introduction. In: Westhead, P., Wright, M. (Eds.), Advances in Entrepreneurship, vol. I. Edward Elgar Publishing, Aldershot.

Wiklund, J., Shepherd, D.A., 2003. Knowledge-based resources, entrepreneurial orientation, and the performance of small and medium-sized businesses. Strat. Manag. J. 24 (13), 1307–1314.

Williams Jr., R.I., Pieper, T.M., Kellermanns, F.W., Astrachan, J.H., 2018. Family firm goals and their effects on strategy, family and organization behavior: a review and research agenda. Int. J. Manag. Rev. 20 (S1), 63–82.

Wilson, K., 2004. Entrepreneurship education at European universities and business schools: results of a joint pilot survey'. Paper presented at the EISB/EFMD Conference in Turku, Finland.

Woo, C.Y., Daellenbach, U., Nicholls-Nixon, C., 1994. Theory building in the presence of 'randomness': the case of venture creation and performance. J. Manag. Studies 31 (4), 507–524.

Wu, C.W., Huarng, K.H., 2015. Global entrepreneurship and innovation in management. J. Bus. Res. 68 (4), 743–747.

Zahra, S.A., 1993. Environment, corporate entrepreneurship and financial performance: an exploratory study. J. Bus. Ventur. 8 (4), 259–285.

Zahra, S.A., Jennings, D.F., Kuratko, D.F., 1999. The antecedents and consequences of firm-level entrepreneurship: the state of the field. Entrepr.: Theory Pract. 24 (2), 45–63.

Zahra, S.A., Randerson, K., Fayolle, A., 2013. Corporate entrepreneurship: where are we? Where can we go from here? Management 16 (4), 357–361.

Zhang, Z., Zyphur, M.J., Narayanan, J., Arvey, R.D., Chaturvedi, S., Avolio, B.J., et al., 2009. The genetic basis of entrepreneurship: effects of gender and personality. Org. Behav. Human Dec. Process. 110 (2), 93–107.

Zott, C., Amit, R., 2007. Business model design and the performance of entrepreneurial firms. Org. Sci. 18 (2), 181–199.

Zott, C., Amit, R., 2010. Business model design: an activity system perspective. Long Range Plan. 43 (2–3), 216–226.

Zott, C., Amit, R., Massa, L., 2011. The business model: recent developments and future research. J. Manag. 37 (4), 1019–1042.

Further reading

Granovetter, M., 1985. Economic action and social structure: the problem of embeddedness. Am. J. Soc. 91 (3), 481–510.

OECD—Organization for Economic Co-operation and Development, 1960. Convention on the Organisation for Economic Co-operation and Development, 14 December, Paris.

The performance of entrepreneurial firms

2.1 Introduction

By the end of the 1980s, some entrepreneurship scholars (Schmitz, 1989; Nooteboom, 1994; Davidsson et al., 1998; Wennekers and Thurik, 1999; Audretsch and Thurik, 2000; Schuh and Triest, 2000; Audretsch and Thurik, 2001; Pagano and Schivardi, 2003; Braunerhjelm, 2010) started considering entrepreneurial (i.e., young and small) firms as the engines of economic growth.[1]

From a theoretical point of view, some scholars (Braunerhjelm, 2010; Hashi and Krasniqi, 2011) support the idea that the reason at the basis of this switch is the application of the *knowledge economy*[2] paradigm to entrepreneurship and the related *knowledge spillover effect*[3] (Acs et al., 1994; Simmie, 2002; Agarwal et al., 2007). As presented by Braunerhjelm (2010), thanks to certain contributions (Romer, 1986; Lucas, 1988), the endogenous process of knowledge creation (typical of the knowledge economy) tried to replace the exogenous one (typical of the neo-classical view).[4]

As a result of the *knowledge spillover effect*, entrepreneurial firms—which are, by definition, "flexible in the face of fluctuating demand and have the potential to

---

[1] As noted by several scholars (Blau, 1987; Wennekers and Thurik, 1999; Audretsch and Thurik, 2001; Grilo and Thurik, 2004), before the affirmation of entrepreneurial firms as the engine of economic growth, attention was mainly addressed toward big companies that undoubtedly drove economic growth worldwide.

[2] This paradigm focuses on the concept of knowledge that, by definition, is characterized by indivisibility, nonrivalry and nonexcludability. Indivisibility stands for the idea that it is not possible to determine costs and benefits linked to each phase of its production process. Nonrivalry, instead, means that who share knowledge still keeps it (differently from what happens with physical goods). Nonexcludability, eventually, means that subjects who did not contribute to its creation can use and exploit it as well. These knowledge characteristics are at the basis of *knowledge spillover effect*.

[3] *Knowledge spillover effect* can be defined as a positive externality (result or impact) that subjects—who are not involved in the knowledge creation process—can get. Put simply, even if subjects do not contribute to creation of new knowledge, they can get to know and use new knowledge since—by definition—it is indivisible, nonrival and nonexcludable. Over the years, scholars have developed the concept of knowledge spillover in reference to management studies (Arrow, 1962; Autio et al., 2004; Huber, 2011; Benassi and Landoni, 2019; Inoue et al., 2019). The reference of knowledge spillover to entrepreneurial firms is rather recent. In this vein, it is important to recall the contributions authored by Audretsch and Lehmann (2006), Audretsch et al. (2006), Audretsch and Keilbach (2007), Acs et al. (2009), Stough and Nijkamp (2009), Agarwal et al. (2010), Plummer and Acs (2014), and Braunerhjelm et al. (2018). In particular, Acs et al. (2013) explicitly talk about Knowledge Spillover Theory of Entrepreneurship—KSTE.

[4] Actually, Braunerhjelm (2010) underlines that a total replacement has never taken place. In reference to entrepreneurship, in fact, the knowledge creation process is still exogenous.

Entrepreneurship Trajectories. DOI: https://doi.org/10.1016/B978-0-12-818650-3.00002-7

act as vehicle for technological and organizational innovation and change" (Hashi and Krasniqi, 2011, p. 457)—could have some advantages in comparison to big companies (Bhidé, 2000; Casson, 2002a,b; Baumol, 2007). For example, they can easily differentiate their offerings, their marketing or placement strategies, and the way they are structured and managed (Baumol, 2004). The above-said is completely true for young firms and only partially true for small ventures (as time passes by, firms develop their routines[5] and so they become less flexible than before). However, generally speaking, entrepreneurial firms[6] can be thought of as being the opposite of big companies (i.e., established ventures).

From an empirical point of view, instead, the reason for this interest switch might be due to the huge contribution that these types of firms made to the US economy (Decker et al., 2016). The noticeable impact that entrepreneurial firms generated, both in terms of job creation and productivity growth, consolidated their relevance. [7]

Since the end of the 1980s and up until the present, the role that entrepreneurial firms have played in relation to economic growth has increased significantly and, thus, many scholars have tried to contribute to the analysis of this phenomenon (Ashcroft et al., 1991; Fritsch, 1997; Audretsch and Fritsch, 1999, 2003; Reynolds, 1999; Braunerhjelm, 2010). However, several aspects related to entrepreneurial firms and to the performance they can achieve need to be properly clarified.

2.2 Problems with prior research

The number of contributions focused on entrepreneurial firms makes the state-of-the-art of entrepreneurial literature such a mess and therefore it is worth proceeding in steps to try to shed some light on the conspicuous literature and get any advancement in an easier way. Accordingly, in the following subsections, attention is focused toward:

1. Defining entrepreneurial firms—Some scholars (Decker et al., 2014) underline the differences occurring between firms if they are evaluated in reference to their age or to their size;

---

[5] Management scholars have largely investigated the concept of routines. In particular, studies about this topic are rooted in the contributions authored by Teece and Pisano (1994) and Teece et al. (1997) and concerning dynamic capabilities. Through dynamic capabilities (Eisenhardt and Martin, 2000; Zollo and Winter, 2002; Winter, 2003; Huy and Zott, 2019), in fact, companies generate new organizational knowledge that is widespread under the shape of routines, that is, new sets of activities or new logics of organization. These routines (and the new knowledge at their basis) can be developed at a company, a group or an individual level.

[6] In reference to dynamic capabilities that entrepreneurial firms can develop, see the contributions authored by Zahra et al. (1999, 2006), Boccardelli and Magnusson (2006), and Teece (2012).

[7] Specific data disclosing the contribution that these firms made to US economy are included in the contributions authored by Decker et al. (2014, 2016).

2. Refining the concept of performance of entrepreneurial firms—The several proposals that have been advanced and shared by entrepreneurship scholars are cited in order to disclose the state-of-the-art of literature; and
3. Reviewing the factors that can affect the performance of entrepreneurial firms—Due to the many contributions proposed by entrepreneurship scholars, it is shown that a plethora of drivers are considered to be at the basis of performance.

2.2.1 Defining entrepreneurial firms

The first aspect that needs to be investigated and discussed deals with the type of ventures that we are going to consider. It is rather obvious that entrepreneurship scholars, policy makers, practitioners, data experts, and people interested in entrepreneurship define entrepreneurial firms in many different ways. Partly, the problem appears to depend on who is speaking about entrepreneurial firms and on the lenses used to observe and define them; partly, the problem also appears to depend on the fact that a clear definition, which can be shared—and hopefully accepted—by all who discuss these types of firms, is missing.

Over the years, several theoretical frameworks have been proposed to identify and investigate entrepreneurial firms (Gartner, 1985, 1988, 1990, 2001; Katz and Gartner, 1988; Gartner and Gatewood, 1992; Giunta, 1993; Buttà, 1995; Larson and Starr, 1993; Woo et al., 1994; Cooper, 1995; Ucbasaran et al., 2001; Sorrentino, 2003; Carlsson et al., 2013; Decker et al., 2014). The main problem, which clearly emerges from the above-cited contributions, concerns the definition of the adjective "entrepreneurial."

In this vein, Davidsson (2016) has recently offered a very interesting reflection about the concept of newness that characterizes entrepreneurship. First, the scholar underlines an existing overlap between entrepreneurship and small business research. This overlap wrongly assumes that entrepreneurial and small firms are under the same dynamics and that, consequently, they try to pursue the same aims (economic and social development). Over the years, empirical evidence has revealed that most small firms are neither innovative nor growth oriented, nor are they inclined to job creation surplus. Instead, these three characteristics are typical of young firms or startups.[8] At this stage, a preliminary and remarkable result consists of the difference between entrepreneurial firms (young firms or startups) and small businesses. However, this distinction might not be sufficient. Several types of entrepreneurial firms (startups or new firms) can come into existence and not all of them actually embody the main aspect of entrepreneurship, i.e. innovation.[9]

At this stage, two contributions need to be recalled and analyzed. The first one is authored by Sorrentino (2003), the second by Decker et al. (2014). Sorrentino

[8] Because of the differences between entrepreneurial and small firms, Davidsson (2016) invites to consider also the difference that passes between policies aiming to support entrepreneurship or small businesses. Because of the different characteristics of their aims, policy makers should define and implement dedicated tools able to support each of them.
[9] See paragraph 1.3 from which the main role of innovation that—in the shape of entrepreneurial opportunities—lies at the basis of entrepreneurship has been derived.

(2003) proposes a very detailed classification of new firms in order to outline which of them can be defined as entrepreneurial. The scholar considers two variables. The former is newness and is meant in an objective way. Newness of firms means that other firms have never carried out the same core activity before. The latter is independence of leadership. This means that new firms can define their strategies autonomously, without any interference by other subjects who are somehow related to them.

By mixing the above two variables (classified according to a high or low level of newness and/or independence of leadership), Sorrentino (2003) argues that entrepreneurial firms are characterized by a high level of newness, which implies that no other firms have carried out the same core activity before, and by a high level of leadership independence, indicating there is no interference by other subjects related to a new firm.

Due to these characteristics, the entrepreneurial firms defined by Sorrentino (2003) differ from those that can result from corporate venturing activities or corporate spin-offs. The latter are characterized by a high level of newness, which implies that no other firms have carried out the same core activity before, and by a low level of leadership independence, as they are the result of corporate venturing activities or represent a corporate spin-off, thus necessarily undergoing an interference by the company from which they derive.

Entrepreneurial firms also differ from those that represent cases of subdivisions or externalizations (outsourcing). Very often, in fact, already existing firms create this type of new firms to improve their own flexibility and efficiency (Sorrentino, 2003, p. 19); however, these firms are certainly not entrepreneurial in a proper way. They are characterized by a low level of newness, resulting from the fact that other firms have already carried out the same core activity before, and by a low level of leadership independence, as their choices depend on the already existing firms creating them.

Eventually, entrepreneurial firms are also different from those that are acquired or inherited. Such firms are characterized by a low level of newness, as their core activities were already carried out prior to their acquisition or inheritance, and by a high level of leadership independence, considering there is no interference by other subjects related to the new firm since new top managers are established.

Thus, the contribution authored by Sorrentino (2003) really helps to define entrepreneurial firms and to differentiate them from other new firms generally understood. Some years later, Decker et al. (2014, p. 5) propose another contribution that aims to classify entrepreneurial firms. According to these scholars, it is appropriate to distinguish between true startups, new establishment of existing businesses, and new firms. Neither new establishment of existing businesses nor new firms—since they are not expressions of entrepreneurship[10]—should be considered when investigating what proper entrepreneurship is.

---

[10] In their contribution, Decker et al. (2016, p. 5) write: "new establishment of firms can take many forms, including simply replacing outdated existing establishments, thus new establishment often do not conform to standard notions of entrepreneurial behavior. For this reason, entrepreneurial research should focus on startups and young firms. It should exclude new businesses emerging from reorganizations such mergers and acquisitions."

Table 2.1 A comparison between new businesses, entrepreneurial firms, and small businesses.

New businesses...	True startups/ entrepreneurial firms...	Small businesses...
... can be formally new but can also carry out already-known activities	... are new and innovative.	... are innovative firms that can be new or already active on the market

Source: Personal elaboration.

From the above-described contributions (Sorrentino, 2003; Decker et al., 2014; Davidsson, 2016), it clearly emerges that entrepreneurial firms are not necessarily small businesses (Davidsson, 2016). Entrepreneurial firms are strongly characterized by innovation (Sorrentino, 2003; Decker et al., 2014) and, thus, they differ from new businesses that could formally be new but, in fact, carry out already implemented activities. In accordance with this, the present volume pays attention to entrepreneurial firms as understood by their proper definition. As such, they need to be both new and innovative (see Table 2.1).

2.2.2 Refining the concept of performance achieved by entrepreneurial firms

The investigation of the performance that entrepreneurial firms (new and innovative ones) can achieve is not easy for two main reasons. The first reason is theoretical. Entrepreneurship scholars, approaching the theme of performance, have adopted different theoretical frameworks rooted in the Resource-Based View, the Industrial Organization Theory, the Evolutionary Economic Perspective, the Transaction Costs Theory, and so on. Due to these different economic backgrounds, entrepreneurship scholars have been able to disclose intriguing results about the performance achieved by new and innovative firms even if, in some cases, soft contradictions or clearly contrasting results have emerged. Of course, the reference to different backgrounds cannot be questioned and, hence, all the results—even if contrasting—need to be taken into consideration.

The second reason why it is not easy to conduct the investigation of the performance achieved by new and innovative firms is empirical and needs to be examined from two different points of view that are strictly connected. The first deals with the heterogeneous nature of the concept (Birley and Westhead, 1990; Murphy et al., 1996; Delmar et al., 2003; OECD, 2008; Braunerhjelm, 2010; Henrekson and Johansson, 2010). By definition, performance is the result of different factors and, therefore, all of them should be considered in its investigation. When using a simple measure of performance, scholars seem to be either missing or ignoring the nature of the investigated phenomenon. The second point is related to the first one. When using a simple measure of performance, results can vary consistently and comparisons cannot be carried out (Brush and Vanderwerf, 1992; Chandler and Jansen, 1992).

The above confirms that both theoretical and empirical aspects make the study of the performance achieved by new and innovative firms a very difficult task. At a tall order, which does not refer to a specific theoretical background and considers multiple measures of performance, performance can be understood in different ways.[11]

For instance, OECD (2008) explicitly lists the core indicators of entrepreneurial performance. These indicators are divided into three particular groups: firm-based, employment-based, and other. The first group (firm-based indicators) includes employer firm birth and death rates, business churn, and survival rates. The second group (employment-based indicators) includes rate of employment, ownership rate of start-ups, and employment in 3- and 5-year old firms. The third group (other indicators) includes growth rate by turnover, value added, productivity, and innovation performance. It could be argued that the third group of indicators does not help in figuring out a precise set of indicators, making the adoption of this classification potentially risky for research proceedings.

According to Audretsch (2003), instead, performance of entrepreneurial firms can be understood as:

1. Innovation;
2. Economic growth (job and wealth creation); and
3. Growth of firms.

At this time, some reflections about the three ways of understanding entrepreneurial performance are appropriate in order to redefine the concept of performance. According to Audretsch (2003), some scholars—adopting a geographical approach—can understand performance of entrepreneurial firms as the rate of innovation that a region or a country can disclose.[12] However, since it is assumed that innovation is at the basis of entrepreneurship, it is not possible to imagine that it can also be at the output (performance) of entrepreneurship as well. Thus, for the present study, innovation can be excluded as a measure of the performance achieved by entrepreneurial firms.

Economic growth (i.e., job and wealth creation) is another indicator that scholars recall (Robson and Bennett, 2000; Wong et al., 2005; Valliere and Peterson, 2009; Braunerhjelm, 2010; Haltiwanger et al., 2013; Decker et al., 2014, 2016) in order to evaluate the performance of entrepreneurial firms. In reference to economic growth, it is appropriate to distinguish between job and wealth creation and analyze each separately.

---

[11] Murphy et al. (1996) present the result of a content analysis referred to articles (published between 1987 and 1993) that investigate the performance of entrepreneurial firms through an empirical research. From their contributions it emerges that entrepreneurial performance can be meant as efficiency, growth, profit, size, liquidity, success/failure, market share, and leverage. Despite achieved results, the contribution is recalled to show that uncertainty about the way of meaning performance is not new in entrepreneurial studies.

[12] See also: Acs et al. (1994); Audretsch (1995, 2003); Audretsch and Feldman (1996).

Despite the undeniable interest in job creation (Birch, 1979; Storey, 1991; Fritsch, 1997; Reynolds, 1999; Armington and Acs, 2004; Anyadike-Danes et al., 2015) and the contributions that confirm the positive impact entrepreneurial firms can have on employment rates (Acs and Armington, 2002; Fritsch and Mueller, 2004; van Stel and Storey, 2004; Baptista et al., 2008; Van Stel and Suddle, 2008; Glaeser and Kerr, 2009), some scholars have carefully collected and analyzed the empirical data about the impact entrepreneurial firms can have on job creation. As a matter of fact, statistical results seem to disprove the positive impact that scholars usually share.

Karahan et al. (2015), for example, rebuild the evolution of labor force (i.e., job creation) generated by startups in the United States. These scholars strongly point out that job creation reached its peak in the late 1970s, subsequently declining continuously for, nearly, the next 30 years.[13] On the strength of empirical data, Karahan et al. (2015) invite others to be cautious when asserting that entrepreneurial firms do contribute to job creation.

Some years later, Decker et al. (2016) share this view as well. After rebuilding specific dynamics of the United States market, taking place in some industries since the year 2000, these scholars call for being careful when proclaiming that entrepreneurial firms can favor job creation, as this might not be true. In this respect, Audretsch and Fritsch (2003)—who investigate the impact entrepreneurial firms can have on the labor market in Germany and compare it with that of the United States—also share the above views (Karahan et al., 2015; Decker et al., 2016) but reach different results. German entrepreneurial startups do not affect job creation in a consistent, positive way. For this reason, they ask for the consideration of long-term results that seem to be more positive than expected.

Of course, it is important to consider some aspects that can partly explain the above result. One such aspect might be related to the innovative industries in which entrepreneurial firms are found and in which new technologies and automation of processes can have a negative effect on the labor force (Acs and Armington, 2002). Another might be linked to a firm's life cycle (Fritsch and Mueller, 2004). Yet another aspect might be related to cultural aspects (Wiklund, 1998; Andersson and Delmar, 2000). For example, entrepreneurial firms in Europe could employ one or two persons, while entrepreneurial firms in United States employ noticeably more persons.

In contrast to the vague results achieved in reference to job creation, the idea that entrepreneurial firms generate a positive effect on wealth creation is confirmed (Utterback et al., 1988; Acs and Audretsch, 1990; Robson and Bennett, 2000; Audretsch, 2002, 2004; Baumol, 2002; Carree et al., 2002; Armington and Acs, 2004; Heirman and Clarysse, 2004; Klapper et al., 2006; Braunerhjelm et al., 2010). Even if wealth creation can be defined and measured in many different ways (such as growth at country level, regional prosperity, index of

---

[13] More precisely, in their study, Karahan et al. (2015) analyse data referring to the United States labor market, over the time span 1979–2007.

productivity), the abovementioned scholars largely agree on the above-cited relationship.[14]

In fact, from empirical data about innovative startups in Italy, a different—contrasting—result comes out (Matricano, 2018). Italian innovative startups actually contribute to job creation but do not create wealth. The reason for this seems to lie in the parameters indicated by the Italian government in order to classify innovative startups as such. These new firms need to invest in R&D activities, assume skilled employees, and hold a patent. The fact that assuming skilled employees is a requisite for classification as an innovative startup has increased job creation; however, innovative startups are not obtaining positive economic results and are, consequently, not contributing to wealth creation.

Despite the relevance that both of the above measures have assumed in reference to entrepreneurship and to the debate about their effective impact, what needs to be underlined here is that job and wealth creation are expressions of economic growth that are generally included in the field of macroeconomics rather than in the field of management. Thus, since they do not fit with the final aim of the present study —that is, to describe entrepreneurship trajectories—attention is moved toward the performance of entrepreneurial firms understood herein as the growth or survival of entrepreneurial firms.

In order to define the meaning of growth in more detail (the third bullet point cited before), an interesting contribution authored by Kemp and Verhoeven (2002) is recalled. These scholars, from an extensive literature review, disclose four research streams focused on growth. The first concerns the effect of an entrepreneurial firm on the economy—specific measures, like Gross National Product (GNP) and employment are considered. The second research stream takes, in the view of Kemp and Verhoeven (2002), a microeconomic perspective. In this case, scholars interested in entrepreneurial growth have paid attention to the "black-box" of firms by trying to investigate their productivity (how resources are managed). The third stream, instead, is focused on entrepreneurial growth as a strategy. Kemp and Verhoeven (2002) clarify what they mean by arguing that interest is focused on the way growth is achieved (market penetration, development, diversification, dimensional growth, acquisition of or cooperation with other firms). The fourth and last research stream looks at the factors that affect a startup's creation and growth.

At this point, a brief comment is necessary. The first research stream falls in the field of macroeconomics rather than management and is, therefore, not included (see also Santarelli and Vivarelli, 2006). The fourth research stream is interesting but only after defining the way in which growth is understood. Thus, it could be argued that both the second and third research streams offer results that are promising for the present study. However, the focus on the "black-box" does not lead to

---

[14] In reference to this, entrepreneurship scholars face some difficulties in identifying and removing external variables that can generate distortive effects on the relationship between entrepreneurial firms and wealth creation.

Table 2.2 Ways of understanding performance of entrepreneurial firms.

Innovation	Economic growth	Growth of firms
According to a geographical approach, the rate of innovation that a region or a country can disclose can be understood as the performance of entrepreneurial firms By assuming that innovation is at the basis of entrepreneurship, this view does not seem very fruitful	Job and wealth creation seem to fall within the field of macroeconomics rather than management. Despite their unquestionable relevance, they are not considered to be indicators of the performance of entrepreneurial firms in the present volume	The view of growth as a strategy that entrepreneurial firms can pursue is embraced in the present study even if some aspects need to be more properly specified

Source: Personal elaboration.

general results because each firm manages its resources in a different way, thus generating different routines for maximizing productivity. Consequently, by exclusion, the view of growth as a strategy to pursue (Fombrun and Wally, 1989; Barnett and Burgelman, 1996; Moreno and Casillas, 2008; Achtenhagen et al., 2010; Coad et al., 2016; Matricano, 2018; Rasmussen et al., 2018) is the one embraced in the present study (see Table 2.2).

Obviously, the above result is partial. Thus far, we have been able to restrict the area of research by excluding some ways of understanding entrepreneurial performance, which either fall in the field of macroeconomics or concern the "black-box," but we still need to proceed with more in-depth investigations to further clarify the direction along which firms can grow.

These choices—oriented toward market penetration, development, diversification, dimensional growth, and acquisition of or cooperation with other firms—cannot be judged as either right or wrong. Each firm can decide its own growth direction (Heshmati, 2001; Garnsey et al., 2006; Hamilton, 2012; Coad et al., 2013).

Critically, even if we assume that each firm can decide its own growth direction, Kemp and Verhoeven (2002)—recalling several contributions on this topic—underline that the choice depends "on an inside-out or outside-in perspective" (Kemp and Verhoeven, 2002, p. 14). For the inside-out perspective, the choice depends on internal factors (competences or resources), while the choice depends on external factors (the environment and the customers) for the outside-in perspective. If so, then the main factors that can affect the growth of entrepreneurial firms need to be reviewed.[15]

---

[15] It is important to notice that this is the fourth stream of research that Kemp and Verhoeven (2002) have derived from their review.

2.2.3   Reviewing the factors that can affect the growth of entrepreneurial firms

Several entrepreneurship scholars have focused their attention on the drivers that can affect the growth of entrepreneurial firms[16] (Katz, 1993; Westhead and Birley, 1995; Johnson et al., 1999; Robson and Bennett, 2000; Sorrentino, 2003; Parente, 2004; Aghion et al., 2007; Brush et al., 2009; Hashi and Krasniqi, 2011; Decker et al., 2014, 2016). The assumption at the basis of the above contributions is that such firms exploit innovation and are, consequently, expected to achieve superior performances.

For instance, Katz (1993) authored one of the most well-known contributions that investigates this topic. According to this scholar, firms hold specific bundles of resources (human, social, physical, organizational, and financial) that they can use as leverage to develop their capabilities.[17] If entrepreneurs can manage this process properly, then they can achieve better performances. Katz (1993) focuses his attention on the importance of combining different resources rather than on the specification of the resources to be considered.

As time passed by, entrepreneurship scholars changed their approach and began listing the possible factors that can affect the performance of entrepreneurial firms. Aghion et al. (2007), for example, find that institutional and policy factors, which can affect the performance of entrepreneurial firms, play a noticeable role. In particular, these scholars invite other researchers not to underestimate the relevance that adjustment costs,[18] administrative costs, labor market regulations, and credit access can assume. The above analysis—which recalls some factors that significantly affect the performance of entrepreneurial firms—is limited to financial aspects and needs to be enlarged.

Brush et al. (2009) enrich this analysis by focusing their attention on three factors that can influence performance: management, marketing, and money. According to them, individual intentions (developed during the start-up phase), stimulation of market demand (since the establishment of the new business), and access to capital (which is very critical in the start-up phase when entrepreneurial firms have no reputation to leverage in order to be financed) seem to exert a relevant impact on the growth of entrepreneurial firms.

Hashi and Krasniqi (2011), after carrying out an extensive review of dedicated literature, identify three groups of variables that can affect the performance of entrepreneurial firms. These three groups concern the entrepreneurs and their innovative capabilities, the main characteristics of the firms (size, age, human capital, and networking capabilities), and some external factors (related to the market,

---

[16] As a matter of fact, entrepreneurship scholars did not investigate this topic in the past. The performance of entrepreneurial firms, in fact, was one of themes characterizing the studied of industrial demography (comparing birth and death rate of entrepreneurial firms). See the contribution authored by Sorrentino (2003).

[17] It is clear the reference to Penrose (1959) and to the theory of growth of firms.

[18] Aghion et al. (2007, p. 734) specify that adjustment costs are "induced by the R&D and/or advertising of incumbent firms."

financial resources, and institutional aspects). In particular, in reference to entrepreneurs and their capabilities, Hashi and Krasniqi (2011, p. 457) highlight the difference between low-level and high-level entrepreneurs. Low-level entrepreneurs—who recall the Kirznerian view of entrepreneurship—are like traders who offer new products and services to customers. On the contrary, high-level entrepreneurs—who recall the Schumpeterian view of entrepreneurship—are more than traders; they aim to introduce innovations in the market.

Another factor that can affect growth of entrepreneurial firms is external support (Westhead and Birley, 1995; Johnson et al., 1999; Robson and Bennett, 2000). Both formal (obtained from banks, lawyers, and government-backed institutions) and informal means of support (obtained from family, relatives, and suppliers) are expected to have a positive impact on the growth of entrepreneurial firms.

As already mentioned, the assumption at the basis of the above contributions is that entrepreneurial firms are expected to achieve superior performances. However, contrary to these expectations, empirical evidence discloses that entrepreneurial firms can also fail (Altman, 1983; Cressy, 2006; Li et al., 2010; Delmar et al., 2013. Decker et al., 2014; Khelil, 2016). Consequently, any trial aiming to predict growth of entrepreneurial firms discloses limited usefulness. From the above review, in fact, it is rather clear that it is not possible to generalize any causal relationship between a specific factor (or a limited group of factors[19]) and growth. Even if several scholars have already noted this result (Delmar, 1997; Delmar and Davidsson, 1998; Birley and Westhead, 1990), the fact that no noticeable step forward has been taken after 20 years of research is quite remarkable (see also: Braunerhjelm, 2010; McKelvie and Wiklund, 2010; Daunfeldt and Halvarsson, 2015; Lee et al., 2016).

2.3 A pragmatic approach to the performance of entrepreneurial firms

The focus on the performance of entrepreneurial firms (understood as growth) and on the review of the factors that can affect it make the undertaking of this study difficult and challenging. In fact, as can be seen from the above-presented review, it appears that much of the debate is developed at a theoretical level. Even if most contributions about the growth of firms leverage empirical data to test probable relationships between the growth drivers and expected outcomes, the definitions, critiques, and clarifications make the debate speculative and, sometimes, far from factual. The reference to specific samples of firms, acting in particular industries and located in certain regions or countries, make it difficult to provide a generalized view of the growth of entrepreneurial firms.

---

[19] Despite the conspicuous amount of contributions proposed in reference to this topic, the categorization proposed by Bouchikhi (1993) and referring to endogenous and exogenous factors in order to create an inclusive framework still seems to be useful.

For the above reasons, at this stage, instead of presenting additional theoretical reflections about what is more or less appropriate for defining the performance of entrepreneurial firms (aiming to propose a new theoretical contribution) and the possible drivers affecting it, a different approach—which can be defined as pragmatic—is adopted.

It is hoped that new insights about the performance of entrepreneurial firms can be derived from a careful reading of the empirical data retrieved from some of the most important entrepreneurial firm databases worldwide.

2.3.1 A review of the official reports on the performances of entrepreneurial firms

In order to follow a pragmatic approach for the study of the performance of entrepreneurial firms—which, hopefully, can lead to generalized results—some official sources of data have been consulted. The aim here does not consist of reporting official data or building statistical models that leverage on them. The reading and analysis of the official data are carried out in order to try to obtain some insights about the performance of entrepreneurial firms that might not have been disclosed before.

The pragmatic approach consists of searching for the performances of entrepreneurial firms in different countries in order to find out if and how this topic is investigated.

At the start, attention is turned toward the phenomenon of entrepreneurship in the US economy. The US Department of Labor publishes data from the Business Employment Dynamics—BED program,[20] a specific program of the US Bureau of Labor Statistics that is focused on young and small businesses.

The official report is divided into four main areas[21] covering:

1. Business establishment age;
2. Establishment survival;
3. Establishment births and deaths; and
4. Firm size.

With respect to business establishment age, the report provides information about new businesses "born" each year and about their associated rates of employment (data are available since 1994). In terms of establishment survival, the report reveals how many firms survive from year to year (in this case, data are also available since 1994). By counting the establishment births and deaths, the official report discloses the number of firms created and closed each year (data are available since 1993). The last report area deals with firm size and data analyze whether firms expand in terms of employment (in this case, data are also available since 1993).

[20] The link to the website is https://www.bls.gov/bdm/.
[21] The link to access these data is https://www.bls.gov/bdm/entrepreneurship/entrepreneurship.htm.

The Government of Canada offers a similar report[22] that is developed by Statistics Canada in collaboration with the Small Business Branch (SBB) of the Innovation, Science and Economic Development Canada (ISED) governmental department. This report is divided into two main areas, dealing with:

1. Firm birth and survival rates; and
2. Job creation and employment.

In the first section, the overall performance of Canadian firms is reported. In particular, data deal with firm births and new firm survival rates. Relevance of this topic is confirmed by a previous report[23] sponsored by the Government of Canada and titled "The State of Entrepreneurship in Canada." Here, the section dealing with an overview of Canada's entrepreneurial performance comprehends four subsections, each dealing with: (a) birth and death rates, (b) survival rates, (c) high-growth firms and gazelles, and (d) R&D expenditures, respectively.

For Europe, empirical data are retrieved from the Eurostat website.[24] Eurostat manages the official statistical data for the EU on several topics. In particular, in terms of the present study, it is possible to find an interesting report titled "Business Demography Statistics" that develops two interesting sections. The first deals with main statistical findings and, in turn, includes four subsections dealing with (a) active enterprises, (b) birth rates, (c) death rates, and (d) enterprise survival rates, respectively. The second deals with high-growth enterprises.

Inside Europe, the Enterprise Research Centre in the United Kingdom – U.K. publishes a report titled "State of Small Business Britain Report"[25] from which relevant information about entrepreneurial firms in U.K. can be derived. In particular, beyond definitions and theoretical aspects, this report also discloses some metrics about the growth of startups (this section analyzes the number of start-ups that do not fail in the first 3 years and that begin the process of initial scaling), the growth of existing businesses (this section deals with the stepping-up of firms created more than 3 years before), high-growth firms, small high-growth firms, and productivity growth. With respect to Italy, instead, some dedicated reports published by Infocamere[26] (the official association of the Italian Chambers of Commerce) deal with entrepreneurial ventures. In the official press releases, the main data presented deal with firms that are active on the market and with birth and death rates (by industry and by region).

At this stage, it is also interesting to mention and analyze the report published by the Organization for Economic Co-operation and Development (OECD). In this report, which was published at the end of 2018 and titled "Entrepreneurship at a glance. Highlights 2018,"[27] the main topics that are investigated deal with new

---

[22] The report can be retrieved from https://www.ic.gc.ca/eic/site/061.nsf/eng/h_03075.html#ex-sum.

[23] The link to the report is https://www.ic.gc.ca/eic/site/061.nsf/eng/h_rd02468.html.

[24] The link to the website is https://www.eui.eu/.

[25] The report can be retrieved from https://www.enterpriseresearch.ac.uk/wp-content/uploads/2018/06/SSBB-Report-2018-final.pdf.

[26] The reports can be retrieved from http://www.infocamere.it/comunicati-stampa.

[27] The report is available at https://www.oecd.org/sdd/business-stats/EAG-2018-Highlights.pdf.

enterprise creations, bankruptcies, job creation by new enterprises, enterprises by size, employment and value added by enterprise size, small and medium enterprises and international trade, compensation of employees by enterprise size, labor productivity and enterprise size, entrepreneurial finance and motivation to set up a business, and venture capital investments.

All the main topics investigated in the official reports published by the above-mentioned governmental or statistical organizations are summarized in Table 2.3.

2.3.2 Discussion about the performances of entrepreneurial firms

The above-cited official reports, whether published by governmental or statistical organizations, can really help to define the performance of entrepreneurial firms that, in relation to present research, stands for the aim of trajectories drawn by entrepreneurs.

Beyond the analysis of data (referring to historical series, measuring the increases/decreases of values, highlighting the gap that can emerge, commenting on the achievable/achieved results, and hypothesizing cause/effect relationships), the official reports and the main topics of interest included inside them (see Table 2.3) can be read at a taller order that does not deal with numbers and percentages but concerns the outputs, the labels, and/or the nomenclature used. From a joint reading of all the reports, it is possible to derive some clear reflections.

Officers interested in entrepreneurial firms pay attention to their birth and death rates. Such analysis gives them an idea of the economic setting (whether it is vibrant and thus new entrepreneurial firms are created, whether it is competitive and thus entrepreneurial firms might fail, whether entrepreneurs are involved and result-oriented or not[28]), while it also provides them with intriguing information about the dynamics that take place in the market at the same time. By comparing the birth and death rates of firms, it is possible to infer the number of startups that survive and that are active on the market (as this is made clear in the report published by Eurostat).

This piece of data seems to be underestimated by entrepreneurship scholars who, as already noted before,[29] are mainly interested in the performance understood as growth and in the factors driving it instead. It is in reference to this last point that

---

[28] Decker et al. (2016) link the results that entrepreneurial firms can achieve to different kinds of entrepreneurs. In particular, they distinguish between subsistence and transformational entrepreneurs. In their view, subsistence entrepreneurs launch a new firm with scarce or even no expectation to get superior performances. More precisely, "subsistence entrepreneurs are small businesses created out of necessity or choice for the entrepreneurs to provide income for themselves and perhaps a few others (in many cases, family members)" (Decker et al., 2016, p. 6). Transformational entrepreneurs, instead, launch new firms with the intention to innovate and grow. Of course, not all the transformational entrepreneurs are likely to succeed in the marketplace (by generating income and work). Thus, in reference to the performances that can be achieved, entrepreneurial firms can show high-growth rates, if entrepreneurs are transformational and they succeed. Other firms can remain active in the marketplace without growing (if subsistence entrepreneurs manage them or if transformational entrepreneurs manage them but they do not succeed). Eventually, firms can fail.

[29] See Section 2.2.3.

Table 2.3 The results emerging from a pragmatic reading of official reports about the performance of entrepreneurial firms.

Country	Source	Topics/Contents
United States	Business Employment Dynamics (BED) program of the Bureau of Labor Statistics (BLS) (www.bls.gov/bdm/ entrepreneurship)	Entrepreneurship and the US Economy 1. Business establishment age 2. Establishment survival 3. Establishment births and deaths 4. Firm size
Canada	Government of Canada (www.ic.gc.ca)	Canadian New Firms: Birth and Survival Rates 1. Firm birth and survival rates: • Overall Performance (this section includes "firm births" and "new firm survival rates")
	Government of Canada (www.ic.gc.ca)	The State of Entrepreneurship in Canada 1. An overview of Canada's entrepreneurial performance: • Birth and death rates • Survival rates • High-growth firms and gazelles • R&D expenditures
Europe	Eurostat (www.ec.europa.eu/eurostat)	Business Demography Statistics 1. Main statistics findings: • Active enterprises in the business economy • Birth rates • Death rates • Enterprise survival rates 2. High-growth enterprises
U.K.	Enterprise Research Centre (www.enterpriseresearch.ac.uk)	State of Small Business Britain Report
Italy	Infocamere (www.infocamere.it)	Press releases: 1. Active firms on the market 2. Birth and death rates (by industry and by region)
Several countries	Organization for Economic Cooperation and Development (OECD) (https://www.oecd.org)	Entrepreneurship at a glance. 2018 Highlights: 1. New enterprise creations 2. Bankruptcies

Source: Personal elaboration.

the official reports analyzed above appear to disclose something even more intriguing. Performance (understood as growth) is not the only issue on which the policy makers, officers, and statisticians focus their attention. Actually, only some reports focus their attention on high-growth firms and gazelles, such as the above-cited report "The State of Entrepreneurship in Canada" or the initial scaling and stepping-up phases analyzed in the report about the U.K. firms.

Of course, this does not mean that high-growth entrepreneurial firms are not important. They stand for a consistent group of firms that follows peculiar dynamics when it is on the market. However, they seem to suggest a wider approach for the data about entrepreneurial startups.

The policy makers, officers, and statisticians interested in startups, in fact, underline that entrepreneurial firms can survive or be active, grow (especially with intensive rates), or fail. Thus, the alternatives to pursue are not dichotomous—the so-called "up or out dynamic" (Haltiwanger et al., 2013; Decker et al., 2014). There are several alternatives to consider: growing, remaining active, or failing.

2.4   Possible outputs of entrepreneurship trajectories

The alternatives proposed above (growing, remaining active, or failing) seem to represent, in a clearer way, the output of entrepreneurial trajectories; hence, attention is going to be focused on each of them.

Both academic research and pragmatic evidence highlight the relevance of firm growth as the main output of entrepreneurship (Davidsson, 1991; Garnsey et al., 2006; Lasch et al., 2007). However, with regards to entrepreneurial firms being properly understood, the concept is taken to the extreme so that, instead of addressing growth, attention is focused toward high-growth (Delmar et al., 2003; Friar and Meyer, 2003; Wong et al., 2005; Davila et al., 2010; Dillen et al., 2019). For this reason, scholars label these ventures as gazelles (Birch and Medoff, 1994; Birch et al., 1995; Henrekson and Johansson, 2010; Parker et al., 2010; Colombelli et al., 2013; Dillen et al., 2019). Obviously, this seems to happen mainly because true startups (entrepreneurial firms properly understood) are new and innovative (Sorrentino, 2003; Decker et al., 2014).

At this stage, it is interesting to provide as clear an explanation of high-growth of entrepreneurial firms as possible. Even if most scholars define high-growth rates of true startups in terms of employees[30] (however, this view is not recalled here

---

[30] It is possible to cite several contributions that define gazelles in reference to job creation: Birch (1981); Birch and Medoff (1994); Birch et al. (1995); Stam (2005); Acs and Mueller (2008); Henrekson and Johansson (2010); Bos and Stam (2013). All the above-cited scholars agree on the assumption that firms can be defined gazelles if they generate at least 20 jobs over a time span ranging from 5 to 10 years.
Decker et al. (2014, pp. 8−9) offer an alternative view and so they define high-growth firms as firms expanding their employment by more than 25% per year.
In this vein, it is worth citing the contribution authored by Acs and Mueller (2008) who propose a categorization based on the number of employees and distinguishing between "mice," small firms with less than 20 employees, "elephants," large firms with more than 500 employees, and "gazelles," the residual category.

because it falls within the macroeconomic impact[31]), there are other scholars who define them in reference to revenue growth (this is the view embraced in this study). Among these scholars, it is worth citing Barringer et al. (2005) who catalog firms as highly-growing only if they show a 3-year compound annual sales growth rate of 80% or above. Birch and Medoff (1994), instead, argue that gazelles are only those firms that continuously show annual sales growth rates of at least 20% over a 4-year period and exceed $100,000 in revenues per year. Furthermore, Autio et al. (2000) argue that gazelles are those firms that increase their sales by at least 50% over three consecutive financial years.

Despite the differences in the growth rates themselves, what matters is the consistent growth that these entrepreneurial firms disclose[32] and that, undoubtedly, make them different from other firms.

On the contrary, entrepreneurial firms can also fail (Smalibone, 1990; Singh et al., 2007; Cardon et al., 2011; Ucbasaran et al., 2013; Olaison and Meier Sørensen, 2014). In this case, even if entrepreneurship scholars have largely investigated this concept (the concept of the liability of newness[33] is widely known), some specifications are necessary before proceeding.

Initially, attention needs to be given to a very important aspect that Beaver (2003) invites us to consider—the proper understanding of failure. In this scholar's opinion, the concept of failure is too often used in a misleading way. Failure, bankruptcy, insolvency, and closure are wrongly considered to be synonymous even if, in fact, they stand for different situations that an entrepreneur can be compelled to face. Without going to a deeper level of analysis, what matters here is the clear distinction between negative cases (bankruptcy and insolvency) that can lead to failure and non-negative cases (closure) that do not lead to failure. Beaver (2003) strongly underlines this difference and invites scholars and practitioners to clarify—case after case—the specific causes that imply the end of a firm.

For the present volume, failure is considered in its negative meaning. It refers to entrepreneurial firms that are pushed out of the market because of an inadequate approach to one of the main issues typical of the entry phase on the market, such as finance, demand forecasting, management, marketing, capitalization, strategy, and planning (see Beaver, 2003, p. 117). We embrace the idea that "failure means that the residual value of the business is low or negative" (Liu et al., 2019, p. 5).

In order to clarify the thickness of failure of entrepreneurial firms, it is appropriate to try to refer to reported percentages. According to Fiet (2001, p. 8), it is possible to "assume that about 20% of nascent entrepreneurs fail each year for the first 5 years of their ventures. Thus, after 5 years, about 33% of those who begin a new

---

[31] Because of the macroeconomic impact that gazelles can generate, several studies investigate the effect in reference to a specific area or region (Li et al., 2016). For example, Harms and Ehrmann (2009) investigate their impact in reference to German; Mohr and Garnsey (2011) analyze it in the UK context; Bavdaž et al. (2009) analyze the Slovenian case while Autio et al. (2000) consider the case of Finland.

[32] Bos and Stam (2013) underline that relevant growth of these firms is not important per se but—above all—for the impact that they generate within the industry they are in.

[33] Stinchcombe (1965) was the first scholar to propose the concept of liability of newness.

venture are still in business." Beyond this generalization, Fiet also underlines that estimations about the failure rates of entrepreneurial firms can vary. One of the parameters that play a relevant role is the industry the startups are in. Boyer and Blazy (2014) studied innovative French microenterprises and found that they were more likely to fail than their noninnovative counterparts. In line with this view, Hyytinen et al. (2015, p. 576) assume that "survival probability of startups engaged in innovativeness is approximately 6−7 percentage points lower than that of other startups" and so they are more inclined to fail. Thus, it seems that the reference to true startups (new and innovative) increases the already high failure rates of new firms.

From the analysis of official reports, a third alternative emerges. It deals with remaining active on the market (Audretsch and Mahmood, 1995; Agarwal, 1997; Strotmann, 2007; Hyytinen et al., 2015; Cabrer-Borrás and Belda, 2018), which is generally understood as survival. Scholars and statisticians, in fact, measure how long (in terms of years) firms are operational on the market.

The idea that firms can be on the market, without growing or failing, needs a clarification because it can be read from very different perspectives. Persisting on the market, in fact, can be a symptom of development that, at least theoretically, is different from growth. According to Sciarelli (1999, p. 146), a noticeable difference exists between the growth and the development of firms, although some scholars tend to consider the words to be synonyms. Growth (which tends toward the extreme concept of high-growth in reference to entrepreneurial firms) stands for a quantitative process that makes the firm expand (for example in terms of size, number of employees, or revenues). Development of firms, instead, is a qualitative process through which the relationship between the firm and its external environment tends to improve.

In order to clarify the relationship between growth and development, Sciarelli (1999) states that in practice firms follow both a qualitative and quantitative process so they pursue both development and growth at the same time. However, in reference to entrepreneurial firms, this scholar maintains that growth implies development (by becoming bigger, a firm can improve its relationship with the external environment) but that development does not necessarily imply growth (if the relationship with the external environment improves, then firms might not aspire to grow in size).

Remaining active on the market, then, can assume a positive meaning if it stands for a qualitative process aiming toward development. At the same time, remaining active on the market can assume a negative meaning if firms that persist on the market are not involved in a development process.

All the performances that entrepreneurial firms can achieve are listed in Table 2.4.

Despite some criticalities that can emerge when conceptualizing firm performance (Denrell et al., 2014; Coad et al., 2016), the aim pursued in this study consists in hypothesizing and categorizing some outputs that entrepreneurial firms can achieve. Through a pragmatic approach, it is rather clear that entrepreneurial firms can grow, develop, survive, or fail.

Table 2.4 The performances that entrepreneurial firms can achieve.

Achieved performance	Definition
Growth (or high-growth)	Growth that entrepreneurial firms can aspire to is amplified in comparison to other firms. Startups, which are new and innovative by definition, expect to achieve superior performances
Development	Development assumes a positive meaning because it stands for a sign of an improvement of relationships with the external environment
Survival	Survival is about persisting on the market and does not imply development (a qualitative process)
Failure	Failure confirms its negative meaning. It is synonymous with bankruptcy and insolvency (entrepreneurial firms are pushed out of the market) and it is in opposition to voluntary closure

Source: Personal elaboration.

A way of understanding growth, development, survival, or failure is necessary to assess the definition of performance of entrepreneurial firms and to interpret entrepreneurial trajectories in the right way.

At this stage, one last specification is appropriate. Throughout the entire analysis, no focus is placed on the individual intentions affecting performance (Hansen and Hamilton, 2011; Douglas, 2013; Dencker and Gruber, 2015). The choice is voluntary and based on the idea that this volume aims to propose entrepreneurship trajectories that can easily generalize what happens when carrying out entrepreneurial phenomena. Of course, it is obvious that entrepreneurs following an entrepreneurial trajectory behave in a certain way, according to the context they are in. This, however, does not reduce the theoretical contribution of a generalized model.

References

Achtenhagen, L., Naldi, L., Melin, L., 2010. Business growth: do practitioners and scholars really talk about the same thing? Entrepr.: Theory Pract. 34 (2), 289–316.

Acs, Z.J., Armington, C., 2002. The determinants of regional variation in new firm formation. Reg. Stud. 36 (1), 33–45.

Acs, Z.J., Audretsch, D.B., 1990. The determinants of small-firm growth in US manufacturing. Appl. Econ. 22 (2), 143–153.

Acs, Z.J., Mueller, P., 2008. Employment effects of business dynamics: mice, gazelles and elephants. Small Bus. Econ. 30 (1), 85–100.

Acs, Z.J., Audretsch, D.B., Feldman, M.P., 1994. R&D spillover and recipient firm size. Rev. Econ. Stat. 100 (1), 336–367.

Acs, Z.J., Braunerhjelm, P., Audretsch, D.B., Carlsson, B., 2009. The knowledge spillover theory of entrepreneurship. Small Bus. Econ. 32 (1), 15–30.

Acs, Z.J., Audretsch, D.B., Lehmann, E.E., 2013. The knowledge spillover theory of entrepreneurship. Small Bus. Econ. 41 (4), 757−774.

Agarwal, R., 1997. Survival of firms over the product life cycle. South. Econ. J. 63 (3), 571−584.

Agarwal, R., Audretsch, D.B., Sarkar, M.B., 2007. The process of creative construction: knowledge spillovers, entrepreneurship, and economic growth. Strat. Entrepr. J. 1 (3−4), 263−286.

Agarwal, R., Audretsch, D., Sarkar, M.B., 2010. Knowledge spillovers and strategic entrepreneurship. Strat. Entrepr. J. 4 (4), 271−283.

Aghion, P., Fally, T., Scarpetta, S., 2007. Credit constraints as a barrier to the entry and post-entry growth of firms. Econ. Policy 22 (52), 732−779.

Altman, E.I., 1983. Why businesses fail. J. Bus. Strategy 3 (4), 15−21.

Andersson, P., Delmar, F., 2000. The characteristics of highgrowth firms and their job contribution. Innovation, Growth and Entrepreneurship. ESBRI, Stockholm.

Anyadike-Danes, M., Hart, M., Du, J., 2015. Firm dynamics and job creation in the United Kingdom: 1998−2013. Int. Small Bus. 33 (1), 12−27.

Armington, C., Acs, Z.J., 2004. Job creation and persistence in services and manufacturing. J. Evol. Econ. 14 (3), 309−325.

Arrow, K., 1962. Economic welfare and the allocation of resources for invention. In: Nelson, R.R. (Ed.), The Rate and Direction of Inventive Activity. Princeton University Press, NJ, pp. 609−626.

Ashcroft, B., Love, J.H., Malloy, E., 1991. New firm formation in the British counties with special reference to Scotland. Reg. Stud. 25 (5), 395−409.

Audretsch, D.B., 1995. Firm profitability, growth, and innovation. Rev. Ind. Org. 10 (5), 579−588.

Audretsch, D.B., 2002. Entrepreneurship: A Survey of the Literature. Enterprise Directorate General. European Commission, EU.

Audretsch, D.B., 2003. Entrepreneurship policy and the strategic management of places. In: Hart, D.M. (Ed.), The Emergence of Entrepreneurship Policy. Cambridge University Press, Cambridge, MA.

Audretsch, D.B., 2004. Sustaining innovation and growth: public policy support for entrepreneurship. Ind. Innov. 11 (3), 167−191.

Audretsch, D.B., Feldman, M.P., 1996. R&D spillovers and the geography of innovation and production. Am. Econ. Rev. 86 (3), 630−640.

Audretsch, D.B., Fritsch, M., 1999. The industry component of regional new firm formation processes. Rev. Ind. Org. 15 (3), 239−252.

Audretsch, D.B., Fritsch, M., 2003. Linking entrepreneurship to growth: the case of West Germany. Ind. Innov. 10 (1), 65−73.

Audretsch, D.B., Keilbach, M., 2007. The theory of knowledge spillover entrepreneurship. J. Manag. Stud. 44 (7), 1242−1254.

Audretsch, D.B., Lehmann, E., 2006. Entrepreneurial access and absorption of knowledge spillovers: strategic board and managerial composition for competitive advantage. J. Small Bus. Manag. 44 (2), 155−166.

Audretsch, D.B., Mahmood, T., 1995. New firm survival: new results using a hazard function. Rev. Econ. Stat. 77 (1), 97−103.

Audretsch, D.B., Thurik, A.R., 2000. Capitalism and democracy in the 21st century: from the managed to the entrepreneurial economy. J. Evol. Econ. 10 (1−2), 17−34.

Audretsch, D.B., Thurik, A.R., 2001. What's new about the new economy? Sources of growth in the managed and entrepreneurial economies. Ind. Corp. Change 10 (1), 267−315.

Audretsch, D.B., Keilbach, M.C., Lehmann, E.E., 2006. Entrepreneurship and economic growth. Oxford University Press.

Autio, E., Arenius, P., Wallenius, H., 2000. Economic impact of gazelle firms in Finland. Helsinki University of Technology Working Paper Series N. 3.

Autio, E., Hameri, A.P., Vuola, O., 2004. A framework of industrial knowledge spillovers in big-science centers. Res. Policy 33 (1), 107–126.

Baptista, R., Escária, V., Madruga, P., 2008. Entrepreneurship, regional development and job creation: the case of Portugal. Small Bus. Econ. 30 (1), 49–58.

Barnett, W.P., Burgelman, R.A., 1996. Evolutionary perspectives on strategy. Strat. Manag. J. 17 (S1), 5–19.

Barringer, B.R., Jones, F.F., Neubaum, D.O., 2005. A quantitative content analysis of the characteristics of rapid-growth firms and their founders. J. Bus. Ventur. 20 (5), 663–687.

Baumol, W.J., 2002. The free-market innovation machine: Analyzing the growth miracle of capitalism. Princeton University Press, Princeton, NJ.

Baumol, W.J., 2004. Entrepreneurial enterprises, large established firms and other components of the free-market growth machine. Small Bus. Econ. 23 (N), 9–21.

Baumol, W.J., 2007. Small frms: why market-driven innovation can't get along without them. Paper presented at IFN conference in Wzxholm.

Bavdaž, M., Drnovšek, M., Dolinar, A.L., 2009. Achieving a response from fast-growing companies: the case of Slovenian gazelles. Econ. Bus. Rev. 11 (3), 187–203.

Beaver, G., 2003. Small business: success and failure. Strat. Change 12 (3), 115–122.

Benassi, M., Landoni, M., 2019. State-owned enterprises as knowledge-explorer agents. Ind. Innov. 26 (2), 218–241.

Bhidé, A.V., 2000. The Origin and Evolution of New Business. Oxford University Press, New York, NY.

Birch, D.L., 1979. The job generation process. Report prepared for the U.S. Department of Commerce, Economic Development Administration. MIT Program on Neighborhood and Regional Change, Cambridge, MA.

Birch, D.L., 1981. Who creates jobs? Public Interest 65, 3–14.

Birch, D.L., Medoff, J., 1994. Gazelles. In: Solmon, L.C., Levenson, A.R. (Eds.), Labor Markets, Employment Policy and Job Creation. Westview Press, Boulder, pp. 159–168.

Birch, D.L., Andew, H., William, P., 1995. Who's Creating Jobs? Cognetics Inc, Boston, MA.

Birley, S., Westhead, P., 1990. Growth and performance contrasts between 'types' of small firms. Strat. Manag. J. 11 (7), 535–557.

Blau, D.M., 1987. A time-series analysis of self-employment in the United States. J. Pol. Econ. 95 (3), 445–467.

Boccardelli, P., Magnusson, M.G., 2006. Dynamic capabilities in early-phase entrepreneurship. Knowledge Process Manag. 13 (3), 162–174.

Bos, J.W., Stam, E., 2013. Gazelles and industry growth: a study of young high-growth firms in The Netherlands. Ind. Corp. Change 23 (1), 145–169.

Bouchikhi, H., 1993. A constructivist framework for understanding entrepreneurship performance. Org. Stud. 14 (4), 549–570.

Boyer, T., Blazy, R., 2014. Born to be alive? The survival of innovative and non-innovative French micro-start-ups. Small Bus. Econ. 42 (4), 669–683.

Braunerhjelm, P., 2010. Entrepreneurship, innovation and economic growth: interdependencies, irregularities and regularities. In: Audretsch, D.B., Flack, O., Heblich, S., Lederer, A. (Eds.), Handbook of Research on Innovation and Entrepreneurship. Edward Elgar, Cheltenham, pp. 161–213.

Braunerhjelm, P., Acs, Z.J., Audretsch, D.B., Carlsson, B., 2010. The missing link: knowledge diffusion and entrepreneurship in endogenous growth. Small Bus. Econ. 34 (2), 105−125.

Braunerhjelm, P., Ding, D., Thulin, P., 2018. The knowledge spillover theory of intrapreneurship. Small Bus. Econ. 51 (1), 1−30.

Brush, C.G., Vanderwerf, P.A., 1992. A comparison of methods and sources for obtaining estimates of new venture performance. J. Bus. Ventur. 7 (2), 157−170.

Brush, C.G., De Bruin, A., Welter, F., 2009. A gender-aware framework for women's entrepreneurship. Int. J. Gender Entrepr 1 (1), 8−24.

Buttà, C., 1995. La genesi dell'impresa: fondamenti cognitivi e decisori. FrancoAngeli, Milano.

Cabrer-Borrás, B., Belda, P.R., 2018. Survival of entrepreneurship in Spain. Small Bus. Econ. 51 (1), 265−278.

Cardon, M.S., Stevens, C.E., Potter, D.R., 2011. Misfortunes or mistakes? Cultural sensemaking of entrepreneurial failure. J. Bus. Ventur. 26 (1), 79−92.

Carlsson, B., Braunerhjelm, P., McKelvey, M., Olofsson, C., Persson, L., Ylinenpää, H., 2013. The evolving domain of entrepreneurship research. Small Bus. Econ. 41 (4), 913−930.

Carree, M., Van Stel, A., Thurik, R., Wennekers, S., 2002. Economic development and business ownership: an analysis using data of 23 OECD countries in the period 1976−1996. Small Bus. Econ. 19 (3), 271−290.

Casson, M., 2002a. Entrepreneurship, business culture and the theory of the firm. In: Acs, Z., Audretsch, B. (Eds.), The International Handbook of Entrepreneurship Research. Spinger Verlagh, Berlin and New York.

Casson, M., 2002b. The Entrepreneur: An Economic Theory. Edward Elgar, Northempton, MA.

Chandler, G.N., Jansen, E., 1992. The founder's self-assessed competence and venture performance. J. Bus. Ventur. 7 (3), 223−236.

Coad, A., Frankish, J., Roberts, R.G., Storey, D.J., 2013. Growth paths and survival chances: an application of Gambler's Ruin theory. J. Bus. Ventur. 28 (5), 615−632.

Coad, A., Segarra, A., Teruel, M., 2016. Innovation and firm growth: does firm age play a role? Res. Policy 45 (2), 387−400.

Colombelli, A., Krafft, J., Quatraro, F., 2013. High-growth firms and technological knowledge: do gazelles follow exploration or exploitation strategies? Ind. Corp. Change 23 (1), 261−291.

Cooper, A.C., 1995. Challenges in predicting new firm performance. In: Bull, I., Thomas, H., Willard, G. (Eds.), Entrepreneurship. Perspectives on Theory Building. Pergamon-Elsevier, Oxford−New York.

Cressy, R., 2006. Why do most firms die young? Small Bus. Econ. 26 (2), 103−116.

Daunfeldt, S.O., Halvarsson, D., 2015. Are high-growth firms one-hit wonders? Evidence from Sweden. Small Bus. Econ. 44 (2), 361−383.

Davidsson, P., 1991. Continued entrepreneurship: ability, need, and opportunity as determinants of small firm growth. J. Bus. Ventur. 6 (6), 405−429.

Davidsson, P., 2016. The field of entrepreneurship research: some significant developments. In: Bögenhold, D., Bonnet, J., Dejardin, M., Garcia Pérez de Lema, D. (Eds.), Contemporary Entrepreneurship. Springer, Cham, pp. 17−28.

Davidsson, P., Lindmark, L., Olofsson, C., 1998. The extent of overestimation of small firm job creation−an empirical examination of the regression bias. Small Bus. Econ. 11 (1), 87−100.

Davila, A., Foster, G., Jia, N., 2010. Building sustainable high-growth startup companies: management systems as an accelerator. Calif. Manag. Rev. 52 (3), 79−105.

Decker, R., Haltiwanger, J., Jarmin, R., Miranda, J., 2014. The role of entrepreneurship in US job creation and economic dynamism. J. Eco. Persp. 28 (3), 3−24.

Decker, R.A., Haltiwanger, J., Jarmin, R.S., Miranda, J., 2016. Where has all the skewness gone? The decline in high-growth (young) firms in the US. Eur. Econ. Rev. 86, 4−23.

Delmar, F., 1997. Measuring growth: methodological considerations and empirical results. In: Donckels, R., Mietinen, A. (Eds.), Entrepreneurship and SME Research: On Its Way to the Next Millenium. Avebury, Aldershot, VA, pp. 199−216.

Delmar, F., Davidsson, P., 1998. A taxonomy of high-growth firms. Front. Entrepr. Res. 18 (1), 399−343.

Delmar, F., Davidsson, P., Gartner, W.B., 2003. Arriving at the high-growth firm. J. Bus. Ventur. 18 (2), 189−216.

Delmar, F., McKelvie, A., Wennberg, K., 2013. Untangling the relationships among growth, profitability and survival in new firms. Technovation 33 (8−9), 276−291.

Dencker, J.C., Gruber, M., 2015. The effects of opportunities and founder experience on new firm performance. Strat. Manag. J. 36 (7), 1035−1052.

Denrell, J., Fang, C., Liu, C., 2014. Perspective: chance explanations in the management sciences. Org. Sci. 26 (3), 923−940.

Dillen, Y., Laveren, E., Martens, R., De Vocht, S., Van Imschoot, E., 2019. From "manager" to "strategist": an examination of the evolving role of persistent high-growth entrepreneurs. Int. J. Entrepr. Behav. Res. 25 (1), 2−28.

Douglas, E.J., 2013. Reconstructing entrepreneurial intentions to identify predisposition for growth. J. Bus. Ventur. 28 (5), 633−651.

Eisenhardt, K.M., Martin, J.A., 2000. Dynamic capabilities: what are they? Strat. Manag. J. 21 (10−11), 1105−1121.

Fiet, J.O., 2001. The theoretical side of teaching entrepreneurship. J. Bus. Ventur. 16 (1), 1−24.

Fombrun, C.J., Wally, S., 1989. Structuring small firms for rapid growth. J. Bus. Ventur. 4 (2), 107−122.

Friar, J.H., Meyer, M.H., 2003. Entrepreneurship and start-ups in the Boston region: factors differentiating high-growth ventures from micro-ventures. Small Bus. Econ. 21 (2), 145−152.

Fritsch, M., 1997. New firms and regional employment change. Small Bus. Econ. 9 (5), 437−448.

Fritsch, M., Mueller, P., 2004. Effects of new business formation on regional development over time. Reg. Stud. 38 (8), 961−975.

Garnsey, E., Stam, E., Heffernan, P., 2006. New firm growth: exploring processes and paths. Ind. Innov. 13 (1), 1−20.

Gartner, W.B., 1985. A conceptual framework for describing the phenomenon of new venture creation. Acad. Manag. Rev. 10 (4), 696−706.

Gartner, W.B., 1988. Who is an entrepreneur? Is the wrong question. Am. Small Bus. J. 12 (4), 11−31.

Gartner, W.B., 1990. What are we talking about when we talk about entrepreneurship? J. Bus. Ventur. 5 (1), 15−28.

Gartner, W.B., 2001. Is there an elephant in entrepreneurship? Blind assumptions in theory development. Entrepr.: Theory Pract. 25 (4), 27−39.

Gartner, W.B., Gatewood, E., 1992. Thus the theory of description matters most. Entrepr.: Theory Pract. 17 (1), 5−10.

Giunta, F., 1993. La Creazione di Nuove Imprese. Uno Schema di Analisi Economico-Aziendale, Cedam, Padova.

Glaeser, E.L., Kerr, W.R., 2009. Local industrial conditions and entrepreneurship: how much of the spatial distribution can we explain? J. Econ. Manag. Strat. 18 (3), 623−663.

Grilo, I., Thurik, R., 2004. Determinants of Entrepreneurship in Europe (October 2004, 12). ERIM Report Series Reference No. ERS-2004-106-ORG. Available at SSRN: https://ssrn.com/abstract = 636815.

Haltiwanger, J., Jarmin, R.S., Miranda, J., 2013. Who creates jobs? Small versus large versus young. Rev. Econ. Stat. 95 (2), 347−361.

Hamilton, R.T., 2012. How firms grow and the influence of size and age. Int. Small Bus. J. 30 (6), 611−621.

Hansen, B., Hamilton, R.T., 2011. Factors distinguishing small firm growers and non-growers. Int. Small Bus. J. 29 (3), 278−294.

Harms, R., Ehrmann, T., 2009. Firm-level entrepreneurship and performance for German gazelles. Int. J. Entrepr. Ventur. 1 (2), 185−204.

Hashi, I., Krasniqi, B.A., 2011. Entrepreneurship and SME growth: evidence from advanced and laggard transition economies. Int. J. Entrepr. Behav. Res. 17 (5), 456−487.

Heirman, A., Clarysse, B., 2004. How and why do research-based start-ups differ at founding? A resource-based configurational perspective. J. Technol. Transf. 29 (3−4), 247−268.

Henrekson, M., Johansson, D., 2010. Gazelles as job creators: a survey and interpretation of the evidence. Small Bus. Econ. 35 (2), 227−244.

Heshmati, A., 2001. On the growth of micro and small firms: evidence from Sweden. Small Bus. Econ. 17 (3), 213−228.

Huber, F., 2011. Do clusters really matter for innovation practices in Information Technology? Questioning the significance of technological knowledge spillovers. J. Econ. Geogr. 12 (1), 107−126.

Huy, Q., Zott, C., 2019. Exploring the affective underpinnings of dynamic managerial capabilities: how managers' emotion regulation behaviors mobilize resources for their firms. Strat. Manag. J. 40 (1), 28−54.

Hyytinen, A., Pajarinen, M., Rouvinen, P., 2015. Does innovativeness reduce startup survival rates? J. Bus. Ventur. 30 (4), 564−581.

Inoue, H., Nakajima, K., Saito, Y.U., 2019. Localization of collaborations in knowledge creation. Ann. Reg. Sci. 62 (1), 119−140.

Johnson, P., Conway, C., Kattuman, P., 1999. Small business growth in the short run. Small Bus. Econ. 12 (2), 103−112.

Karahan, F., Pugsley, B., Sahin, A., 2015. Understanding the 30-year decline in the startup rate: a general equilibrium approach. Unpublished Manuscript, May.

Katz, J.A., 1993. The dynamics of organizational s emergence: a contemporary group formation perspective. Entrepr.: Theory Pract. 17 (2), 97−101.

Katz, J.A., Gartner, W., 1988. Properties of emerging organizations. Acad. Manag. Rev. 13 (3), 429−441.

Kemp, R.G.M., Verhoeven, W.H.J., 2002. Growth Patterns of Medium-sized, Fast-growing Firms: The Optimal Resource Bundles for Organisational Growth and Performance. SCALES, Zoetermeer.

Khelil, N., 2016. The many faces of entrepreneurial failure: insights from an empirical taxonomy. J. Bus. Ventur. 31 (1), 72−94.

Klapper, L., Laeven, L., Rajan, R., 2006. Entry regulation as a barrier to entrepreneurship. J. Fin. Econ. 82 (3), 591−629.

Larson, A., Starr, J.A., 1993. A network model of organization formation. Entrepr.: Theory Pract. 17 (2), 5—15.

Lasch, F., Le Roy, F., Yami, S., 2007. Critical growth factors of ICT start-ups. Manag. Decision 45 (1), 62—75.

Lee, C., Hallak, R., Sardeshmukh, S.R., 2016. Innovation, entrepreneurship, and restaurant performance: a higher-order structural model. Tourism Manag. 53, 215—228.

Li, S., Shang, J., Slaughter, S.A., 2010. Why do software firms fail? Capabilities, competitive actions, and firm survival in the software industry from 1995 to 2007. Inform. Syst. Res. 21 (3), 631—654.

Li, M., Goetz, S.J., Partridge, M., Fleming, D.A., 2016. Location determinants of high-growth firms. Entrepr. Reg. Dev. 28 (1—2), 97—125.

Liu, Y., Li, Y., Hao, X., Zhang, Y., 2019. Narcissism and learning from entrepreneurial failure. J. Bus. Ventur. Available on line at. Available from: https://www.sciencedirect.com/science/article/pii/S0883902617309345.

Lucas, R.E., 1988. On the mechanisms of economic development. J.Mon. Econ. 22 (1), 3—42.

Matricano, D., 2018. Le startup innovative in Italia: Gli aspetti manageriali e il loro impatto sulla performance. G Giappichelli Editore.

McKelvie, A., Wiklund, J., 2010. Advancing firm growth research: a focus on growth mode instead of growth rate. Entrepr.: Theory Pract. 34 (2), 261—288.

Mohr, V., Garnsey, E., 2011. How do high-growth firms grow? Evidence from Cambridge, UK. Econ. Manag. Fin. Markets 6 (4), 29—59.

Moreno, A.M., Casillas, J.C., 2008. Entrepreneurial orientation and growth of SMEs: a causal model. Entrepr.: Theory Pract. 32 (3), 507—528.

Murphy, G.B., Trailer, J.W., Hill, R.C., 1996. Measuring performance in entrepreneurship research. J. Bus. Res. 36 (1), 15—23.

Nooteboom, B., 1994. Innovation and diffusion in small firms: theory and evidence. Small Bus. Econ. 6 (5), 327—347.

OECD, 2008. A Framework for Addressing and Measuring Entrepreneurship. OECD Statistics Working Paper. OECD Publishing, Paris. STD/DOC(2008)2.

Olaison, L., Meier Sørensen, B., 2014. The abject of entrepreneurship: failure, fiasco, fraud. Int. J. Entrepr. Behav. Res. 20 (2), 193—211.

Pagano, P., Schivardi, F., 2003. Firm size distribution and growth. Scand. J. Econ. 105 (2), 255—274.

Parente, R., 2004. Creazione e sviluppo dell'impresa innovativa. G. Giappichelli. Torino.

Parker, S.C., Storey, D.J., Van Witteloostuijn, A., 2010. What happens to gazelles? The importance of dynamic management strategy. Small Bus. Econ. 35 (2), 203—226.

Penrose, E., 1959. The Theory of the Growth of the Firm. Basil Blackwell and Mott, Oxford.

Plummer, L.A., Acs, Z.J., 2014. Localized competition in the knowledge spillover theory of entrepreneurship. J. Bus. Ventur. 29 (1), 121—136.

Rasmussen, C.C., Ladegård, G., Korhonen-Sande, S., 2018. Growth Intentions and board composition in high-growth firms. J. Small Bus. Manag. 56 (4), 601—617.

Reynolds, P.D., 1999. Creative destruction: source or symptom of economic growth. In: Acs, Z.J., Carlsson, B., Karlsson, C. (Eds.), Entrepreneurship, Small and Medium-sized Enterprises and the Macroeconomy. Cambridge University Press, pp. 97—136.

Robson, P.J., Bennett, R.J., 2000. SME growth: the relationship with business advice and external collaboration. Small Bus. Econ. 15 (3), 193—208.

Romer, P., 1986. Increasing returns and long run growth. J. Pol. Econ. 94 (5), 1002—1037.

Santarelli, E., Vivarelli, M., 2006. Entrepreneurship and the process of firms' entry, survival and growth. IZA discussion paper N. 2475.

Schmitz Jr., J.A., 1989. Imitation, entrepreneurship, and long-run growth. J. Pol. Econ. 97 (3), 721−739.

Schuh, S., Triest, R.K., 2000. The role of firms in job creation and destruction in US manufacturing. New Engl. Econ. Rev. 29−44.

Sciarelli, S., 1999. Economia e Gestione dell'Impresa. CEDAM, Padova, IT.

Simmie, J., 2002. Knowledge spillovers and reasons for the concentration of innovative SMEs. Urban Stud. 39 (5−6), 885−902.

Singh, S., Corner, P., Pavlovich, K., 2007. Coping with entrepreneurial failure. J. Manag. Org. 13 (4), 331−344.

Smalibone, D., 1990. Success and failure in new business start-ups. Int. Small Bus. J. 8 (2), 34−47.

Sorrentino, M., 2003. Le Nuove Imprese. Economia delle Nuove Iniziative Imprenditoriali, Cedam, Padova.

Stam, E., 2005. The geography of gazelles in the Netherlands. Tijdschrift voor economische en sociale geografie 96 (1), 121−127.

van Stel, A., Storey, D., 2004. The link between firm births and job creation: is there a Upas tree effect? Reg. Stud. 38 (8), 893−909.

van Stel, A., Suddle, K., 2008. The impact of new firm formation on regional development in the Netherlands. Small Bus. Econ. 30 (1), 31−47.

Stinchcombe, A.L., 1965. Organizations and social structure. In: March, J. (Ed.), Handbook of Organizations. Randy McNally, Chicago, IL.

Storey, D.J., 1991. The birth of new firms—does unemployment matter? A review of the evidence. Small Bus. Econ. 3 (3), 167−178.

Stough, R., Nijkamp, P., 2009. Knowledge spillovers, entrepreneurship and economic development. Ann. Reg. Sci. 43 (4), 835−838.

Strotmann, H., 2007. Entrepreneurial survival. Small Bus. Econ. 28 (1), 87−104.

Teece, D.J., 2012. Dynamic capabilities: routines versus entrepreneurial action. J. Manag. Stud. 49 (8), 1395−1401.

Teece, D.J., Pisano, G., 1994. The dynamic capabilities of firms: an introduction. Ind. Corp. Change 3 (3), 537−556.

Teece, D.J., Pisano, G., Shuen, A., 1997. Dynamic capabilities and strategic management. Strat. Manag. J. 18 (7), 509−533.

Ucbasaran, D., Westhead, P., Wright, M., 2001. The focus of entrepreneurial research: contextual and process issues. Entrepr.: Theory Pract. 25 (4), 57−80.

Ucbasaran, D., Shepherd, D.A., Lockett, A., Lyon, S.J., 2013. Life after business failure: the process and consequences of business failure for entrepreneurs. J. Manag. 39 (1), 163−202.

Utterback, J.M., Meyer, M., Roberts, E., Reitberger, G., 1988. Technology and industrial innovation in Sweden: a study of technology-based firms formed between 1965 and 1980. Res. Policy 17 (1), 15−26.

Valliere, D., Peterson, R., 2009. Entrepreneurship and economic growth: evidence from emerging and developed countries. Entrepr. Reg. Dev. 21 (5-6), 459−480.

Wennekers, A.R.M., Thurik, A.R., 1999. Linking entrepreneurship and economic growth. Small Bus. Econ. 13 (1), 27−55.

Westhead, P., Birley, S., 1995. Employment growth in new independent owner-managed firms in Great Britain. Int. Small Bus. 13 (3), 11−34.

Wiklund, J., 1998. Small firm growth and performance: entrepreneurship and beyond. Doctoral dissertation, Internationella Handelshögskolan, Jonkoping.

Winter, S.G., 2003. Understanding dynamic capabilities. Strat. Manag. J. 24 (10), 991−995.

Wong, P.K., Ho, Y.P., Autio, E., 2005. Entrepreneurship, innovation and economic growth: evidence from GEM data. Small Bus. Econ. 24 (3), 335—350.

Woo, C.Y., Daellenbach, U., Nicholls-Nixon, C., 1994. Theory building in the presence of 'randomness': the case of venture creation and performance. J. Manag. Stud. 31 (4), 507—524.

Zahra, S.A., Kuratko, D.F., Jennings, D.F., 1999. Guest editorial: entrepreneurship and the acquisition of dynamic organizational capabilities. Entrepr.: Theory Pract. 23 (3), 5—10.

Zahra, S.A., Sapienza, H.J., Davidsson, P., 2006. Entrepreneurship and dynamic capabilities: a review, model and research agenda. J. Manag. Stud. 43 (4), 917—955.

Zollo, M., Winter, S.G., 2002. Deliberate learning and the evolution of dynamic capabilities. Org. Sci. 13 (3), 339—351.

The business model

3

3.1 The business model: an overlapping concept

The concept of business model is not new in management literature.[1] As noted by Demil and Lecocq (2010, p. 227), "the term business model has flourished in the managerial literature since the end of the 90 s." Since then, however, academics have devoted scarce attention to this topic of research (Osterwalder et al., 2005; Zott and Amit, 2010; DaSilva and Trkman, 2014; Klang et al., 2014).

According to some scholars (Hedman and Kalling, 2003; Voelpel et al., 2004, 2005; Lindman, 2007; Casadesus-Masanell and Ricart, 2010; McGrath, 2010; George and Bock, 2011; Arend, 2013; Baden-Fuller and Mangematin, 2013; DaSilva and Trkman, 2014; Spieth et al., 2014), the main reason for such scarce attention seems to lie in the overlapping with other long-established management concepts that cannot be put aside so easily.

The most common overlap occurs between the notions of business model, strategy, and tactics. According to Casadesus-Masanell and Ricart (2010), business model refers to the logic of firms, the way they work to create value. Strategy, which follows the setting up of the business model, refers to the choices that firms put into practice to operationalize the business model. Eventually, tactics refer to the residual choices. Beyond the dissimilarities between strategy and tactics (which are not going to be analyzed here), what matters is the difference between the business model and the strategy/tactics that concerns two different levels of analysis. A business model represents a kind of logic, that is, the system and principles at the basis of a firm's value creation. It stands for a holistic and theoretical approach to what firms are going to do. Strategy/tactics, instead, are the practical translations of what is included in the business model.

Another concept that overlaps with the business model is competitive advantage that, generally speaking, describes the firms' position within an industry.[2] Since the concepts of competitive advantage and business model can overlap (actually, the concept of competitive advantage and its description is expected to be included in

---

[1] Actually, as noted by DaSilva and Trkman (2014), Bellman, Clark, Malcom, Craft and Ricciardi were the first ones to use the term business model in their article "On the construction of a multistage, multi-person business game" published in 1957 while Jones (1960) was the first one to use the term business model in the title of his article.

[2] Competitive advantage is a typical issue of strategic management studies. Among the scholars who contributed to its affirmation it is possible to cite Chandler (1962), Hofer and Schendel (1978), Ansoff (1979) and, of course, Porter (1985, 1996).

Entrepreneurship Trajectories. DOI: https://doi.org/10.1016/B978-0-12-818650-3.00003-9

the business model), the business model has not been able to disclose and affirm its relevance (McGrath, 2010).

Another example can be related to the venture's revenue model (Zott and Amit, 2010; George and Bock, 2011). As noted by Zott and Amit (2010), a noticeable difference exists between these concepts. A business model is a set of activities that aim toward value creation for all the parties involved. The venture's revenue model, instead, is related to its pricing strategy and, in practice, comes after the business model has been defined. Of course, and this is a very important aspect that is worth underlying, the creation of value is something more than setting a price. Regardless, despite the clear and unequivocal difference, the concepts are wrongly perceived and are, sometimes, assumed to be synonyms.

Yet another example is linked to the relationship between the terms business model and business concept (Hedman and Kalling, 2003; Voelpel et al., 2005). Even if some scholars confuse the two, they are clearly distinct. The business concept is at the basis of—and thus it precedes—the business model.

Examples of concepts that overlap with the business model might be more and more (Lindman, 2007; DaSilva and Trkman, 2014). What matters here is that scholars reach the same conclusion: the limited relevance of business model in management studies is the result of its overlap with other management notions. According to the above review, it is clear that certain already existing management concepts, which are closely related to the concept of business model and, in fact, precede or follow its set up, have impeded its affirmation.

3.2   Defining the business model

Only over the last decade, there has been a radical change in management studies[3] and the concept of business model has been reaffirming its relevance (Baden-Fuller and Morgan, 2010; Chesbrough, 2010; Demil and Lecocq, 2010; McGrath, 2010; Thompson and MacMillan, 2010; Zott and Amit, 2010; Zott et al., 2010, 2011; Baden-Fuller and Mangematin, 2013; DaSilva and Trkman, 2014; Wirtz et al., 2016; Saebi et al., 2017). Management scholars have started recognizing the business model as a stand-alone concept and, consequently, as an autonomous field of research. However, because of its novelty, it still needs to be properly defined.

In this vein, one of the main problems of a business model is its definition. Several scholars have tried to formulate brief definitions of the business model and some of these definitions are included in Table 3.1.

From the above definitions, it clearly results that, despite differences in the nomenclature used, the definitions of a business model are similar and focused on the aim to achieve: the creation of value. For this reason, Saebi et al. (2017) do not offer any brief definition but refer to a business model by underlying the structure of a value chain and the importance of a value proposition for capturing value. In

---

[3] See the contribution of DaSilva and Trkman (2014) who rebuild the ongoing of papers published on business model.

Table 3.1 Some definitions of the business model.

Author(s)	Definition
Zott and Amit (2010)	A business model "enables the firm, in concert with its partners, to create value and also to appropriate a share of value" (p. 216)
Demil and Lecocq (2010)	A business model refers to "the articulation between different components or building blocks to produce a proposition that can generate value for consumers and thus for the organization" (p. 227)
Gambardella and McGahan (2010)	A business model is "an organization's approach to generating revenue at a reasonable cost" (p. 263)
Casadesus-Masanell and Ricart (2010)	A business model is "the logic of the firm, the way it operates and how it creates value for its stakeholder" (p. 196)

Source: Personal elaboration.

sum, it emerges that value creation and capture are the concepts at the basis of business models.

Other scholars, rather than proposing new definitions, have focused their attention on the activities that business models should include. Chesbrough and Rosenbloom (2002, pp. 533–534) have carried out one of the first trials to catalog the functions that should be included in a business model. These functions are:

- Articulation of value proposition;
- Identification of market segment and specification of revenue generation model;
- Definition of value chain;
- Definition of revenue mechanisms;
- Estimation of cost structure and profit potential;
- Description of the position of the firm in the value network; and
- Formulation of competitive strategy.

Despite the different approach, focusing on activities rather than looking for a definition, the idea that a business model is a set of functions oriented toward value is confirmed. This is also confirmed by another stream of research that has paid attention to the components of business models, the parts or sections to be included in it.

After reviewing several proposals that management scholars[4] have advanced about the business model, Zott and Amit (2010, p. 217) underline how they all seem to convey the idea that a business model is an "activity system." Activities stand for the engagement of human, physical, and/or capital resources in order to achieve an overall objective that, generally speaking, stands for value creation.

---

[4] Zott and Amit (2010), in their paper, review some previous contributions authored by Afuah and Tucci (2001), Afuah (2004), Chesbrough and Rosenbloom (2002), Eismann (2002), Johnson et al. (2008), and Mitchell and Coles (2003). All these scholars have offered interesting view of business model that have conveyed into the one proposed by Zott and Amit (2010).

According to these scholars, two sets of parameters need to be considered in business models. They are "design elements," such as content, structure, and governance, and "design themes," such as novelty, lock-in, complementarities, and efficiency. As specified by the above scholars, in reference to "design elements," content refers to specific/selected activities that are carried out; structure, instead, concerns how the specific/selected activities are carried out; and governance deals with the subjects involved who perform the specific/selected activities. With regards to "design themes," Zott and Amit (2010) mean novelty as a new activity, structure, and governance. They define lock-in as the possibility to bond third parties. They describe complementarities as the possibility to carry out several activities together, as a system. Finally, they also define efficiency as an approach that aims to select and manage activity, structure, and governance in an efficient way.

From a different point of view, rooted in the Penrosian view of a firm as a bundle of resources,[5] Demil and Lecocq (2010) include three core components in business models: resources and competences, organizational structure, and proposition for value delivery. Resources and competences can be both internal and external. They combine one another and characterize each firm. The organizational structure, instead, deals with the activities to be carried out and can be modified until the point that firms involve their stakeholders in dedicated networks (Nenonen and Storbacka, 2010). The proposition for value delivery deals with the way firms deliver created value to their customers.

McGrath (2010) considers two core components of the business model instead. The first is the unit of business (i.e., what customers pay for). The second is the process or the set of operations that can lead to profitability.

For sure, the above review helps neither to define, in a clear and univocal way, the business model nor to identify its main components.[6] It definitely does help to realize the scope that business models aim toward—that is, value creation (see Table 3.2)—and how complex the study of a business model is.

As it clearly emerges from Table 3.2, beyond the different definitions, dissimilar functions, and distinctive components that scholars have proposed in reference to a business model, they all largely share the idea that a business model aims toward value creation. Whatever the perspective adopted to study the topic, the result that scholars and, above all, entrepreneurs and managers expect to achieve thanks to a business model is to create value.

---

[5] The resource based-view (RBV) assumes that firms are bundles of resources that necessarily differ from each other (Penrose, 1959). According to this, each firm needs to set up its business model. In this vein, the contribution authored by DaSilva and Trkman (2014) needs to be cited. The scholars consider RBV as relevant in the studies on business model even if they argue "RBV alone cannot explain the complexity of business model" (DaSilva and Trkman, 2014, p. 382). In their view, in fact, beyond resources, it is important to consider the transactions that are put into practice in order to create value. For this reason, they enlarge the theoretical framework and include transaction cost economics (Meyer et al., 1992; Williamson, 1975, 1983) as well.

[6] According to Demil and Lecocq (2010, pp. 243−244), "a complete list of all the possible elements which a business model may be configured is unforeseeable."

Table 3.2 Different topics investigated by management scholars in reference to business models.

Definitions	Functions	Components/parts
A business model enables... (Zott and Amit, 2010) A business model is the articulation of different components /building blocks to... (Demil and Lecocq, 2010) A business model is a mechanism toward... (Gambardella and McGahan, 2010) A business model is the logic of the firm toward... (Casadesus-Masanell & Ricart, 2010) A business model deals with value chain, value proposition in order to... (Saebi et al., 2017)	The functions that Chesbrough and Rosenbloom (2002) include in a business model refer to: 1. Value proposition 2. Market and revenue generation model 3. Value chain 4. Revenue mechanisms 5. Cost structure and profit 6. Value network 7. Competitive strategy; and aim to...	"Design elements" and "Design themes" able to...(Zott and Amit, 2010) "Resources and competences," "organizational structure" and "proposition for value delivery" in order to... (Demil and Lecocq, 2010) "Unit of business" and "process/set of operations" taking to... (McGrath, 2010)
	... value creation	

Source: Personal elaboration.

3.3   Setting up the business model

After clarifying that the main aim of a business model is value creation—on which management scholars largely agree—it is imperative to move attention toward another critical point dealing with the setting up of a business model.

Even if entrepreneurs or general managers are aware of the scope they can achieve through their business model, this does not mean that its definition (of functions and/or of components/parts to be included in it) and its implementation (putting functions and/or components/parts into practice) are easy tasks to carry out. The main difficulties seem to be related to the business model nature (Baden-Fuller and Morgan, 2010; Demil and Lecocq, 2010).

To begin with, it is appropriate to recall the contribution authored by Baden-Fuller and Morgan (2010). These scholars approach the theme from an intriguing perspective that falls halfway between theory and practice and, hence, their contribution really seems to stand for the connection point between defining a business model and implementing it. They recall the difference between taxonomy and typology. Taxonomy is instrumental for the identification of classes or types of functions, components, or parts of a business model. By leveraging a bottom-up approach that, by definition, is based on observations and empirical work it is possible to derive classes or types. Typology, instead, leads to the identification of the types of functions, components, or parts of a business model. These result from a top-down approach that is based on conceptual and theoretical conjectures. None of the approaches' results are more relevant than those of another, thus scholars argue that business models are "ideal types" (Baden-Fuller and Morgan, 2010, p. 161) that fall halfway between taxonomy and typology.

In the view proposed by Baden-Fuller and Morgan (2010), the nature of a business model is rather difficult to explain. Accordingly, setting up a business model is a challenge because the functions, components, or parts to be included in it result from empirical observations (bottom-up approach) and theorizing (top-down approach).

As a matter of fact, difficulties related to a business model do not deal only with the dichotomy of empiricism/theorizing in reference to the functions, components, or parts to be included. Relevant difficulties also deal with the business model evolution. As noted by Demil and Lecocq (2010), the concept of a business model can be read from two different perspectives: static and transformational.

Basically, the static perspective highlights the fact that a business model summarizes and discloses how value is created. On the contrary, the transformational perspective underlines the always-changing nature of a business model, which is instrumental for the competition on the market and the creation of value.

Both perspectives have strengths and weaknesses. The main strength of the static perspective is the possibility to catalog different business models and to understand the way each organization creates value. At the same time, however, a static approach does not allow for the realization of whether and how business models evolve in order to compete on the market. The transformational perspective allows for the evolution of business models to be captured (and this stands for a strength) even if paying attention to the changes rather than the components of a business model ends up being a weakness, as attention is not focused on the components of a business model.[7]

From the above, it is clear that the nature and evolution of a business model are difficult to frame. Setting up a business model necessarily implies huge risks that, if not properly managed, can destroy value rather than create it.

3.3.1 Innovation, adaptation, and experimentation

Setting up a business model is not an ultimate choice (Johnson, 2018). Entrepreneurs and top managers, in fact, can evaluate several alternatives before setting it up (business model innovation) and, above all, they can consider new and different options after setting it up (business model adaptation).

---

[7] Demil and Lecocq (2010) recall the view proposed by Yip (2004) and Teece (2007). In order to support this limitation of transformational perspective, they also recall other contributions authored by Raff (2000), Winter and Szulanski (2001) and Johnson et al. (2008) that focus on the evolution of business models rather than on their main components.

Saebi et al. (2017) clarify the difference between business model innovation and adaptation. Business model innovation (which can be due to both internal and external factors) takes place when firms aim to disrupt the ongoing market conditions. Accordingly, a business model comprehends innovative aspects that can modify the state-of-the-art. Business model adaptation, instead, takes place when firms aim to respond to external, environmental changes. In this case, firms can set up a new business model that can be non-innovative and can simply react to changes that have occurred. Due to the above-described differences, business model innovation and adaptation are analyzed separately.

Business model innovation mainly concerns high-tech industries in which the changes occurring are internal, that is, firms generate them. In these industries, the value of groundbreaking technology is unknown until it is commercialized (Chesbrough, 2010). As a result of the newness of the technology (Pateli and Giaglis, 2005), it is possible that none of the existing business models can be used to commercialize it. Consequently, a process aiming to set up an innovative business model begins. This process is very challenging because it is unclear how to proceed and what results can be expected. Scholars only agree on the fact that firms are successful if they can fit novelty (for example, new technology to be commercialized) into an innovative business model (see also Amit and Zott, 2012; Desyllas and Sako, 2013; Massa and Tucci, 2013; Velu and Jacob, 2016; Wirtz and Daiser, 2017; Foss and Saebi, 2018).

Business model adaptation,[8] instead, begins with the idea that business models are "permanently in a state of transitory disequilibrium" (Demil and Lecocq, 2010, p. 240) and need to be modified. Put simply, business model components are modified in order to make them fit more with the market (Demil and Lecocq, 2010; Saebi et al., 2017; Haas, 2018). The insight at the basis of this view is that uncertain, fast-moving, and unpredictable environments cause several deep changes[9] that force firms to adapt their business models (Saebi et al., 2017).

Similarly to innovation, business model adaptation is also not easy and, of course, can fail. According to Saebi et al. (2017), this can happen for two main reasons. The first is related to changes. Scholars are still debating whether positive or negative changes drive firms to adapt their business models. Positive or negative changes in the market imply a proactive or a reactive approach, respectively, to be taken by firms, which can affect adaptation in different ways and drive toward results that differ from the ones expected. The second reason is linked to path-dependency. The way firms acted in the past necessarily affects the way they are going to act in the future (i.e., to respond to external changes). The proposal to focus attention on business model modularity goes along this view and tries to solve the problem of business model adaptation to the external context (Schön, 2012).

---

[8] As noted by Saebi et al. (2017), scholars talk about business model evolution, learning, adaptation, and erosion. All these words are considered as synonyms.

[9] Some examples of the changes that can take place in the market refer to stakeholders, to regulatory forces, and to the introduction of new technologies onto markets. For other examples, see Saebi et al. (2017).

Table 3.3 Business model innovation, adaptation, and experimentation.

Business model innovation...	Business model adaptation...
...takes place when firms aim to disrupt the ongoing market conditions and...	...takes place when components are modified to make them fit more with the market and...
... can be carried out through a discovery-driven approach that is based on incremental learning and related validations (business model experimentation)	

Source: Personal elaboration.

Beyond differences emerging between business model innovation and adaptation (Saebi et al., 2017), it is clear that in both cases the creation and delivery of value through a business model is risky. Achieved results can totally differ (in positive and negative terms) from the expected ones.[10]

A very interesting contribution, proposed in order to try to solve the above problem, deals with the experimentation of business models (Chesbrough, 2010; McGrath, 2010). Respectively, these scholars investigate experimentation in reference to business model innovation (Chesbrough, 2010) and to business model evolution, that is, adaptation (McGrath, 2010). What is said above gives strengths to the experimentation in reference to business models. The view of these scholars is rooted in the idea that uncertain, fast-moving, and unpredictable environments do not allow for the foreseeing of their possible evolutions. Hence, the reference to innovation or adaptation when setting up a business model can only be considered as a result of experimentation,[11] standing for a discovery-driven approach that consists of proceeding through incremental learning and related validations (checkpoints) in order to reduce costs and risks.[12] Experimentation makes the business model "highly path-dependent and unlikely to be determinable a priori" (McGrath, 2010, p. 255) but also more able to fit with probable market changes, if the process is carried out properly (see Table 3.3).

The idea of experimentation in reference to business models (Chesbrough, 2010; McGrath, 2010) seems to reconcile what was said above. Experimentation considers the dichotomy of empiricism/theorizing (Baden-Fuller and Morgan, 2010), the static and transformational perspectives (Demil and Lecocq, 2010), and the concepts of business model innovation and adaptation (Saebi et al., 2017). Therefore experimentation might represent the way to approach, and hopefully to solve, the

---

[10] According to DaSilva and Trkman (2014), in order to reduce risks or outperform, managers have to (1) choose the right business model; (2) execute the business model in an excellent way; (3) develop and strengthen the dynamic capabilities of the firm; and (4) modify the business model—effectively and timely—when it is necessary.

[11] McGrath (2010) underlines that (1) business model experimentation takes place across as well as within firms; (2) business model evolution is highly path-dependent; and (3) it is not possible to know in advance which design will win.

[12] Of course, the strategic orientation that firms disclose in reference to business model adaptation plays a relevant role (Saebi et al., 2017).

criticalities emerging in reference to the setting up[13] of business models. Shyly, the concept of experimentation seems to drive toward the concept of dynamic capabilities[14] that can shape the business model according to a strategic perspective (Achtenhagen et al., 2013; Andries et al., 2013; Cavalcante, 2014; Teece, 2018). Regardless, as Teece (2018, p. 42) underlines, "pioneering a new business model is not always a path to advantage." Risks related to experimenting and dynamic capabilities (which can take to pioneering business models) are too high and need to be properly evaluated.

Partly in line with the above, Chesbrough (2007) proposes a business model framework, which does not discuss experimentations in a straightforward way but - somehow - recalls that concept. According to the scholar, firms should evaluate their business models to try to improve them. This means moving from basic to advanced business models. In his contribution, Chesbrough lists six types of business models as follows:

1. An undifferentiated business model (firms selling commodities use this type of business model);
2. A business model with some differentiation (firms show some degree of differentiation in their products or services);
3. A segmented business model (firms show a high degree of differentiation in their products or services);
4. An externally aware business model (firms implement relationships with external partners to start new projects; implicitly, the business model needs to change);
5. A business model that integrates an innovation process (firms experiment with their business models); and
6. A business model based on an open and adaptive platform (firms model their value chain and adapt it to emerging needs).

From the above, it derives that beyond the differences—related to time, nature of changes, and pursued aims—innovation, adaptation, and experimentation confirm the always-changing nature of the business model.

3.4 Factors affecting the setting up of a business model

Despite the ongoing debates about the dichotomy empiricism/theorizing (Baden-Fuller and Morgan, 2010), the static and transformational perspectives (Demil and Lecocq, 2010), and the concepts of business model innovation and adaptation (Saebi et al., 2017), scholars tend to agree about the fact that some factors do affect the setting up of business models.

---

[13] Baden-Fuller and Morgan (2010) propose a very intriguing comparison between business models and living organisms. Business models need to change in order to fit with competitive setting. Consequently, they can be thought as real-life examples to study. The scholars write: "business models are to management what organisms are to biology" (Baden-Fuller and Morgan, 2010, p. 163).

[14] Of course, there is a clear reference to the theory about dynamic capabilities proposed by Teece, Pisano, and Shuen in 1997.

These factors depend neither on the theory that lies at the basis of a business model nor on the mindset of entrepreneurs or top managers. They are objective factors that, as such, determine the setting up of a business model. Specifically, they are the industry the firm is in and the firm's age.

3.4.1 Relevance of industry

The idea that industries play a relevant role when entrepreneurs are going to set up (or managers are going to modify) their business models can be found in several contributions that rebuild specific case studies and attempt to generalize the achieved results (Demil and Lecocq, 2010; McGrath, 2010; Zott and Amit, 2010; Baden-Fuller and Haefliger, 2013; Saebi et al., 2017; DaSilva, 2018). Teece (2010) is the scholar who mainly contributed to the affirmation of this idea when he opposed traditional industries and information/Internet industries.

According to him, it is of great importance to consider the industry the firm is in when investigating the setting up (or subsequent modification) of its business model. With respect to traditional industries, it is clearly underlined that business models must morph over time, as changing markets, technologies, and legal structures dictate and/or allow. It seems that the reference to an industry is an aspect that implies opportunities and threats that cannot be ignored.[15] In information/Internet industries, in fact, firms have always implemented challenging business models because of the dynamics that take place inside them (information is difficult to price and, consequently, new, unexpected, and unpredictable business models are set up or modified).

Further theoretical contributions seem to confirm the theoretical opposition between the traditional and information/Internet industries even if they do not compare the industries—just like Teece (2010) does. A contribution that is worth recalling in this vein is the one authored by Saebi et al. (2017). In their empirical research about business model adaptation, these scholars exclude some industries[16] that, from their point of view, can impede the generalization of achieved results. This somewhat implies that noticeable differences exist between industries. Other scholars, instead, focus their attention only on specific industries[17] but confirm Teece's view in the end.

---

[15] In this vein, Sanchez and Ricart (2010) propose a very interesting contribution concerning low-income markets.

[16] In the contribution of Saebi et al. (2017), the industries excluded from the survey are: agriculture, forestry, electricity, water-related industries, financial services, insurance industry, public administration, education, health and social work, sewage and refusal disposal, activities of membership organizations, cultural and sporting activities, and extra-territorial organizations. In particular, some of these industries are excluded because of "their close connections to, and funding from, the public sector" (Saebi et al., 2017, p. 572).

[17] See the contribution of McGrath (2010) who provides several examples of changes to business model such as: LEGO group, some social networks (such as Twitter, Facebook, My Space, and LinkedIn), Xerox, Southwest Airlines and Dell.

Zott and Amit (2010), for instance, analyze the case of FriCSo, an engineering company in the field of friction reduction. Since their core activity can be used in the machine manufacturing, automobile, or shipbuilding industries, it is very important for them to define their business model in an appropriate way. It is possible to define different business models, according to the way in which the business idea and its possible applications are understood. This means that high-tech industries can have different business models, that is, the unexpected and unpredictable ones.

The above result is in line with the idea that a business model is of great relevance in reference to technology-based companies,[18] related to ICT sectors in general (Froud et al., 2009; Aspara et al., 2011) and to the Internet industry in particular (Mahadevan, 2000; Chen, 2003; Pateli and Giaglis, 2004; Kshetri, 2007; DaSilva and Trkman, 2014; Doganova and Eyquem-Renault, 2009).

Demil and Lecocq (2010) analyze the case of the Arsenal Football Club. According to their analysis, it is clear that the Arsenal Football Club has modified its business model in order to achieve a satisfying performance (in terms of firm results). However, changes made have not modified the business model in a radical way. A football club, in fact, is in an industry where the football players, sponsors, and fans have a determinant role in achieving success, thus this role cannot be modified even if the business model changes. From the case study it emerges that, despite the depth of the changes made, the business model is respected and the changes are not radical.

A very recent stream of research is focused on the relevance of sustainable business models, which deal with industries that are strongly based on the concept of eco-efficiency, eco-innovation, and corporate social responsibility (Bocken et al., 2014; Lewandowski, 2016; Linder and Williander, 2017; Geissdoerfer et al., 2018; Manninen et al., 2018). Here, the business model takes on specific characteristics that assume a great value in those industries but that are not, at least up until now, commonly shared in other industries.

Regardless, the above review underlines the differences that can exist between industries even if, as already mentioned, the experimentation of business models can lead to new versions of business models that might consistently differ from previous ones. For this reason, scholars primarily pay attention to the age of firms, as this is an objective factor that can really affect the setting up or the modification of a business model.

3.4.2   Relevance of firm age

The conjecture that a business model can completely change in accordance with the age of a firm is widely embraced by scholars (Fiet and Patel, 2008; Chesbrough, 2010; Demil and Lecocq, 2010; McGrath, 2010; Sosna et al., 2010; Teece, 2010, 2018; Zott and Amit, 2010; Saebi et al., 2017), who underline this in their contributions very often. In fact, while some scholars focus their interest only on startups or

---

[18] Euchner and Ganguly (2014) cite the cases of companies that have developed new business models such as Netflix, Dell and the Apple iTunes.

on established firms—by driving readers to derive the tacit implications—other scholars openly compare startups and established firms in order to highlight the differences between them.

Among the scholars who address their interest toward startups, it is suitable to cite Teece (2010) and McGrath (2010). The former argues that it is over the start-up phase that entrepreneurs define the design or architecture of the value creation, delivery, and capture mechanisms, that is, their business model (Teece, 2010). This scholar clearly states that the ideal business model never comes to existence during the start-up phase. The latter claims that new firms define their business models in accordance with their core activities and, thus, they can define all the main characteristics of their business models (McGrath, 2010). Hence, it is clear that entrepreneurs who are launching their startups can evaluate several alternatives before selecting the one that fits their core activity the most. Even if not explicitly maintained, this means that established firms do not have the same possibility.

Scholars who focus their attention on established firms confirm this. According to Saebi et al. (2017), established firms try to adapt their business models but can fail in this endeavor. Put simply, established firms have fewer alternatives than the startup firms do, because they are already on the market and could, therefore, only attempt to adjust their business models. Similarly, Demil and Lecocq (2010) argue that established firms could face changes in their cost/revenue structures (which can be due to new productive inputs, to the reengineering of an organizational process, or to the internalization/externalization of a value chain activity), needing to modify their business models as a result. Also, in this case, it is possible to begin certain processes that aim to change business models by leveraging some drivers or facilitators, but the alternatives are limited in number. In this vein, Chesbrough (2010) underlines that barriers to changing business models of established firms are authentic. Dedicated tools might be helpful but their contribution can be limited. Even if the above scholars do not compare established firms and startups, it is clear that cited difficulties can be applied to established firms and not to startups.

The difference between startups and established firms—a difference that is indirectly derived by going through the above contributions—is clearly expressed by other scholars.[19] Zott and Amit (2010, p. 217) argue that the design of a business model is a key decision for an entrepreneur who creates a new firm and a crucial—perhaps more difficult—task for general managers who are charged with rethinking their old model to make their firm fit for the future. Once the template is set, the activities are in place, and the resources have been developed and honed, that template will be difficult to change, due to forces of inertia and resistance to change.

Furthermore, McGrath (2010) states that incumbents might leverage the experimentation of a business model because of their contractual power on the market

[19] Among the several contributions, it is relevant to cite the one proposed by Nair and Blomquist (2019) who describe the phases through which business model develops. They are business model validation, business model development, and business model scalability. These phases mark the passage from entrepreneurial firms to bigger (or even established) firms.

and of their resources. However, empirical cases[20] show that only true startups can benefit from changes in the market. These firms are more inclined to experiment with new business models rather than established firms, which keep their business models as they are, if they work well on the market, instead.

Similarly, Teece (2018) argues that startups find the setting up of their business models to be easier than mature firms find the transformation of their business models to be. This is true because startups have fewer established assets and procedures to re-engineer. Recently, Nair and Blomquist (2019) have confirmed this idea. According to these scholars, a business model passes through four phases[21]: perceptions of the team around a scalable idea, validation of the business model, development of the business model, and business model scalability. Since entrepreneurial firms begin with the perceptions connected to a scalable idea and then they go through the validation and development processes in order to reach business model scalability, they are more likely to modify their business model than the establishes firms are (see also Mason and Spring, 2011; Hacklin and Wallnöfer, 2012; Barquet et al., 2013). The latter might already be in the phase of business model scalability and, consequently, changes to the business model might be difficult to make.

While it may seem that startups have a lot of advantages that established firms do not, this is true only to a certain extent. The business models of startups, in fact, are strongly influenced by their founders' education and previous work experiences (Sosna et al., 2010). This means that all the alternatives evoked before are restricted because of the profile and the background of entrepreneurs. Similarly to what happens to established firms (which suffer organizational inertia and lock-in effects), startups might also face some obstacles when setting up their business models (see Table 3.4).

From the above, two interesting results are obtained. The first is the relevance of the business models of startups, which can be selected among several possibilities

Table 3.4 Obstacles to the setting up of business models.

Established firms...	Entrepreneurial firms...
...might be more inclined to modify their business models because of their contractual power on the market and of their resources...	...might be more inclined to modify their business models because their structures are more flexible...
...however, they cannot easily modify their business models because of established assets and reengineering procedures	...however, they cannot easily modify their business models because they depend on their founders' education and previous work experience

Source: Personal elaboration.

---

[20] In her contribution, McGrath (2010) analyzes the Internet-based industries.

[21] Even if the scholars refer to Swedish business incubators and to their ability to set up a business model, the phases can be easily generalized to all entrepreneurial firms.

(as previously mentioned, in some industries the business models of startups can be unexpected and unpredictable). The second is the reference to the entrepreneurs' individual characteristics that probably affect the setting up of business models.

As already noted in reference to the performance of entrepreneurial firms,[22] the individual characteristics of entrepreneurs and their entrepreneurial intentions are not considered herein because the aim of this volume is to draw entrepreneurship trajectories that are objective in nature and that do not depend on entrepreneurial profiles. For this reason, in the next sections, attention is focused on the business models of startups without any reference to the characteristics of the entrepreneurs setting them up. Even if this might be detrimental to the analysis (i.e., the effect of the entrepreneurs' individual characteristics not being considered), the choice is justified by the cognitive aim pursued by this volume.

3.5   Entrepreneurial firms and their business models

Although the relevance that business models can have for entrepreneurial firms is clear, studies about business models and entrepreneurial firms have always proceeded along distinct paths (Trimi and Berbegal-Mirabent, 2012). The practice of combining these streams is so recent that some scholars underline the fact that there was no consistent framework to refer to until recently (George and Bock, 2011).

Among the contributions focused on the business models of entrepreneurial firms (Morris et al., 2005; McGrath, 2010; Sosna et al., 2010; Zott and Amit, 2010), it is worth recalling the one authored by Zott and Amit (2007) who, starting from their previous study (Amit and Zott, 2001), attempt to refer the concept of a business model to entrepreneurial firms exclusively.

Beyond the reference to entrepreneurial firms, the choice to recall the contribution by Zott and Amit (2007) is also due to the fact that these scholars introduce the concept of design themes[23] of business model. They try to drive attention toward specific configurations of a business model. Rather than defining the contents of business models or enlisting the activities included in them or the parts constituting them, they focus their attention on the theme—that is, on the idea at the basis of business models. This means interpreting a business model from a larger perspective that reduces the relevance of each of its individual parts but underlines the relevance of the approach at its basis at the same time. Implicitly, this means that the details of a business model are sacrificed in favor of a broader approach to or a general view of a business model. In reference to entrepreneurial firms, which have not defined their business model yet (Teece, 2010, 2018) and can modify it with fewer constraints than incumbent firms (McGrath, 2010), this approach seems more fitting. Thus it is adopted hereinafter.

Amit and Zott (2001) identify four design themes that can refer to business model. They are novelty, lock-in, complementarities, and efficiency. If the design

[22] See Section 2.4.
[23] The concept of "design themes" was already cited in Section 3.2.

Table 3.5 Design themes.

Established firms	Entrepreneurial firms
Amit and Zott (2001, 2015) enlist these four alternative design themes: 1. Novelty 2. Lock-in 3. Complementarities 4. Efficiency	Zott and Amit (2007) reduce the alternatives to two when they investigate entrepreneurial firms: 1. Novelty 2. Efficiency

Source: Personal elaboration.

theme is novelty, then the business model is focused on new activities and new ways of linking and managing them. The dominant design concerns novelty and all that is new for a firm. If the design theme is lock-in, then the business model is focused on activities able to pull stakeholders and implement long-lasting relationships with them. If the design theme is complementarities, then the business model is focused on bundling activities and exchanges. Finally, if the design theme is efficiency, then the business model focuses on cost-reducing transactions and activities in order to improve economic efficiency.

Even if the scholars enlist four design themes, specify their characteristics, and validate them (Amit and Zott, 2001, 2015), it is the scholars themselves who reduce the optional design themes when discussing entrepreneurial firms[24] (Zott and Amit, 2007) and focus their attention on the design themes related to novelty and efficiency (see Table 3.5).

In their analysis, these scholars specify that the design themes of business models that are focused on novelty and efficiency are neither mutually exclusive nor uncontaminated (efficiency design elements can refer to novelty-related issues and vice-versa) and, moreover, they are not even exhaustive (novelty- and efficiency-centered business models can include some aspects of lock-in and complementarities design themes).

Unthinkingly, business models designed around novelty exploit the concept of newness. They can include new ways of understanding an entrepreneurial opportunity, of designing and managing economic transactions, of linking external parties, of referring to the external market—by new products or services (Björkdahl and Holmén, 2013). The only constant is the reference to something new that consistently differs from what the firm (or other firms) did before.[25]

---

[24] In their contribution (Zott and Amit, 2007, p. 182), the scholars write: "we identify two critical themes of business model design − efficiency centered and novelty centered—and offer hypotheses about the impact of business model design themes on the performance of the focal entrepreneurial firm." Even if they do not question about the relevance that the other design themes (lock-in and complementarities) can have, they focus their attention only on the design themes related to efficiency and novelty when talking about entrepreneurial firms.

[25] According to the scholars, e-Bay and Dell are some examples of business models designed around novelty.

At this stage, a sequence of reflections naturally flows. First, it is implicit that firms setting up a novelty-centered business model are innovative firms who offer something new to the market. The idea of setting up a business model oriented toward novelty needs to be rooted in the innovation that such firms want to exploit. Subsequently, a firm can transpose the concept of newness into their business model as well. Second, the higher the degree of business model novelty is, the higher the performance that these firms can achieve would be.[26] Once customers, suppliers, and stakeholders generally meant have been locked-in because of the novelty offered to them, it is not easy for them to switch to another firm. This means that firms with a business model designed around novelty can expect superior performances. Actually, Zott and Amit (2007) empirically demonstrate that business models designed around novelty positively affect the performance of entrepreneurial firms.

On the contrary, business models designed around efficiency leverage imitation rather than innovation (conveyed in a business model designed around novelty). By leveraging imitation, it is clear that such firms try to pursue a different aim, consisting of reducing transaction costs[27] through simplified or repetitive transactions with the same stakeholders (Meyer et al., 1992), and to create value—which is at the basis of the transaction cost theory (Williamson 1975, 1983). The idea that business models designed around efficiency leverage imitation rather than innovation might drive toward the assumption that this business model theme is not suitable for entrepreneurial firms (which, by definition, are young and innovative). In fact, during the times of paucity and in uncertain and risky contexts, entrepreneurial firms might be interested in efficiency-centered business models; hence, their relevance cannot be excluded *a priori*.

The fact that business models designed around efficiency can also be of some value to entrepreneurial firms recalls the idea that design themes are neither mutually exclusive nor uncontaminated (as mentioned earlier, efficiency design elements can refer to novelty-related issues and vice-versa). For this reason, Zott and Amit (2007) propose a business model design theme that is created by mixing novelty and efficiency themes (see also Zott and Huy, 2007). In the view of these scholars, novelty and efficiency can be complementary and can have a positive impact on performance when used together. Firms that aim to exploit novelty can also leverage efficiency and firms that aim to exploit efficiency can also leverage novelty. Thus it results that efficiency and novelty are two concepts that can nurture each other. However, the results that can be achieved by mixing efficiency and novelty themes are not straightforward. On the one hand, firms can create more value if they focus on both rather than only on one (i.e., efficiency or novelty). On the other hand, the mix between efficiency and novelty can become stuck between innovation and imitation, which might cause unsatisfactory results. All the types of business models that entrepreneurial firms can implement are listed in Table 3.6.

---

[26] See also the contribution authored by Lambert and Davidson (2013).

[27] According to the scholars, Amazon is a good example of business model designed around efficiency since it aims to disclose its transaction transparency (Zott and Amit, 2007, p. 185).

Table 3.6 Business model types that entrepreneurial firms can implement.

Business model types	Definition
Novelty-centered	They include new ways of understanding an entrepreneurial opportunity, of designing and managing economic transactions, of linking external parties, of referring to the external market
Efficiency-centered	They try to pursue a different aim, consisting of reducing transaction costs through simplified or repetitive transactions with the same stakeholders, in order to create value
Mixed	Novelty and efficiency can be complementary. Firms can aim to exploit novelty by leveraging efficiency or they can aim to exploit efficiency by leveraging novelty

Source: Personal elaboration.

3.6 Concluding remarks

Despite achievable results, in terms of satisfactory or unsatisfactory performance that firms can reach through their business models, the contribution authored by Zott and Amit (2007) identifies three alternative themes that entrepreneurial firms can evaluate when they set up their business models. These alternatives are designed around novelty, efficiency, or both (see Table 3.6).

A major aspect that is worth underlining concerns the fact that design themes do not analyze the specific components of a business model. On the contrary, they simply express the concept at their basis (such as innovation, cost reduction, or both). Since they can be easily generalized, these themes are very suitable for proposing entrepreneurship trajectories.

As previously mentioned, this volume aims to propose entrepreneurship trajectories that can easily generalize what happens when carrying out entrepreneurial phenomena. Accordingly, the choice to focus attention on the concepts at the basis of entrepreneurial firms' business models rather than on the specific components included in the business model seems the most appropriate one.

Novelty and efficiency are generalized concepts to which all firms (including entrepreneurial ones) can refer. In this vein, the impulsive reference to two main competitive strategies (differentiation and cost leadership[28]) confirms the relevance of these concepts. At the same time, the reference to these theories rooted in the field of strategic management provides another important insight.[29] Strategic management scholars define the alternatives to be addressed with no reference to the individual characteristics of the managers implementing them (whether they are more or less inclined toward risk). Thus, by transposing these concepts to the field of entrepreneurship, it is possible to preserve the idea that the individual

---

[28] Differentiation and cost leadership are two well-known competitive strategies proposed by Porter (1985).

[29] In this vein, see the contributions authored by Zott and Amit (2008, 2013).

characteristics of entrepreneurs setting up their business models can be temporarily put aside, without, of course, denying their relevance.

At this stage, one question about entrepreneurial firms and their business models comes out. As shown, business models depend on the industry, on the age of firms, or on the individual profile of the entrepreneurs setting them up only to a certain extent. So, what do business models strictly depend on?

In order to answer this question, it is not correct to think about the aim that entrepreneurs/managers pursue by leveraging business models (i.e., value creation). Attention should be addressed toward the ancestors of business models instead. It is important to investigate the causes that might affect the choice between a business model designed around novelty, efficiency, or both. This issue has been scarcely investigated by scholars who—*au contraire*—have largely investigated the impact and the result of a business model (Magretta, 2002; Shafer et al., 2005).

According to Zott and Amit (2010, p. 217), "the overall objective of a focal firm's business model is to exploit a business opportunity by creating value for parties involved." This specific statement discloses what could lie at the basis of a business model by driving attention toward entrepreneurial opportunities.

In view of the fact that entrepreneurial opportunities can vary across and within industries, can have different origins, and can be exploited in different ways, it seems reasonable to investigate them and to clarify their role in reference to entrepreneurship trajectories.

References

Achtenhagen, L., Melin, L., Naldi, L., 2013. Dynamics of business models; strategizing, critical capabilities and activities for sustained value creation. Long Range Plann. 46 (6), 427–442.

Afuah, A., 2004. Business Models: A Strategic Management Approach. Irwin/McGraw-Hill, New York, NY.

Afuah, A., Tucci, C.L., 2001. Internet Business Models and Strategies: Text and Cases.. McGraw-Hill, New York, NY.

Amit, R., Zott, C., 2001. Value creation in e-business. Strat. Manag. J. 22 (6–7), 493–520.

Amit, R., Zott, C., 2012. Creating value through business model innovation. MIT Sloan Manag. Rev. 53 (3), 41–49.

Amit, R., Zott, C., 2015. Crafting business architecture: the antecedents of business model design. Strat. Entrepr. J. 9 (4), 331–350.

Andries, P., Debackere, K., Van Looy, B., 2013. Simultaneous experimentation as a learning strategy: business model development under uncertainty. Strat. Entrepr. J. 7 (4), 288–310.

Ansoff, I., 1979. The changing shape of the strategic problem. In: Schendel, D., Hofer, C. (Eds.), Strategic management: A new view of business policy and planning: 37-44. Little Brown and Co, Boston.

Arend, R.J., 2013. The business model: present and future: beyond a Skeumorph. Strat. Org. 11 (4), 390–402.

Aspara, J., Lamberg, J.A., Laukia, A., Tikkanen, H., 2011. Strategic management of business model transformation: lessons from Nokia. Manag. Decision 49 (4), 622−647.

Baden-Fuller, C., Haefliger, S., 2013. Business models and technological innovation. Long Range Plann. 46 (6), 419−426.

Baden-Fuller, C., Mangematin, V., 2013. Business models: a challenging agenda. Strat. Org. 11 (4), 418−427.

Baden-Fuller, C., Morgan, M.S., 2010. Business models as models. Long Range Plann. 43 (2−3), 156−171.

Barquet, A.P.B., de Oliveira, M.G., Amigo, C.R., Cunha, V.P., Rozenfeld, H., 2013. Employing the business model concept to support the adoption of product−service systems (PSS). Ind. Market. Manag. 42 (5), 693−704.

Bellman, R., Clark, C.E., Malcolm, D.G., Craft, C.J., Ricciardi, F.M., 1957. On the construction of a multi-stage, multi-person business game. Oper. Res. 5 (4), 469−503.

Björkdahl, J., Holmén, M., 2013. Business model innovation: the challenges ahead. Int. J. Prod. Dev. 18 (3/4), 213−225.

Bocken, N.M., Short, S.W., Rana, P., Evans, S., 2014. A literature and practice review to develop sustainable business model archetypes. J. Clean. Prod. 65, 42−56.

Casadesus-Masanell, R., Ricart, J.E., 2010. From strategy to business models and onto tactics. Long Range Plann. 43 (2−3), 195−215.

Cavalcante, S.A., 2014. Preparing for business model change: the "pre-stage" finding. J. Manag. Govern. 18 (2), 449−469.

Chandler, A.D., 1962. Strategy and Structure: Chapters in the History of the Industrial Enterprise. MIT Press, Cambridge, MA.

Chen, S., 2003. The real value of "e-business models.". Bus. Horiz. 46 (6), 27−33.

Chesbrough, H., 2007. Business model innovation: it's not just about technology anymore. Strat. Leadership 35 (6), 12−17.

Chesbrough, H., 2010. Business model innovation: opportunities and barriers. Long Range Plann. 43 (2−3), 354−363.

Chesbrough, H., Rosenbloom, R.S., 2002. The role of the business model in capturing value from innovation: evidence from Xerox Corporation's technology spin-off companies. Ind. Corp. Change 11 (3), 529−555.

DaSilva, C.M., 2018. Understanding business model innovation from a practitioner perspective. J. Bus. Models 6 (2), 19−24.

DaSilva, C.M., Trkman, P., 2014. Business model: what it is and what it is not. Long Range Plann. 47 (6), 379−389.

Demil, B., Lecocq, X., 2010. Business model evolution: in search of dynamic consistency. Long Range Plann. 43 (2−3), 227−246.

Desyllas, P., Sako, M., 2013. Profiting from business model innovation: evidence from Pay-As-You-Drive auto insurance. Res. Policy 42 (1), 101−116.

Doganova, L., Eyquem-Renault, M., 2009. What do business models do? Innovation devices in technology entrepreneurship. Res. Policy 38 (10), 1559−1570.

Eismann, R.T., 2002. Internet Business Models. McGraw-Hill Irwin, New York, NY.

Euchner, J., Ganguly, A., 2014. Business model innovation in practice. Res.Technol. Manag. 57 (6), 33−39.

Fiet, J.O., Patel, P.C., 2008. Forgiving business models for new ventures. Entrepr.: Theory Pract. 32 (4), 749−761.

Foss, N.J., Saebi, T., 2018. Business models and business model innovation: between wicked and paradigmatic problems. Long Range Plann. 51 (1), 9−21.

Froud, J., Johal, S., Leaver, A., Phillips, R., Williams, K., 2009. Stressed by choice: a business model analysis of the BBC. Br. J. Manag. 20 (2), 252−264.

Gambardella, A., McGahan, A.M., 2010. Business-model innovation: general purpose technologies and their implications for industry structure. Long Range Plann. 43 (2−3), 262−271.

Geissdoerfer, M., Morioka, S.N., de Carvalho, M.M., Evans, S., 2018. Business models and supply chains for the circular economy. J. Clean. Prod. 190, 712−721.

George, G., Bock, A.J., 2011. The business model in practice and its implications for entrepreneurship research. Entrepr.: Theory Pract. 35 (1), 83−111.

Haas, Y., 2018. A qualitative approach to business model dynamics. J. Bus. Models 6 (2), 37−43.

Hacklin, F., Wallnöfer, M., 2012. The business model in the practice of strategic decision making: insights from a case study. Manag. Decision 50 (2), 166−188.

Hedman, J., Kalling, T., 2003. The business model concept: theoretical underpinnings and empirical illustrations. Eur. J. Inform. Syst. 12 (1), 49−59.

Hofer, C.W., Schendel, D., 1978. Strategy formulation: Analytical concepts. St. Paul, MN: West.

Johnson, M.W., 2018. Reinvent Your Business Model. Harvard Business Review Press, Boston, MA.

Johnson, M.W., Christensen, C.M., Kagermann, H., 2008. Reinventing your business model. Harvard Bus. Rev. 86 (12), 57−68.

Jones, G.M., 1960. Educators, electrons, and business models: a problem in synthesis. Acc. Rev. 35 (4), 619−626.

Klang, D., Wallnöfer, M., Hacklin, F., 2014. The business model paradox: a systematic review and exploration of antecedents. Int. J. Manag. Rev. 16 (4), 454−478.

Kshetri, N., 2007. Barriers to e-commerce and competitive business models in developing countries: a case study. Electron. Comm. Res. Appl. 6 (4), 443−452.

Lambert, S.C., Davidson, R.A., 2013. Applications of the business model in studies of enterprise success, innovation and classification: an analysis of empirical research from 1996 to 2010. Eur. Manag. J. 31 (6), 668−681.

Lewandowski, M., 2016. Designing the business models for circular economy: towards the conceptual framework. Sustainability 8 (1), 1−28.

Linder, M., Williander, M., 2017. Circular business model innovation: inherent uncertainties. Bus. Strat. Environ. 26 (2), 182−196.

Lindman, M.T., 2007. Remarks on the quality of the construction of business concepts. Eur. Bus. Rev. 19 (3), 196−215.

Magretta, J., 2002. Why business model matters. Harvard Bus. Rev. 80 (5), 86−92.

Mahadevan, B., 2000. Business models for Internet-based e-commerce: an anatomy. Calif. Manag. Rev. 42 (4), 55−69.

Manninen, K., Koskela, S., Antikainen, R., Bocken, N., Dahlbo, H., Aminoff, A., 2018. Do circular economy business models capture intended environmental value propositions? J. Clean. Prod. 171, 413−422.

Massa, L., Tucci, C.L., 2013. Business Model Innovation. The Oxford Handbook of Innovation Management. Oxford University Press, Oxford, pp. 420−441.

Mason, K., Spring, M., 2011. The sites and practices of business models. Ind. Market. Manag. 40 (6), 1032−1041.

McGrath, R.G., 2010. Business models: a discovery driven approach. Long Range Plan. 43 (2−3), 247−261.

Meyer, M., Milgrom, P., Roberts, J., 1992. Organizational prospects, influence costs, and ownership changes. J. Econ. Manag. Strat. 1 (1), 9−35.

Mitchell, D., Coles, C., 2003. The ultimate competitive advantage of continuing business model innovation. J. Busi.Strat. 24 (5), 15−21.

Morris, M., Schindehutte, M., Allen, J., 2005. The entrepreneur's business model: toward a unified perspective. J. Bus. Res. 58 (6), 726−735.

Nair, S., Blomquist, T., 2019. Failure prevention and management in business incubation: practices towards a scalable business model. Technol. Anal. Strat. Manag. 31 (3), 266−278.

Nenonen, S., Storbacka, K., 2010. Business model design: conceptualizing networked value co-creation. Int. J. Qual. Service Sci. 2 (1), 43−59.

Osterwalder, A., Pigneur, Y., Tucci, C.L., 2005. Clarifying business models: origins, present, and future of the concept. Commun. Assoc. Inform. Systems 16 (1), 1−25.

Pateli, A.G., Giaglis, G.M., 2004. A research framework for analysing eBusiness models. Eur. J. Inform. Syst. 13 (4), 302−314.

Pateli, A.G., Giaglis, G.M., 2005. Technology innovation-induced business model change: a contingency approach. J. Orga. Change Manag. 18 (2), 167−183.

Penrose, E., 1959. The Theory of the Growth of the Firm. Basil Blackwell and Mott, Oxford.

Porter, M.E., 1985. Competitive Advantage: Creating and Sustaining Superior Performance.. The Free Press, New York, NY.

Porter, M.E., 1996. What is strategy? Harvard Bus. Rev. 74, 61−79.

Raff, D.M.G., 2000. Superstores and the evolution of firm capabilities in American bookselling. Strat. Manag. J. 21 (10−11), 1043−1059.

Saebi, T., Lien, L., Foss, N.J., 2017. What drives business model adaptation? The impact of opportunities, threats and strategic orientation. Long Range Plann. 50 (5), 567−581.

Sanchez, P., Ricart, J.E., 2010. Business model innovation and sources of value creation in low-income markets. Eur. Manag. Rev. 7 (3), 138−154.

Schön, O., 2012. Business model modularità: a way to gain strategic flexibility? Control. Manag. 56 (2), 73−78.

Shafer, S.M., Smith, H.J., Linder, J.C., 2005. The power of business models. Bus. Horiz. 48 (3), 199−207.

Sosna, M., Trevinyo-Rodríguez, R.N., Velamuri, S.R., 2010. Business model innovation through trial-and-error learning: the Naturhouse case. Long Range Plann. 43 (2−3), 383−407.

Spieth, P., Schneckenberg, D., Ricart, J.E., 2014. Business model innovation: state of the art and future challenges for the field. R&D Management 44 (3), 237−247.

Teece, D.J., 2007. Explicating dynamic capabilities: the nature and microfoundations of (sustainable) enterprise performance. Strat. Manag. J. 28 (13), 1319−1350.

Teece, D.J., 2010. Business models, business strategy and innovation. Long Range Plann. 43 (2−3), 172−194.

Teece, D.J., 2018. Business models and dynamic capabilities. Long Range Plann. 51 (1), 40−49.

Teece, D.J., Pisano, G., Shuen, A., 1997. Dynamic capabilities and strategic management. Strat. Manag. J. 18 (7), 509−533.

Thompson, J.D., MacMillan, I.C., 2010. Business models: creating new markets and societal wealth. Long Range Plann. 43 (2−3), 291−307.

Trimi, S., Berbegal-Mirabent, J., 2012. Business model innovation in entrepreneurship. Int. Entrepr. Manag. J. 8 (4), 449−465.

Velu, C., Jacob, A., 2016. Business model innovation and owner—managers: the moderating role of competition. R&D Manag. 46 (3), 451−463.

Voelpel, S.C., Leibold, M., Tekie, E.B., 2004. The wheel of business model reinvention: how to reshape your business model to leapfrog competitors. J. Change Manag. 4 (3), 259−276.

Voelpel, S., Leibold, M., Tekie, E., Von Krogh, G., 2005. Escaping the red queen effect in competitive strategy: sense-testing business models. Eur. Manag. J. 23 (1), 37−49.

Williamson, O.E., 1975. Markets and Hierarchies: Analysis and Antitrust Implication − A Study in the Economics of Internal Organizations. Free Press, MacMillan, New York, NY.

Williamson, O.E., 1983. Credible commitments: using hostage to support axchange. Am. Econ. Rev. 73 (4), 519−540.

Winter, S.G., Szulanski, G., 2001. Replication as strategy. Org. Sci. 12 (6), 730−743.

Wirtz, B.W., Daiser, P., 2017. Business model innovation: an integrative conceptual framework. J. Bus. Models 5 (1), 14−34.

Wirtz, B.W., Pistoia, A., Ullrich, S., Göttel, V., 2016. Business models: origin, development and future research perspectives. Long Range Plann. 49 (1), 36−54.

Yip, G.S., 2004. Using strategy to change your business model. Bus. Strat. Rev. 15 (2), 17−24.

Zott, C., Amit, R., 2007. Business model design and the performance of entrepreneurial firms. Org. Sci. 18 (2), 181−199.

Zott, C., Amit, R., 2008. The fit between product market strategy and business model: implications for firm performance. Strat. Manag. J. 29 (1), 1−26.

Zott, C., Amit, R., 2010. Business model design: an activity system perspective. Long Range Plann. 43 (2−3), 216−226.

Zott, C., Amit, R., 2013. The business model: a theoretically anchored robust construct for strategic analysis. Strat. Org. 11 (4), 403−411.

Zott, C., Huy, Q., 2007. Symbolic emphasizing: how entrepreneurs use symbolism to acquire resources. Admin. Sci. Q. 52 (1), 70−105.

Zott, C., Amit, R., Massa, L., 2010. The business model: theoretical roots, recent developments, and future research. IESE Bus. School − Univ. Navarra 1−43.

Zott, C., Amit, R., Massa, L., 2011. The business model: recent developments and future research. J. Manag. 37 (4), 1019−1042.

Further reading

Bellman, R., Clark, C.E., Malcolm, D.G., Craft, C.J., Ricciardi, F.M., 1957. On the construction of a multi-stage, multi-person business game. Oper. Res. 5 (4), 469−503.

Brettel, M., Strese, S., Flatten, T.C., 2012. Improving the performance of business models with relationship marketing efforts: an entrepreneurial perspective. Eur. Manag. J. 30 (2), 85−98.

Cavalcante, S.A., Kesting, P., Ulhøi, J., 2011. Business model dynamics and innovation: (re) establishing the missing linkages. Manag. Decision 49 (8), 1327−1342.

Entrepreneurial opportunities

4

4.1 The identification of entrepreneurial opportunities

Before analyzing the origins of entrepreneurial opportunities or, from the opposite point of view, the way entrepreneurial opportunities are identified (i.e., recognized, discovered, or created), it is necessary to first define the boundaries of the research field accurately. Even if the exploitation of entrepreneurial opportunities undoubtedly lies in the economic field,[1] the same is not true of the identification of entrepreneurial opportunities. The act of identification, in fact, goes beyond economic borders into different research fields. This is due to several reasons.

The first reason is the decisive role played by reality. It is the *incipit* from which the entrepreneurial process begins. An opportunity, in fact, is literally defined as "an amount of time or a situation in which something can be done" (Merriam-Webster's English Dictionary). An entrepreneurial opportunity, instead, can be defined as "a feasible, profit-seeking, potential venture that provides an innovative new product or service to the market, improves on an existing product/service, or imitates a profitable product/service in a less-then-saturated market" (Singh, 2001, p. 11). This definition makes such opportunities referable to many research fields. They can be born in every possible context and there is no exclusively economic origin of opportunities.

The second reason results from individuals' involvement with reality. It is simply through the actions of individuals that opportunities come into existence. In order to make this happen, basically, an agent does not refer only to economic parameters. In most cases, opportunities are the result of individual differences.

The third and last reason can be found in the output of identification phase. Opportunities, at that point, are not entrepreneurial. They need to be evaluated accurately to define whether they can yield a profit or not. Some of them, in fact, can be far from exploitable in the market.

Overall, the assumption that the identification of opportunities does not strictly lie in the economic field of research but also moves among the psychological, social, and cognitive research fields seems to be a valid starting point for the following analysis. The underlying rationale of this analysis is straightforward because it concerns the evolution of the approaches to opportunity identification, according to both an empirical and a theoretical perspective.

---

[1] Many entrepreneurship scholars (Shane and Venkataraman, 2000; Casson and Wadeson, 2007; Plummer et al., 2007; Sleptsov and Anand, 2008) refer to the economic evaluations that entrepreneurs need to carry out before deciding whether to exploit or not an entrepreneurial opportunity.

Entrepreneurship Trajectories. DOI: https://doi.org/10.1016/B978-0-12-818650-3.00004-0

The evolution of the individual-opportunity nexus (Shane, 2003) can be clarified by recalling three different approaches that have been proposed over the years.[2] They are the neoclassical, the Austrian, and the contemporary approach.

All of them are based on the individual intent to earn a profit (Shane and Venkataraman, 2000; Mueller, 2007; Hmielesky and Baron, 2008; Ucbasaran et al., 2008) but each looks at the determinant factor, which is the one leading the individual toward the identification of an entrepreneurial opportunity, as exogenous or endogenous.

The external origins of opportunities start from the idea that reality exists by itself. All changes that can happen in a noneconomic setting, for example, in the technological, political, or social setting, can be a source of new entrepreneurial opportunities. These changes take place continually and create newer and newer opportunities. They are objective and always awaiting to be taken (i.e., recognized or discovered).

On the contrary, by admitting the internal origins of opportunities, a "differential access to existing information" (Shane, 2003, p. 20) is required to identify opportunities. In this case, it is not important to determine what causes them. All that matters is that, by leveraging individual capabilities, opportunities can come into existence (i.e., they are created).

As can be noticed, even if both theories consider information as existing, the approach is different. In fact, by admitting that all contextual changes provide new information, it is implicitly affirmed that individuals do not play a decisive role. Actually, it seems possible to argue that they do not even play any role in reference to the birth of entrepreneurial opportunities. Instead, if it is considered that individuals use the information they possess, the *locus* of opportunity birth is internal.

McMullen and Shepherd (2006, p. 133) make an interesting contribution to the understanding of this difference when they discuss the notions of "third-person opportunity" and "first-person opportunity." The former type of opportunity is the one that exists for anyone; the latter is one meant for a specific economic agent. In other words, it means that everyone can grasp third-person opportunities but only one individual is able to grasp a first-person opportunity.[3] Accordingly, the role of individuals radically changes—to such an extent that it seems possible that individuals will go beyond the act of recognition or discovery toward the creation of an opportunity by shaping reality in accordance with their will.

---

[2] In reference to the individual-opportunity nexus, it is interesting to recall two contributions: the former authored by Eckhardt and Shane (2013) who analyze objective and subjective aspects of entrepreneurship and integrate them in the original individual-opportunity nexus; the latter authored by Davidsson (2015) who proposes a reconceptualization of entrepreneurial opportunities and the entrepreneurship nexus.

[3] Smith et al. (2009) propose a similar distinction when they divide opportunities in codified and tacit. The first are a "well-documented, articulated or communicated profit-seeking situation in which a person seeks to exploit market inefficiency in a less-than-saturated market," instead the second are a "profit-seeking situation that is difficult to codify, articulate or communicate in which a person seeks to exploit market inefficiency in a less-than-saturated market" (p. 44). See also Gaglio (2004) and McMullen (2015).

Table 4.1 The elements used for differentiating entrepreneurial opportunities.

Domain or subject	Explanations	External conditions
What How	Why	Who Where When

Source: Personal elaboration.

This brief synthesis about the external or internal origins of entrepreneurial opportunities is just a premise from which to study the neoclassical, the Austrian, and the contemporary approaches in a more formal way. To frame each approach, it is necessary to begin with an analysis of the main scholars who support each theory; only then will it be possible to make some conjectures about the peculiar elements of each approach.

In general terms, the frameworks used to mark the peculiar elements of each approach are subjected to both an empirical and a theoretical perspective in this study.[4] It means that the first level of analysis deals with the ever-changing empirical world in which entrepreneurial action takes place (Spedale and Watson, 2014). The second level of analysis, instead, concerns assumptions about the objective or subjective nature of entrepreneurial phenomenon. More specifically, the analysis of the empirical perspective is based on a list of six key elements proposed by Companys and McMullen (2007) in reference to Whetten's theory (1989). These six elements that are going to be considered are: what, how, why, who, where, and when.[5]

In order to proceed with determining the most influential element, Whetten (1989) proposes dividing them into three categories. The first, comprehending what and how, contributes to determine the domain or subject of theory and provides a detailed description of the entrepreneurial phenomenon. The second category consists of why and gives explanations for it. The third one, based on the analysis of who, where, and when, analyzes the conditions in which entrepreneurial action takes place instead. The groups of elements are shown in Table 4.1.

Obviously, the empirical perspective seeks to determine which element influences the entrepreneurial process the most. The inquiry starts with the assumption that one key element is a determinant over the others, which still contribute to the process itself, of course. When focusing on each of the three approaches, this study demonstrates that the determinant element tends to change over time.

---

[4] McMullen and Shepherd (2006) propose another approach to create an "action framework" when they leverage the pragmatic and the conceptual perspectives.

[5] Recalling Whetten's theory about journalistic questions (1989), Companys and McMullen try to explain each of the six key elements. In fact, "what" is used to identify variables, constructs and concepts able to explain a phenomenon; "how" can inquire the relation existing between factors; "why" is the element that justifies the phenomenon; "when" is the temporal factor; "where" is the contextual factor; and "who" defines the subject involved. As it will be clear, the original classification proposed by Companys and McMullen (2007) is quite different. This is due to the fact that they focus their attention on different schools of entrepreneurial opportunities (p. 304) – that are: the economic, the cultural cognitive, and the sociopolitical schools- rather than on the neoclassical, the Austrian, and the contemporary approaches.

The analysis of the theoretical perspective, instead, deals with the assumptions about the ontology (studies about the nature of being, existence, or reality), epistemology (studies about the nature and limitations of knowledge), and human nature (studies about the thoughts, feelings, and actions of human beings) that characterize each approach.[6] In fact, by relating these assumptions to all the intermediate cases existing along a continuous line moving from an objectivist to a subjectivist approach in social sciences (Morgan and Smircich, 1980), profound differences emerge.

After the results drawn using an empirical and a theoretical perspective-based analysis are highlighted, the neoclassical, the Austrian, and the contemporary approaches serve to provide the basis for a general view of the identification of entrepreneurial opportunities starting an entrepreneurial process.

4.2   The neoclassical approach

Going through several theories proposed over the years, it is possible to make reference to three main approaches that constitute turning points in entrepreneurial studies. The first of these to be considered is the neoclassical one. It was born with Say's proposal (1803), grew with Knight's theory (1921), and reached a considerable development with Schumpeter's contribution[7] (1934), lasting for some years afterward.

Having their roots in the neoclassical economic theory, the scholars embracing this approach are aware of the fact that the market system is based on *equilibrium* (actually, it is a never-reached status of a equilibrium).[8] They take for granted that demand and supply interact with one another until producers can sell all the goods to consumers at a certain price. For each product, moreover, there is always a market in which the economic exchange takes place.[9]

The perfect rationality attributed to economic agents is one of the most important hypothesis on which the neoclassical theory is built. Both consumers and producers are able to make decisions "precisely, without contradictions and in real time"

---

[6] The assumptions about ontology and human nature are very easy to understand. The choice to insert also epistemology is due to the fact that the way an individual determines what knowledge is and the way it is learnt are strictly connected with the other two topics. When describing the three approaches, the importance of epistemology will be clear.

[7] Even if Schumpeter is one of the first scholars belonging to the Austrian school, since he studied there, his theory about the individual-opportunity nexus makes him much more neoclassical than Austrian. Waters (1994) can really help to understand the boundary position assigned to Schumpeter when he says: "to Schumpeter neoclassical principles are useful elements to begin to explain an economy, but they do only that. The valid and more complex explanation goes beyond the static micro principles of the conventional science to a dynamic and evolutionary one" (p. 258). The Schumpeterian vision of opportunity seems to be rooted in the neoclassical theory that is why the evolutionary part of his theory will be sacrificed according to the aim of the present work.

[8] Schumpeter's view (1934) starts from the idea of a market characterized by *equilibrium* but, actually, it is an unreachable *status*. All the continuous innovations, in fact, move the market away from *equilibrium* itself (as noticed, among the others, by McMullen et al., 2007, p. 280) so that, before *equilibrium* could happen, the market is pushed far away again and so on.

[9] Examples of markets, in which both demand and supply already exist, include arbitrage and franchises (Sarasvathy et al., 2005).

(Mazzoni, 2007, p. 108). Setting consumers aside, the role that producers[10] can play is not that relevant. They can obtain the same information as everyone else in the market and, consequently, differences between producers are not supposed to exist. There is no reference to something that could be characteristic of one producer or entrepreneur and not of another.

The neoclassical approach, fundamentally, seems to be based on a contradiction. On the one hand, there is no chance of identifying new entrepreneurial opportunities but, on the other hand, economic history recalls that, of course, new entrepreneurial opportunities have been identified and exploited in markets, because of the role of the entrepreneurs who aim to satisfy new consumers' needs (McDaniel, 2005).

In a context like the one described above, certain questions about the origins of entrepreneurial opportunities arise forcefully. Taking for granted that (1) demand and supply can always reach *equilibrium* (or tend to it), (2) there is always a market in which economic exchanges take place, and (3) all individuals (both producers and consumers) are supposed to be very similar, it is reasonable to assume that the sources of entrepreneurial opportunities cannot be sought in the economic environment and — at the same time — they do not depend on individuals.

Schumpeter (1934) solves the question about the origins of entrepreneurial opportunities by proposing three sources of innovation:

1. technological changes;
2. political and regulatory changes; and
3. social and demographic changes.

Despite all the possible comments based on the similarities or differences between sources of innovation,[11] what clearly emerges is that "technological, political, social, regulatory and other types of change offer a continuous supply of new information about different ways to use resources" (Shane and Venkataraman, 2000, p. 221). Entrepreneurial opportunities, consisting of combining existing resources in alternative ways, are supposed to come forth in a noneconomic setting. In fact, neoclassical "opportunities do not exist as part of the market" (McMullen et al., 2007, p. 281) but "exist outside the economic sphere" (Buenstorf, 2007, p. 325). In this context, "the ability to alter governance mechanism via resource mobilization becomes an important source of competitive advantage" (Companys and McMullen, 2007, pp. 306–307), as it is the way to exploit entrepreneurial opportunities.

The assumption that entrepreneurial opportunities exist in the noneconomic sphere generates an important question concerning the individuals who can exploit them. It is really important to remark here the fact that no particular feature is attributed to individuals. In fact, even if entrepreneurs know about technological, political, social, regulatory, and other types of change, the reference is always to external

---

[10] The neoclassical theory focuses only on consumers and producers in the market so, by referring to producers, it is possible to include also entrepreneurs.

[11] For a detailed comparison, see also Shane (2003, p. 23 ss.).

knowledge (of opportunities existing somewhere else) but not to internal knowledge[12] (meant as a quality that an individual is supposed to possess or not).

The analysis of the neoclassical approach is not developed to determine where opportunities exactly lie before being identified but to highlight that they are supposed to exist on their own. By maintaining that opportunities are supposed to exist as standing alone, it is possible to state that they are supposed to exist beyond economic boundaries. They exist because they derive from other settings (political, technological, or social) and can be exploited in the economic environment in which the perspective "to earn entrepreneurial profit will provide an incentive to many economic actors" (Shane, 2003, p. 221).

The previous recognition in the neoclassical approach helps to fix some interesting key points in this theory. First, it seems possible to suppose that entrepreneurial opportunities just need to be recognized—not discovered or created[13] (Sarasvathy et al., 2005). Entrepreneurs only need to take an external innovation into the economic field to be sure they can exploit it. Nothing more than a simple act, consisting of bringing something already invented or created in another context to the economic one, is required.

The second key point, derived from the previous one, deals with external causes that generate opportunities being stronger and more determinant than both economic rules and roles of individuals.

The third key point concerns the role of entrepreneurs being reduced to a minimum level because they are only supposed to be the *interface* (McMullen et al., 2007, p. 281) between other fields and the economic one. In fact, it consists of having the knowledge of changes that have occurred in other fields and then of finding the resources and the means necessary to begin the entrepreneurial process.

As anticipated in the previous section, the interpretation offered by the neoclassical approach toward the origins of entrepreneurial opportunities is a necessary premise to develop a more in-depth analysis from both an empirical and a theoretical perspective.

From an empirical perspective, the analysis is based on the six elements proposed by Companys and McMullen (2007): what, how, why, who, where, and when.

The best way to find the one changing element, which is able to determine an entrepreneurial opportunity, and to subsequently analyze its implications for entrepreneurs, consists of proceeding using a process of elimination. As proposed earlier, all the elements point out different aspects of a theory: what and how provide descriptions; why gives explanations; and who, where, and when express limitations. The description of the neoclassical approach can be considered static. The

---

[12] Differences about knowledge, meant as qualities an individual has in contrast to the others, is a topic characterizing von Hayek's view (1945) in the Austrian approach.

[13] It is important to note that Sarasvathy et al. (2005) offer three different definitions about the first step of the entrepreneurial process. The distinction between the act of "recognition" (neoclassical), the act of "discovery" (Austrian) and the act of "creation," will be kept in this chapter to underline the differences between the different approaches but, generally, when talking about the discovery phase there is no direct reference to the Austrian approach. See also Alvarez and Barney about the difference between the discovery and creation of opportunity (2007, 2008, 2010).

Table 4.2 The element determining entrepreneurial opportunities in the neoclassical approach.

Elements	Definitions
What	...is used to identify the variables, constructs, and concepts able to explain a phenomenon
How	...is used to inquire about the relations existing between factors
	This is the changing element determining entrepreneurial opportunities in the neoclassical approach. What can determine the recognition of an entrepreneurial opportunity is the change in data about material resources and the emphasis that is placed on how problems are solved
Why	...is the element that justifies the phenomenon
When	...is the temporal factor
Where	...is the contextual factor
Who	...defines the subject involved

Source: Personal elaboration.

explanations (why) are given by changes that do not fall in the economic sphere. There is nothing to suppose about limitations: the place (where), the time/situation (when), and the individuals (who) do not need any specification. All the neoclassical entrepreneurial processes consist of introducing new combinations into the market (what) but—and this is the changing element—they depend on mobilizing/obtaining resources (how). In other words, what can determine the recognition of an entrepreneurial opportunity is the "change in data about material resources" (Companys and McMullen, 2007, p. 303). According to these scholars, the "emphasis is placed on how problems are solved" (p. 305). In the neoclassical approach, in fact, changes in data about material resources are of great importance (see Table 4.2).

From a theoretical perspective, instead, attention must be paid to ontology, epistemology, and human nature according to Morgan and Smircich's work (1980). The theoretical perspective provides the means to capture—metaphorically speaking—the essence of the neoclassical approach.

In terms of ontology, the neoclassical reality[14] can be defined as "a concrete structure," "a machine," or "a closed system" (Morgan and Smircich, 1980, pp. 492–493). Since everything seems to be predetermined, the individual[15] is only a "responder" (Morgan and Smircich, 1980, p. 492) to external reality.

---

[14] Morgan and Smircich (1980, p. 495) provide a more complex description of neoclassical reality: "The social world is a hard, concrete, real thing out there, which affects everyone in one way or another. It can be thought of as a structure composed of a network of determined relationships between constituent parts. Reality is to be found in the concrete behavior and relationship between these parts. [...] Reality by definition is that which is external and real. The social world is as concrete and real as the nature world."

[15] Also in this case, to understand better, Morgan and Smircich (1980, p. 495) provide a wider description: "Human beings are product of the external forces in the environment to which they are exposed. Stimuli in their environment condition them to behave and respond to events in predictable and determinate ways. A network of causal relationships links all the important aspects of behavior to context. Though human perception may influence this process to some degree, people always respond to situation in a lawful (i.e., rule-governed) manner."

The necessity of dealing with epistemology is now comprehensible because the limited role attributed to individuals does not allow them to have a deeper understanding. The epistemological stance is simply that of constructing a positivist science in which there is no insight. This is the best way to sum up what entrepreneurs are supposed to do in order to identify an entrepreneurial opportunity.

In the end, a very clear synthesis of the neoclassical approach is given by Sarason et al. (2006), according to who "an apprehendable reality exists, driven by natural laws [...] the aim of research should be to identify causal explanations and fundamental laws that explain regularities in human social behavior" (p. 300).

4.3   The Austrian approach

Another approach, which constitutes a turning point in entrepreneurial studies, is the Austrian one, thus called because it originated from and mainly developed in the Austrian school.[16] This approach has its roots in von Hayek's (1945) and von Mises' (1949) theories, finding its best representative in Kirzner (1973). However, many years later, it is still a valid approach supported by scholars such as Baumol (1993), Casson (1982), Khilstrom and Laffont (1979), Brealey and Myers (1988), Evans and Jovanovic (1989), and, eventually, by Shane and Venkataraman (2000).

The origins of this new approach can be traced to the deep and radical changes, both social and cultural,[17] that took place between the end of the 19th century and the beginning of the 20th century. Scholars lost their certainties about the perfect mechanism that the market was supposed to follow. All that had been hypothesized about the agents' perfect information was broken down and uncertainty[18] became

---

[16] The Austrian School originated in Vienna in the early 20th century.

[17] The most important social event that characterized the ending of the 19th century was the Great Depression. Its effects where so dramatic that made people lost faith in the neoclassical economic rules. Some other important changes also happened in the theoretical field where the new theories proposed by Chamberlin (1933) and Coase (1937).

[18] According to Knight (1921), it is possible to distinguish three kinds of uncertainty. The first kind of uncertainty is referable to "a future whose distribution exists and is known." All the events, which are expected to happen in the future, are already known so the individual can easily reduce this kind of uncertainty through diversification. Economic agents, in fact, can evaluate different scenarios, foresee all the possible events and choose accordingly. This kind of uncertainty is very easy to reduce. The second kind of uncertainty, instead, is generated by "a future whose distribution exists but is not known in advance." This kind of uncertainty is due to the fact that future events can be hypothesized after several trials but they can never be formalized. Reducing uncertainty, in this case, is not easy. An individual, in fact, is not supposed to foresee what is going to happen so all the changes are seen as if they would happen for the first time. The third kind of uncertainty, the most difficult one to face, is the one that Knight explicitly calls "true uncertainty." It is referred to a future that is unknown and unknowable. The only reason why entrepreneurs decide to bear this uncertainty is that they expect to earn entrepreneurial profits.
The last kind of uncertainty is the one connected to entrepreneurial studies and so the most inquired. Some other scholars, following Knight's view of "true uncertainty," have related uncertainty to the impossibility of foreseeing future events (Pennings, 1981; Pfeffer and Salancik, 1978; Duncan, 1972) or future outcomes (Schmidt and Cummings, 1976; Downey and Slocum, 1975; Duncan, 1972).

the main feature of the Austrian approach. In such a negative scenario, an important change occurred in economic studies. The concept of *equilibrium* became no longer acceptable, as it was in the neoclassical approach. Hence, the concept of *equilibrium* was replaced by the concept of *disequilibrium*.

The presence of uncertainty and the consequent *disequilibrium* in the market compels scholars to rethink the role of the entrepreneur. According to Kirzner (1973), entrepreneurs are the only ones able to move the market system out of the *disequilibrium* toward the *equilibrium* again. This new economic setting works in the opposite manner to that of the neoclassical one. Also, in this case, it persists that this is just a trial toward the *equilibrium* again that is never attained. The new way of interpreting both the market forces and the role of individuals involved in economic issues leads toward considering the origins of opportunities from a different point of view.

What seems to characterize the Austrian approach is the idea that the existence of external reality, typically a neoclassical notion, still remains valid; however, entrepreneurs, who are now acting to achieve *equilibrium* again by starting from a *disequilibrium status*, are considered positively. They are positively evaluated because of the existing information they hold and their differential access to it, which they can put into practice. Shane (2003) underlines the idea that "new information is important in explaining the existence of entrepreneurial opportunities" (p. 20). In a market characterized by *disequilibrium*, gaps and imperfections can temporarily occur and require to be filled. These gaps and imperfections, consisting of the fact that "information is imperfectly distributed [and] all economic actors do not receive new information at the same time," as noted by Shane and Venkataraman (2000, p. 221), are the factors that give birth to Austrian entrepreneurial opportunities. In fact, Shane (2003) notes, "Kirzner argued that the existence of opportunities requires only differential access to existing information" (p. 20).

By relying on the idea of existing information, it is possible to maintain that the Austrian approach follows the beaten track previously defined by the neoclassical scholars. Of course, there are some differences that necessarily occur. In fact, "while the Kirznerian [and so the Austrian] entrepreneur discovers and pursues opportunities that exist within markets, the Schumpeterian [and so neoclassical] entrepreneur discovers opportunities that exist outside the economic sphere and

---

Others, on the contrary, have identified uncertainty with the missing information about the cause–effect nexus (Lawrence and Lorsch, 1967).

A clearer definition of uncertainty has been proposed by Hmielesky and Baron (2008) who recall Knight's definition and maintain that "a state of uncertainty occurs when the probabilities of decision outcomes cannot be estimated, because the necessary information is unknowable in the present" (2008, p. 289). In particular, implications due to uncertainty are very relevant in reference to entrepreneurial opportunities (Duncan, 1972; Downey and Slocum, 1975). To be able to face uncertainty, in fact, individuals cannot follow "relatively complete and unchanging" strategies but they should follow "emergent and changing" strategies (Alvarez and Barney, 2007, p. 17). In this vein, the debate about the nexus risk and uncertainty comes out. Some scholars (Hmielesky and Baron, 2008; Knight, 1921) propose viewing uncertainty and risk as two different concepts. While other scholars (Gifford, 2005; Khilstrom and Laffont, 1979) consider uncertainty as implying risk. Gifford, for example, analyze the role of "uncertainty and the accompanying risk" (2005, p. 37).

pursues these opportunities by bringing them into the marketplace" (Buenstorf, 2007, p. 325). In both cases, opportunities exist on their own. However, the market provides them in the former case, while it is a noneconomic sphere that provides them in the latter.

In this vein, Drucker (1985)—who tried to disclose the probable sources of entrepreneurial opportunities—offered a very important contribution, giving more strength to the Austrian approach. According to this scholar, the sources of entrepreneurial opportunities are:

1. the unexpected;
2. incongruities;
3. process needs;
4. industry market and structures;
5. demographic changes;
6. changes in public perception; and
7. new technology and scientific findings.

The above sources are divided into two main groups.[19] The first consists of internal sources and the second of external ones. The purpose here is to determine whether opportunities exist on their own or not, resulting in the conclusion that an objective reality still seems to exist.[20] By admitting that "opportunities are created by earlier entrepreneurial errors which have resulted in shortages, surplus, misallocated resources" (Kirzner, 1997, p. 70), the question about the origins of opportunities seems definitively solved.

The contrast between the neoclassical and Austrian approaches is very useful to determine, first, the role of entrepreneurs and, subsequently, the different ways of accessing entrepreneurial opportunities.

With regards to the role of entrepreneurs, while the neoclassical view is based on the assumption that an entrepreneurial opportunity reveals itself in new combinations (Schumpeter, 1911) generated by the demand and supply factors that "exist rather obviously" (Sarasvathy et al., 2005), the Austrian approach redefines the role of entrepreneurs by giving them a more determinant part during the identification phase. The aim of Austrian entrepreneurs, in fact, is no longer about bringing "new combinations" of already existing factors into the market but about "new products for well-known needs and desires, as well as new applications for existing technologies" (Buenstorf, 2007, pp. 326–327). It implies that either the demand or the

---

[19] Drucker's distinction about internal and external sources considers the venture as the boundary between the two sides. At a larger extent, the venture can be seen as the means to distinguish what is economic from what is not.

[20] Sarasvathy et al.'s (2005) difference between the act of "recognition" (neoclassical), the act of "discovery" (Austrian) and the act of "creation," is confirmed by Kirzner who maintains that: "the notion of discovery, midway between that of deliberately produced information in standard search theory [neoclassical], and that of sheer windfall gain generated by pure chance [contemporary], is central to the Austrian approach" (1997, p. 72).

supply factors are absent in the market,[21] as noted by Sarasvathy et al. (2005), and that they need to be discovered.

Several proposals have been made to identify the different ways of accessing entrepreneurial opportunities (the second aspect cited above). They are: imperfect knowledge (von Hayek, 1945), asymmetric beliefs (von Mises, 1949), and differences in entrepreneurial alertness (Kirzner, 1973). Von Hayek's imperfect knowledge is clearly expressed when he maintains that:

> The economic problem of society is thus not merely a problem of how to allocate given resources — if given is taken to mean given to a single mind which deliberately solves the problem set by these data. It is rather a problem of how to secure the best use of resources known to any of the members of society, for ends whose relative importance only these individuals know. Or, to put it briefly, it is a problem of the utilization of knowledge not given to anyone in its totality (1945, pp. 519–520).

Thus this scholar highlights that knowledge of specific circumstances is incomplete. Hence, several differences can arise between individuals so that only some of them are able to recognize opportunities not available to others.[22]

The new market concept, in contrast with the neoclassical view, results from the importance given by von Hayek (1945) to knowledge and is subsequently enriched by von Mises' view of "the market as an entrepreneurially driven process" (Kirzner, 1997, p. 67), which is "driven by the daring, imaginative, speculative actions of entrepreneurs who see opportunities for pure profit in the conditions of disequilibrium" (p. 68). Accordingly, asymmetric beliefs are the causes giving birth to entrepreneurial opportunities.

The Austrian approach to imperfect knowledge is very different from the neoclassical one. In fact, as explained by Kirzner (1997, p. 62):

> For the Austrian approach imperfect information is seen as involving an element which cannot be fitted at all into neoclassical model, that of sheer (i.e., unknown) ignorance. [...] Sheer ignorance differs from imperfect information in that the discovery which reduces sheer ignorance is necessarily accompanied by the element of surprise — one had not hitherto realized one's ignorance.

This view is best explained in the Kirznerian theory that is based on the concept of "alertness." Here, "the pure entrepreneur [is] a decision-maker whose

---

[21] Sarasvathy et al. (2005) provide two examples to understand these kinds of market. The first refers to cures for diseases. It is a market where demand exists but supply has to be discovered. The second, instead, consists of new technological applications at personal computers. In this market supply exist but demand still has to be discovered.

[22] By looking at Hayek's theory, and at all the theories proposed later, Kirzner underlines that "Austrian emphasis on the entrepreneur is fundamental. Whereas each neoclassical decision maker operates in a world of given price and output data, the Austrian entrepreneur operates to change price/output data. In this way, as we shall see, the entrepreneurial role drives the ever-changing process of the market" (1997, p. 70).

entire role arises out of his alertness to hitherto unnoticed opportunities" (Kirzner, 1973, p. 39).

The consequences resulting from the relevance of alertness seem to have enabled the Austrian approach to survive for a long time. Baumol (1993) supports the idea that entrepreneurship cannot be the consequence of a process in which mechanical behaviors depend on a predetermined set of alternatives, thus openly rejecting the neoclassical model. Other scholars have developed the concept of differential accesses. Casson (1982) underlines the belief that entrepreneurs have unique information so that they can decide in a way that no one else would ever do. Some other scholars, such as Khilstrom and Laffont (1979), Brealey and Myers (1988), Evans and Jovanovic (1989), and, in recent years, Forbes (2005) and Klein (2008), highlight the role of knowledge in creating differences between individuals. Eventually, Shane and Venkataraman (2000) reaffirm that "although recognition of entrepreneurial opportunity is a subjective process, the opportunities themselves are objective phenomena that are not known to all parties at all times" (p. 220), underlining again the role of knowledge.

These previous interpretations of the Austrian approach help fix some interesting key points of this theory.

First, it seems possible to suppose that entrepreneurial opportunities need to be discovered (Sarasvathy et al., 2005). An individual needs to leverage on differential accesses to existing entrepreneurial opportunities in order to exploit them. This process becomes a little more complicated if compared to the neoclassical approach because knowledge and/or alertness are the new factors stimulating entrepreneurship.

The second key point (strictly connected to the first one) deals with the role of external causes generating entrepreneurial opportunities. In the Austrian approach, external causes are not considered to be very strong and determinant, leaving a more important role to the entrepreneurs who are able to discover entrepreneurial opportunities.

The third key point reevaluates the role of entrepreneurs. Currently, it consists of certain elements (i.e., knowledge and/or alertness) that can make the entrepreneurial process begin.

As previously noted, after identifying the key elements of the Austrian approach toward the origins of entrepreneurial opportunities, it is possible to proceed with the analysis from both an empirical and a theoretical perspective.

After describing the entire Austrian approach (starting from the origins and arriving at the present-day interpretations), it is now time for the analysis of its key elements,[23] as proposed by Companys and McMullen (2007). For this approach, the analysis must proceed by exclusion too.

The description of the Austrian approach is based on the following assumptions. A particular set of individuals (who), in an economic environment (where) during a

---

[23] It is important to recall that: what and how provide description; why gives explanations; and who, where, and when express limitations.

Table 4.3 The element determining entrepreneurial opportunities in the Austrian approach.

Elements	Definitions
What	...is used to identify the variables, constructs, and concepts able to explain a phenomenon
How	...is used to inquire about the relations existing between factors
Why	...is the element that justifies the phenomenon
When	...is the temporal factor
Where	...is the contextual factor
Who	...defines the subject involved
	This is the changing element that determines entrepreneurial opportunities in the Austrian approach. It is sufficient to think about the complexity of interactions that entrepreneurs need to develop to obtain necessary resources and information and about the way in which others can be mobilized and organized to exploit opportunities

Source: Personal elaboration.

certain time (when), is supposed to act because of gaps and imperfections (explanations, why). The information (what) is supposed to exist on its own and all the aspiring entrepreneurs are aware of changes in data about material resources (how) sooner or later. According to the above, "who" stands for the changing element that determines an entrepreneurial opportunity (see Table 4.3). Of course— as underlined by Companys and McMullen (2007)—"who" stands for "a set of individuals" (i.e., the entrepreneurs). It is sufficient to think about the individual characteristics that entrepreneurs need to develop in order to disclose temporary gaps in the markets, to mobilize and organize resources to exploit opportunities.[24]

The empirical assumptions just made have certain implications on the theoretical perspective regarding ontology, epistemology, and human nature, as classified by Morgan and Smircich (1980). The Austrian approach, on the imaginary line connecting objectivist to subjectivist approaches, can be imagined at a hypothetical half-way point on the line. In fact, the objective reality and the subjective importance of individuals drive scholars (Morgan and Smircich, 1980, p. 495) to see reality as a concrete process.[25]

---

[24] It recalls the concept of combinative capabilities which Kogut and Zander (1992) referred to firms.

[25] In reference to the objective reality and the subjective importance of individuals, Morgan and Smircich (1980, p. 495) write: "The social world is an evolving process, concrete in nature, but ever changing in detailed form. Everything interacts with everything else and it is extremely difficult to find determinate causal relationships between constituent processes. At best, the world expresses itself in terms of general and contingent relationships between its more stable and clear-cut elements. The situation is fluid and creates opportunities for those with appropriate ability to mold and exploit relationships in accordance with their interests. The world is in part what one makes of it: a struggle between various influences, each attempting to move toward achievement of desired ends."

The passage from a totally objective reality to an objective/subjective one is underlined when reading the role attributed to entrepreneurs.[26] They are considered to be "adaptive agents" (Morgan and Smircich, 1980, p. 495).

In the end, the epistemological assumption of the Austrian approach is seen as referable to studies of systems, processes, and changes. According to the interpretation of the Austrian approach by Sarason et al. (2006),[27] it is possible to say that there exists "an objective reality, but [it is] imperfectly apprehendable because of basically flawed human intellectual mechanisms" (p. 300).

The conclusion reached is that the Austrian approach cannot neglect the existence of objective opportunities but recognizes a certain importance of the individual as well.

4.4 The contemporary approach

In the last few years, many scholars (Sarasvathy et al., 2005; Aldrich and Ruef, 2006; Sarason et al., 2006; Alvarez and Barney, 2007, 2008, 2010; Miller, 2007; Dimov, 2011; Alvarez et al., 2014; Ramaglou and Zyglidopoulos, 2015; Ramaglou and Tsang, 2016) have started studying the relationship between individuals and opportunities in accordance with changes occurring in the economic environment.[28] Their aim is to analyze the way entrepreneurs attempt to face the evolving reality and to propose a new model to interpret it. The well-known economic crisis began in 2008, the difficulties arising for both existing and emerging markets, and the continuous and radical changes in social and political fields, are all factors that influence entrepreneurship, its origins, and its features. From this perspective, the neoclassical and the Austrian approaches have been totally overtaken. They can no longer fully describe what is happening in the economic field. Nothing can be defined as given. An external reality, whether economic or not, is difficult to admit and, even more importantly, it is very complex to study.

The new approach, the contemporary one (Sarasvathy et al., 2005), begins with the assumption that sometimes both demand and supply of a market do not even exist[29] before a new entrepreneurial opportunity comes into existence, implying that they have to be created[30]. By admitting that entrepreneurs are supposed to

---

[26] Morgan and Smircich (1980, p. 495) describe entrepreneurs as: "Human beings exist in an interactive relationship with their world. They influence and are influenced by their context or environment. The process of exchange that operates here is essentially a competitive one, the individual seeking to interpret and exploit the environment to satisfy important needs, and hence survive. Relationship between individuals and environment express a pattern of activity necessary for survival and well-being of the individual."

[27] When referring to the Austrian approach, Sarason et al. (2006) refer to it as postpositivist approach. It is useful to underline the so many referenced to the Neoclassical approach (the positivist one).

[28] The passage to "virtual economy" and the growing interest in "economic systems" is what influences economic studies.

[29] For a list of ventures that created both demand and supply see Sarasvathy et al. (2005, p. 146).

[30] The approach is taken from Buchanan and Vanberg (1991) who "suggest that markets are creative processes in which agents create new goods in unforeseeable ways" (Buenstorf, 2007, p. 327).

create both the demand and the supply for a nonexisting market, it seems plausible to assume that they also have to create an entrepreneurial opportunity. The causal reasoning, in other words, is developed according to the paradigm that maintains that an entrepreneurial opportunity gives birth to a new market, made up of demand and supply. The approach intended here completely modifies the way in which the individual-opportunity nexus is interpreted and radically changes the roles of reality and of the individual by reducing the importance of the first and increasing the relevance of the second.[31]

Determining the origins of entrepreneurial opportunities becomes more complex after reducing the importance of reality. For example, Gartner et al. (2001) maintain that opportunities are enacted phenomena with no existence that is independent of individuals who envision and/or exploit them. This view is then further developed by the structuration theory, based on the idea that there is "a reciprocal relationship between agency and structure, and as such offers a perspective that specifically articulates the relationship between agent (entrepreneur) and structure (opportunity) as a duality. A duality, as opposed to a dualism, presents two constructs that cannot exist, or be understood, separate from each other" (Sarason et al., 2006, p. 289).

The neoclassical and Austrian dualism and, with it, the influence that an individual could or could not have on reality are definitely overcome. The individual-opportunity nexus is based on a dynamic interaction that never stops. Furthermore, Buenstorf (2007) underlines the idea that "opportunities are understood as the logical outcomes of dynamic economic processes" (p. 324).

At this point, of course, an important question is to wonder about the way entrepreneurial opportunities are created. Interactions with other individuals are seen as "social structures that constrain and enable entrepreneurs in the venturing process" (Sarason et al., 2006, p. 287). A set of relationships is the place in which entrepreneurial opportunities lay until entrepreneurs find them. The role of entrepreneurs becomes crucial in the new approach. They are supposed to be "purposeful, knowledgeable, reflexive and active" (p. 290). They do not recognize or discover opportunities but are able to create them.[32]

Accordingly, the sources of entrepreneurial opportunities in this approach are different from the ones related to the neoclassical and to the Austrian approaches.

---

[31] Actually, an even more extreme approach is proposed by Klein who maintains "opportunities are best characterized neither as discovered or created, but imagined. [...] the concept of opportunity imagination emphasizes that gains (and losses) do not come into being objectively until entrepreneurial action is complete (i.e., until final goods and services have been produced and sold)" (2008, p. 181). The approach followed here, as mentioned earlier, is based on a multistage selection process that necessarily is in contrast, and automatically excludes, a whole view of it.

[32] As proposed by Sarasvathy et al. (2005), opportunities can be the result of the act of "recognition" (Neoclassical approach), of the act of "discovery" (Austrian approach) or, eventually, of the act of "creation" (contemporary approach).

As proposed by Companys and McMullen[33](2007), the possible sources are divided into two categories:

1. producers (e.g., cultural communities and robust design); and
2. consumers (e.g. fads and user practices).

The sources identified above disclose that "changes in interpretations are considered to be the source of entrepreneurial opportunity" (p. 306). In other words, the source is subjective, depending on the way in which reality is considered and evaluated as a starting point for the opportunity creating process. Accordingly, the role of economic agents must fit with the new aim they envisage. Entrepreneurs need to have the ability to intervene in the world or to refrain from intervention and should be able to deploy a range of causal power, including that of influencing others.

One of the main capabilities that entrepreneurs need to leverage is the ability to observe and understand what they are doing while they are doing it. In fact, as proposed by Sarason et al. (2006), "knowledgeable entrepreneurs are empowered to act in a manner that influences opportunities and to reflexively monitor the impact of their actions leading to actions that reinforce, modify or create new opportunities" (p. 292). The main turning point in entrepreneurial theories is that opportunities are not separate from entrepreneurs because the latter build and shape them.

In this case, it also seems very useful to try and fix the key points of the contemporary approach. First, opportunities only need to be created (Sarasvathy et al., 2005). Entrepreneurs need to create the supply and demand of a market that does not yet exist. The process is very complicated because everything depends on entrepreneurs. The second key point, inquiring about the role of external reality, demonstrates its decreasing importance, as opportunities are now not supposed to exist on their own. The third key point analyzes the role of entrepreneurs, which has now reached its peak. Everything is the result of entrepreneurial action that is capable of generating a new entrepreneurial opportunity and, subsequently, an entire market in order to enable economic exchanges to take place.

After identifying the key elements of the contemporary approach toward the origins of entrepreneurial opportunities, it is time to proceed with its analysis from both an empirical and a theoretical perspective.

The empirical perspective, contemplating the analysis of the key elements (what, how, why, who, where, and when) proposed by Companys and McMullen (2007), is useful for a more in-depth understanding.

The description of the contemporary approach is based on the following assumptions. Given a particular set of individuals (who), in an economic environment (where) during a certain time (when), the descriptive elements (what and how) are supposed to be the same. The ever-changing element that determines entrepreneurial action is "why," meant to be understood as "changes in interpretations of data"

---

[33] The scholars, actually, propose different sources also for the neoclassical and the Austrian approach. For the first group they propose knowledge, structural holes, and political factors (like deregulation of a market). For the second, instead, they talk about capabilities (product and factor innovation) and information (latent needs).

Table 4.4 The element determining entrepreneurial opportunities in the contemporary approach.

Elements	Definitions
What	...is used to identify the variables, constructs, and concepts able to explain a phenomenon
How	...is used to inquire about the relations existing between factors
Why	...is the element that justifies the phenomenon
	This is the changing element determining entrepreneurial opportunities in the contemporary approach. Emphasis is placed on changes in data interpretations by entrepreneurs and on how strategic issues or problems are defined
When	...is the temporal factor
Where	...is the contextual factor
Who	...defines the subject involved

Source: Personal elaboration.

(Companys and McMullen, 2007, p. 303). According to the scholars, the "emphasis is placed on how strategic issues or problems are defined" (p. 305) by individuals. The "why" element, of course, stresses again the importance of entrepreneurs who, only by their actions, create entrepreneurial opportunities (see Table 4.4).

The theoretical perspective regarding ontology, epistemology, and human nature, listed by Morgan and Smircich (1980), mirrors the empirical assumptions just cited. The contemporary approach can be considered at the opposite end of the neoclassical approach because it reduces, at *minimum*, the importance of an existing, autonomous reality[34] and conveys the assumption that everything is supposed to be the result of a subjective process (Morgan and Smircich, 1980, p. 495). The contemporary approach shows off the role of entrepreneurs.[35] They are considered to be the "creators of their realities" (Morgan and Smircich, 1980, p. 495).

In the end, the epistemological assumption aims to understand how a social reality is created (see also Wood and McKinley, 2010). The conclusion is that the

---

[34] According to Morgan and Smircich (1980, p. 495), "The social world is a continuous process, created afresh in each encounter of everyday life as individuals impose themselves on their world to establish a realm of meaningful definition. They do so through the medium of language, labels, actions, and routines, which constitute symbolic modes of being in the world. Social reality is embedded in the nature and use of these modes of symbolic action. The realm of social affairs thus has no concrete status of any kind; it is a symbolic construction. Symbolic modes of being in the world, such as through the use of language, may result in the development of shared, but multiple realities, the status of which is fleeting, confined only to those moments in which they are actively constructed and sustained."

[35] As for the description of entrepreneurs Morgan and Smircich (1980, p. 495) write: "Human beings create their realities in the most fundamental ways, in an attempt to make their world intelligible to themselves and to others. They are not simply actors interpreting their situations in meaningful ways, for there are no situations other than those which individuals bring into being through their own creative activity. Individuals may work together to create a shared reality, but that reality is still a subjective construction capable of disappearing the moment its members cease to sustain it as such. Reality appears as real to individuals because of human acts of conscious or unwitting collusion."

contemporary approach reduces the importance of objective opportunities and thus that of an objective reality. On the contrary, the contemporary approach attributes primary importance to the individual and to all the subjective factors that not only contribute but also determine the origins of entrepreneurial opportunities.

4.5 Reflections on the identification of entrepreneurial opportunities

To stress the way opportunities are identified (Holcombe, 2003; Alvarez and Barney, 2007; Zahra, 2008; Martin and Wilson, 2016), it can be useful to sum up the above analysis about the neoclassical, the Austrian, and the contemporary approaches, as shown in Table 4.5.

From Table 4.5, a case emerges in which there are no entrepreneurial opportunities. In fact, if there is no external reality and an individual does not possess any quality, there is no chance for new entrepreneurial opportunities to come into existence. Of course, this is an extreme case, purely theoretical, obtained through an attentive classification of all possible variables. As already stated in the previous sections, the various combinations of individual qualities with external reality generate three possible cases.

The first case, the neoclassical one, is characterized by the predominance of the external reality over individual qualities. Neoclassical entrepreneurs, according to the Schumpeterian view, are just a means able to introduce innovations into the economic field. According to this approach, the entrepreneurial process seems to be objective and to occur without a relevant participation of the individuals involved.

The individuals involved, who are able to pursue opportunities that derive from the external reality, characterize the Austrian approach. The combination of both individual qualities (e.g., Kirznerian alertness) and an existing reality determines new entrepreneurial opportunities and makes the entrepreneurial process begin.

The last case, the contemporary one, criticizes the two previous ones and underlines the relevance of the individuals over the reality. Entrepreneurs, by acting, create entrepreneurial opportunities that have not necessarily existed before.

To proceed with the analysis of the identification phase, it is suitable to attempt to capture some features that disclose deep differences between the three approaches in the clearest manner. At the first level of analysis, there are some

Table 4.5 A comparison of the different approaches to identifying entrepreneurial opportunities.

	Existing external reality	Nonexisting external reality
Individual qualities	Austrian approach	Contemporary approach
No individual qualities	Neoclassical approach	No entrepreneurial opportunities

Source: Personal elaboration.

Table 4.6 A comparison between the neoclassical, Austrian, and contemporary approaches.

	Neoclassical (positivist)	Austrian (postpositivist)	Contemporary (reflexive)
Existence of opportunity	Exist by themselves (concrete structure)	Exist by themselves (concrete process)	Must be created (social construction)
Role of individuals	Responder	Adaptor	Creator
Relationship between an individual and an opportunity	Dualism (opportunities prevail)	Dualism (individuals prevail)	Duality
The way the process is carried out	Systematic research	Discovery	Serendipity

Source: Adapted from Sarasvathy, S.D., Dew, N., Velamuri, S.R., Venkataraman, S., 2005. Three views of entrepreneurial opportunity. In: Acs, Z.J., Audretsch, D.B. (Eds.), Handbook of Entrepreneurship Research: An Interdisciplinary Survey and Introduction. Springer, New York, p. 146.

differences that can contribute to a comparison between the three approaches. These differences could be[36]:

- Focus of interest: While the neoclassical approach looks at the entire system, the Austrian approach looks at the process in which individuals and reality interact. The contemporary approach, eventually, looks at the individual decision to create opportunities.
- Unit of competition: In the neoclassical approach, entrepreneurs compete for resources because they have to be able to obtain them (how). In the Austrian approach, they compete for the strategies that would enable them to discover opportunities instead (who). In the contemporary approach, they compete to create values that depend on nonexisting opportunities (why).

Beyond the already mentioned topics, some other ones are also treated, as shown in Table 4.6. These topics focus on differences in terms of the existence of opportunities, the role of individuals, the relationship between an individual and an opportunity, and the way the process is carried out.

All the above contents, except the way the process is carried out, have already been discussed in previous sections. Since there is a strong need for a true understanding of what happens in the identification phase, it is suitable to highlight the last topic that underlines the different ways in which entrepreneurs do act. Afterward, it is possible to make some assumptions about the identification phase in general.

The ways in which entrepreneurs[37] carry out their research process can be classified as systematic research (Shaver and Scott, 1991), act of discovery (Kaish and Gilad, 1991; Kirzner, 1997), or serendipity (Buenstorf, 2007).

---

[36] For a more exhaustive list of possible topics useful to compare the three approaches see also Sarasvathy et al. (2005).

[37] For a more accurate analysis of these processes see Shane (2000).

The neoclassical approach, based on the assumption that opportunities are objective and only need to be recognized, seems to be the case in which systematic research is the most fruitful. In a context characterized by perfect information, as highlighted by Smith et al. (2009), "implicit [...] is the assumption that the object of the search is readily identifiable" (p. 44). The object of the search—that is, entrepreneurial opportunities—exists on its own; thus it is possible to obtain a positive result from the research simply by defining the fields of search (technological, social, or political) and analyzing them.

This kind of process has been criticized by Kirzner (1997), who admits that it "can be undertaken for a piece of missing information, but only because the searcher is aware of the nature of what he does not know, and is aware with greater or lesser certainty of the way to find out the missing information" (p. 71). The Kirznerian view points out the differences between the neoclassical and the Austrian approaches and underlines the passage from systematic research to that of the discovery process.

According to this scholar, no one can be aware of what part of knowledge, what gap, or what information is needed—therefore systematic research cannot be used. Moreover, it seems that "it might be expected that a time consuming search process would identify it [an opportunity] sooner or later" (Kirzner, 1997). However, this does not seem true because an Austrian entrepreneur is not supposed to know what the object of the search is. The impossibility of listing the probable ways to discover opportunities is confirmed by the fact that the Austrian approach focuses on the elements[38] and not on the ways in which to find entrepreneurial opportunities. The idea that seems to emerge is that "different types of opportunities are related with different identification processes" (Smith et al., 2009, p. 45), changing from time to time. What the neoclassical and the Austrian approaches have in common is individual intention leading to the identification of entrepreneurial opportunities. As noted by Krueger et al. (2000), what is important is that entrepreneurs do not act according to an external *stimulus* but because of their own entrepreneurial intentions.

Of course, these approaches are in antithesis with the contemporary approach, which is based on serendipity. In this case "opportunities may also arise from the entrepreneur's own activity without this activity being directed toward entrepreneurial purposes" (Buenstorf, 2007, p. 328). Entrepreneurial opportunities, according to the contemporary approach, are created and the act of thinking of a process with no starting point and with no specific purpose can be understood as similar to that of the creation of new opportunities (Cornelissen and Clarke, 2010). The continuous refining of a personal way of approaching the external environment takes entrepreneurs in a nonpredefined direction. This is when serendipity takes place.

4.6 Concluding remarks

At this stage, before concluding the discussion about entrepreneurial opportunities, it is appropriate to recall Shane's (2003) contribution, according to which

---

[38] See the Austrian approach analyzed in Section 4.3.

entrepreneurs identify opportunities due to two groups of factors that can be identified as "access to information" or "information corridors," on the one hand, and
"cognitive capabilities" on the other (p. 45). By looking at the discovery of
entrepreneurial opportunities as the resultants of these different factors (typical of
the Austrian approach), in particular, it becomes much easier to explain why some
individuals can discover opportunities but not others (Baron, 1998; Mitchell et al.,
2000, 2008; Shane and Venkataraman, 2000; Casson, 2003; Forbes, 2005;
Anderson and Nichols, 2007; Gartner et al., 2008).

The first group of factors includes life experiences, social networks, and information search processes (Shane, 2003). Life experiences refer to everything that is
derived from a previous job function or everyday experience that could really make
it easier for an individual to discover a new opportunity (Ucbasaran et al., 2003).
Additionally, social networks can really help an individual, as "information is likely
to be spread across a variety of people" (Shane, 2003, p. 49), and individuals
involved in search processes are more likely to find new opportunities. All these
factors contribute the information that individuals possess before beginning the
search process (Venkataraman, 1997; Sleptsov and Anand, 2008). Some other scholars prefer referring, in a more general way, to prior knowledge[39] (Shane, 2000),
tacit or codified (Smith et al., 2009), or experiential knowledge (Lamont, 1972;
Corbett, 2005; Foss and Foss, 2008) about locations, potential markets, sources of
capital, employees, and ways to organize. Prior-knowledge is a necessary prerequi-
site for beginning the process and its main strength is that it derives from "idiosyn-
cratic life experiences" (Shane, 2000, p. 451). Thus it differs from one individual to
another[40] and, necessarily, leads to the discovery of different opportunities.

The second group of factors, identified as cognitive capabilities, is based on
absorptive capacity,[41] intelligence, and cognitive properties instead (Shane, 2003).
They are all individual features and thus, necessarily, must differ from one individual to another.

Access to information can be seen as the result of the experiences from which
individuals could learn something new and develop new information. On the contrary, cognitive capabilities can be interpreted as an example of innate qualities that
an individual can either possess or not, such as intelligence or cognitive properties.[42] Predominance of cognitive capabilities, typical of the neoclassical approach,
seems to oppose access to information, which can be characteristic of the contemporary approach.

---

[39] The concept of prior knowledge distances itself from von Hayek (1945) who focuses on knowledge in
a certain place and at a given time. Prior knowledge here is to mean the causes generating knowledge.

[40] As Roberts (1991) maintains, in fact, prior knowledge is the result of work experience, education, and
other means. It influences the way an individual can understand, realize, and act. Of course it implies
that prior knowledge cannot be replicated.

[41] See Cohen and Levinthal (1990).

[42] Even if there is no clear reference to the nature versus nurture debate, the list of individual differences
proposed by Shane (2003, p. 45 ss.) leads to recognize these two categories. The factors included in
both the groups are typically meant as representative of natural or nurtured factors.

The three types of opportunities that entrepreneurs can identify (through the act of recognition, discovery, or creation) completely differ from one another. As already explained above, noticeable dissimilarities exist between them in reference to their origins and, nowadays, scholars are actively involved in this debate (Sarasvathy, 2001; Short et al., 2010; Hansen et al., 2009, 2011; Alvarez and Barney, 2013; Suddaby et al., 2015; Wood, 2016; Braver and Danneels, 2018; Foss and Klein, 2018; Alvarez and Barney, 2019; Rastkhiz et al., 2019).

According to this, is it likely to expect that different ways of exploiting identified entrepreneurial opportunities can be defined? In addition, is it likely to expect that different outcomes can emerge in reference to their exploitation on the market? The investigation of the feasible links between entrepreneurial opportunities, business models, and growth paths is the research focus lying at the basis of this volume.

References

Aldrich, H.E., Ruef, M., 2006. Organizations Evolving, second ed. Sage, Thousand Oaks, CA.

Alvarez, S.A., Barney, J., 2007. Discovery and creation: alternative theories of entrepreneurial action. Strat. Entrepr. J. 1 (1−2), 11−26.

Alvarez, S.A., Barney, J., 2008. Opportunities, organizations, and entrepreneurship. Strat. Entrepr. J. 2 (3), 171−173.

Alvarez, S.A., Barney, J.B., 2010. Entrepreneurship and epistemology: the philosophical underpinnings of the study of entrepreneurial opportunities. Acad. Manag. Ann. 4 (1), 557−583.

Alvarez, S.A., Barney, J.B., 2013. Epistemology, opportunities, and entrepreneurship: comments on Venkataraman et al. (2012) and Shane (2012). Acad. Manag. Rev. 38 (1), 154−157.

Alvarez, S.A., Barney, J.B., 2019. Has the concept of opportunities been fruitful in the field of entrepreneurship? Acad. Manag. Persp. Available from: https://doi.org/10.5465/amp.2018.0014.

Alvarez, S.A., Barney, J.B., McBride, R., Wuebker, R., 2014. Realism in the study of entrepreneurship. Acad. Manag. Rev. 39 (2), 227−233.

Anderson, M.H., Nichols, M.L., 2007. Information gathering and changes in threats and opportunity perception. J. Manag. Stud. 44 (3), 367−387.

Baron, R., 1998. Cognitive mechanisms in entrepreneurship: why and when entrepreneurs think differently than other people. J. Bus. Ventur. 13 (4), 275−294.

Baumol, W., 1993. Formal entrepreneurship theory in economics: existence and bond. J. Bus. Ventur. 8 (3), 197−210.

Braver, L., Danneels, E., 2018. Propensities return us to the discovery-creation debate about entrepreneurial opportunities. Acad. Manag. Rev. 43 (4), 812−815.

Brealey, R., Myers, S., 1988. Principles of Corporate Finance. McGraw Hill, New York.

Buchanan, J.M., Vanberg, V.J., 1991. The market as a creative process. Econ. Philos. 7 (2), 167−186.

Buenstorf, G., 2007. Creation and pursuit of entrepreneurial opportunities: an evolutionary perspective. Small Bus. Econ. 28 (4), 323−337.

Casson, M., 2003. The Entrepreneur: An Economic Theory, second ed., first ed. in 1982 Edward Elgar Publishing, Cheltenham, UK.

Casson, M., Wadeson, N., 2007. Entrepreneurship and macroeconomic performance. Strat. Entrepr. J. 1 (3–4), 239–262.

Chamberlin, E.H., 1933. The Theory of Monopolistic Competition. Harvard University Press, Cambridge, MA.

Coase, R.H., 1937. The nature of the firm. Economica 4 (16), 386–405.

Cohen, W.M., Levinthal, D.A., 1990. Absorptive capacity: a new perspective on learning and innovation. Admin. Sc. Quart 35 (1), 128–152.

Companys, Y.E., McMullen, J.S., 2007. Strategic entrepreneurs at work: the nature, discovery, and exploitation of entrepreneurial opportunities. Small Bus. Econ. 28 (4), 301–322.

Corbett, A.C., 2005. Experiential learning within the process of opportunity identification and exploitation. Entrepr.: Theory Pract. 29 (3), 473–491.

Cornelissen, J.P., Clarke, J.S., 2010. Imagining and rationalizing opportunities: inductive reasoning and the creation and justification of new ventures. Acad. Manag. Rev. 35 (4), 539–557.

Davidsson, P., 2015. Entrepreneurial opportunities and the entrepreneurship nexus: a reconceptualization. J. Bus. Ventur. 30 (5), 674–695.

Dimov, D., 2011. Grappling with the unbearable elusiveness of entrepreneurial opportunities. Entrepr.: Theory Pract. 35 (1), 57–81.

Downey, H.K., Slocum, J.W., 1975. Uncertainty: measures, research, and sources of variation. Acad. Manag. J. 18 (3), 562–578.

Drucker, P.F., 1985. Innovation and Entrepreneurship. Harper & Row, New York.

Duncan, R.B., 1972. Characteristics of organizational environments and perceived environmental uncertainty. Admin. Sci. Q. 17 (3), 313–327.

Eckhardt, J.T., Shane, S.A., 2013. Response to the commentaries: the individual-opportunity (IO) nexus integrates objective and subjective aspects of entrepreneurship. Acad. Manag. Rev. 38 (1), 160–163.

Evans, D., Jovanovic, B., 1989. An estimated model of entrepreneurial choice under liquidity constraints. J. Pol. Econ. 97 (4), 808–827.

Forbes, D.P., 2005. Are some entrepreneurs more overconfident than others? J. Bus. Ventur. 20 (5), 623–640.

Foss, K., Foss, N.J., 2008. Understanding opportunity discovery and sustainable advantage: the role of transaction costs and property rights. Strat. Entrepr. J. 2 (3), 191–207.

Foss, N.J., Klein, P., 2018. Entrepreneurial opportunities: who needs them? Acad. Manag. Persp. Available from: https://doi.org/10.5465/amp.2017.0181.

Gaglio, C.M., 2004. The role of mental simulation and counterfactual thinking in the opportunity identification processes. Entrepr.: Theory Pract. 28 (6), 533–552.

Gartner, W.B., Carter, N.M., Hills G.E., 2001. The language of opportunity. Paper presented at the Movements of Entrepreneurial Workshop, Stockholm, Sweden.

Gartner, W.B., Shaver, K.G., Liao, J., 2008. Opportunities as attributions: categorizing strategic issues from an attributional perspective. Strat. Entrepr. J. 2 (4), 301–315.

Gifford, S., 2005. Risk and uncertainty. In: Acs, Z.J., Audretsch, D.B. (Eds.), Handbook of Entrepreneurship Research: An Interdisciplinary Survey and Introduction. Springer, New York.

Hansen, D.J., Shrader, R., Monllor, J., 2009. Composite definitions of entrepreneurial opportunity and their operationalizations: toward a typology. Front. Entrepr. Res. 29 (17), 1–15.

Hansen, D.J., Shrader, R., Monllor, J., 2011. Defragmenting definitions of entrepreneurial opportunity. J. Small Bus. Manag. 49 (2), 283–304.

von Hayek, F.A., 1945. The use of knowledge in society. Am. Econ. Rev. 35 (4), 519−530.

Hmielesky, K.M., Baron, R.A., 2008. Regulatory focus and new venture performance: a study of entrepreneurial opportunity exploitation under conditions of risk versus uncertainty. Strat. Entrepr. J. 2 (4), 285−299.

Holcombe, R.G., 2003. The origins of entrepreneurial opportunities. Rev. Austrian Econ. 16 (1), 25−43.

Kaish, S., Gilad, B., 1991. Characteristic of opportunities search of entrepreneurs versus executives: sources, interests and general alertness. J. Bus. Ventur. 6 (1), 45−61.

Khilstrom, R., Laffont, J., 1979. A general equilibrium entrepreneurial theory of firm formation based on risk aversion. J. Pol. Econ. 87 (4), 719−748.

Kirzner, I.M., 1973. Competition and Entrepreneurship. The University of Chicago Press, Chicago and London.

Kirzner, I.M., 1997. Entrepreneurial discovery and the competitive market process: an Austrian approach. J. Econ. Lit. 35 (1), 60−85.

Klein, P.G., 2008. Opportunity discovery, entrepreneurial action and economic organization. Strat. Entrepr. J. 2 (3), 175−190.

Knight, F.H., 1921. Risk, Uncertainty and Profit. August M. Kelley, New York.

Kogut, B., Zander, U., 1992. Knowledge of the firm, combinative capabilities and the replication of technology. Org. Sci. 3 (3), 383−397.

Krueger, J.R., Norris, F., Reilly, M., Carsrud, A., 2000. Competing model of entrepreneurial intention. J. Bus. Ventur. 15 (5−6), 411−432.

Lamont, L., 1972. What entrepreneurs learn from experience. J. Small Bus. 10 (July), 254−260.

Lawrence, P.R., Lorsch, J.W., 1967. Organization and Environment. Harvard University Press, Boston, MA.

Martin, L., Wilson, N., 2016. Opportunity, discovery and creativity: a critical realist perspective. Int. Small Bus. J. 34 (3), 261−275.

Mazzoni, C., 2007, Le Relazioni Impresa-Settore-Mercati. Il Rapporto Micro-Macro nella Teoria dell'Impresa, Carocci Editore, Roma.

McDaniel, B.A., 2005. A contemporary view of Joseph A. Schumpeter's theory of the. Entrepr. J. Econ. Issues 39 (2), 485−489.

McMullen, J.S., 2015. Entrepreneurial judgment as empathic accuracy: a sequential decision-making approach to entrepreneurial action. J. Inst. Econ. 11 (3), 651−681.

McMullen, J.S., Shepherd, D.A., 2006. Entrepreneurial action and the role of uncertainty in the theory of the entrepreneur. Acad. Manag. Rev. 31 (1), 132−152.

McMullen, J.S., Plummer, L.A., Acs, Z.J., 2007. What is an entrepreneurial opportunity? Small Bus. Econ. 28 (4), 273−283.

Miller, K.D., 2007. Risk and rationality in entrepreneurial processes. Strat. Entrepr. J. 1 (1−2), 57−74.

von Mises, L., 1949. Human Action: A Treatise on Economics. Yale University Press, New Haven, CT.

Mitchell, R.K., Smith, B., Seawright, K., Morse, E., 2000. Cross-cultural cognitions and the venture creation process. Acad. Manag. Rev. 43 (5), 974−993.

Mitchell, R.K., Mitchell, J.R., Smith, J.B., 2008. Inside opportunity formation: enterprise failure, cognition, and the creation of opportunities. Strat. Entrepr. J. 2 (3), 225−242.

Morgan, G., Smircich, L., 1980. The case for qualitative research. Acad. Manag. Rev. 5 (4), 491−500.

Mueller, P., 2007. Exploiting entrepreneurial opportunities: the impact of entrepreneurship on growth. Small Bus. Econ. 28 (4), 355−362.

Pennings, M.P., 1981. Strategically independent organization. In: Nystrom, P., Starbuck, W. (Eds.), Handbook of Organizational Design Volume 1: Adapting Organizations to Their Environments. Oxford University Press, Oxford.

Pfeffer, J., Salancik, G.R., 1978. The External Control of Organization: A Resource Dependent Perspective. Harper and Row Publishers Inc, New York.

Plummer, L.A., Haynie, J.M., Godesiabois, J., 2007. An essay on the origins of entrepreneurial opportunity. Small Bus. Econ. 28 (4), 363–379.

Ramaglou, S., Zyglidopoulos, S., 2015. The constructivist view of entrepreneurial opportunities: a critical analysis. Small Bus. Econ. 44 (1), 71–78.

Ramoglou, S., Tsang, E.W., 2016. A realist perspective of entrepreneurship: opportunities as propensities. Acad. Manag. Rev. 41 (3), 410–434.

Rastkhiz, A.S.E., Dehkordi, M., Farsi, J.Y., Azar, A., 2019. A new approach to evaluating entrepreneurial opportunities. J. Small Bus. Enterpr. Devel. 26 (1), 67–84.

Roberts, E., 1991. Entrepreneurs in High Technology: Lessons from MIT and Beyond. Oxford University Press, New York.

Sarason, Y., Dean, T., Dillard, J.F., 2006. Entrepreneurship as the nexus of individual and opportunity: a structuration view. J. Bus. Ventur. 21 (3), 286–305.

Sarasvathy, S.D., 2001. Causation and effectuation: toward a theoretical shift from economic inevitability to entrepreneurial contingency. Acad. Manag. Rev. 26 (2), 243–264.

Sarasvathy, S.D., Dew, N., Velamuri, S.R., Venkataraman, S., 2005. Three views of entrepreneurial opportunity. In: Acs, Z.J., Audretsch, D.B. (Eds.), Handbook of Entrepreneurship Research: An Interdisciplinary Survey and Introduction. Springer, New York.

Say, J.B., 1803. A Treatise on Political Economy: Or, the Production, Distribution and Consumption of Wealth. Augustus M. Kelley, New York (printed version of 1964).

Schmidt, S.M., Cummings, L.L., 1976. Organizational environment, differentiation and perceived environmental uncertainty. Decision Sci. 7 (3), 447–467.

Schumpeter, J.A., 1911. The Theory of Economic Development: An Inquiry Into Profits, Capital, Credit, Interest and Business Cycle, 1934 ed. Harvard University Press, Cambridge, MA.

Shane, S., 2000. Prior knowledge and the discovery of entrepreneurial opportunities. Org. Sci. 11 (4), 448–469.

Shane, S., 2003. A General Theory of Entrepreneurship. The Individual-Opportunity Nexus. Edward Elgar Publishing, Cheltenham, UK.

Shane, S., Venkataraman, S., 2000. The promise of entrepreneurship as a field of research. Acad. Manag. Rev. 25 (1), 217–226.

Shaver, K.G., Scott, L.R., 1991. Person, process, and choice: the psychology of new venture creation. Entrepr.: Theory Pract. 16 (2), 23–46.

Short, J.C., Ketchen, D.J., Shook, C.L., Ireland, R.D., 2010. The concept of opportunity in entrepreneurship research: past accomplishments and future challenges. J. Manage. 36 (1), 40–65.

Singh, R., 2001. A comment on developing the field of entrepreneurship through the study of opportunity recognition and exploitation. Acad. Manag. Rev. 26 (1), 10–12.

Sleptsov, A., Anand, J., 2008. Exercising entrepreneurial opportunities: the role of information-gathering and information-processing capabilities of the firm. Strat. Entrepr. J. 2 (4), 357–372.

Smith, B.R., Matthews, C.H., Schenkel, M.T., 2009. Differences in entrepreneurial opportunities: the role of tacitness and codification in opportunity identification. J. Small Bus. Manag. 47 (1), 38–57.

Spedale, S., Watson, T.J., 2014. The emergence of entrepreneurial action: at the crossroads between institutional logics and individual life-orientation. Int. Small Bus. J. 32 (7), 759–766.

Suddaby, R., Bruton, G.D., Si, S.X., 2015. Entrepreneurship through a qualitative lens: insights on the construction and/or discovery of entrepreneurial opportunity. J. Bus. Ventur. 30 (1), 1–10.

Ucbasaran, D., Westhead, P., Wright, M., Binks, M., 2003. Does entrepreneurial experience influence opportunity identification? J. Private Equity 7 (1), 7–14.

Ucbasaran, D., Westhead, P., Wright, M., 2008. Opportunity identification and pursuit, does an entrepreneur's human capital matter? Small Bus. Econ. 30 (2), 153–173.

Venkataraman, S., 1997. The distinctive domain of entrepreneurship research: an editor's perspective. In: Katz, J., Brockhouse, R. (Eds.), Advances in Entrepreneurship, Firm Emergence, and Growth, vol. 3. JAI Press, Greenwich, CT, pp. 119–138.

Waters, W.A., 1994. The social economics of Joseph A. Schumpeter. Rev. Soc. Econ. 52 (4), 256–259.

Whetten, D.A., 1989. What constitutes a theoretical contribution? Acad. Manag. Rev. 14 (4), 490–495.

Wood, M.S., 2016. Misgiving about dismantling the opportunity construct. J. Bus. Ventur. Insights 7, 21–25.

Wood, M.S., McKinley, W., 2010. The production of entrepreneurial opportunity: a constructivist perspective. Strat. Entrep. J. 4 (1), 66–84.

Zahra, S.A., 2008. The virtuous cycle of discovery and creation of entrepreneurial opportunities. Strat. Entrepr. J. 2 (3), 243–257.

Further reading

Alvarez, S.A., Barney, J.B., Anderson, P., 2013. Forming and exploiting opportunities: the implication of discovery and creation process for entrepreneurial and organizational research. Org. Sci. 24 (1), 301–317.

Sarasvathy, S.D., 2008. Effectuation: Elements of Entrepreneurial Expertise. Edward Elgar Publishing Limited, Cheltenham, UK.

Entrepreneurship trajectories

5

5.1 The approach for drawing entrepreneurship trajectories

This research study started with a review of the main themes addressed by scholars in entrepreneurship literature (Audretsch et al., 2015; Welter et al., 2017; Kuckerts and Prochotta, 2018; Kuratko and Morris, 2018) in order to disclose the *leitmotiv* of entrepreneurship. This begins with the role of innovation that (in the shape of entrepreneurial opportunities) lies at the basis of entrepreneurship and ends with the impact of entrepreneurship (which is measured by considering achievable and achieved performances).

By embracing the idea that entrepreneurial opportunities and achieved performances can be the boundaries of entrepreneurial phenomena, then the right approach to their study seems to consist of considering entrepreneurship as a practice, an organizational process, or a journey (Eckhardt and Shane, 2003, 2013; Shane, 2003; Companys and McMullen, 2007; McMullen et al., 2007; Eckhardt and Ciuchta, 2008; Foss and Foss, 2008; Johannisson, 2008, 2011; Cha and Bae; 2010; Davidsson, 2015, 2016).

Entrepreneurs—putting into practice a process and experiencing a journey—are expected to be interested in the trajectory to be addressed. By definition, a trajectory is the path followed when an individual or an object moves from one place to another. It is the result of the intertwining of unexpected events with purposeful decisions.

The approach adopted in previous chapters goes backward: it began with the entrepreneurial performance that can be achieved (Birley and Westhead, 1990; Murphy et al., 1996; Delmar et al., 2003; OECD, 2008; Braunerhjelm, 2010; Henrekson and Johansson, 2010), passed through the business model (Amit and Zott, 2001; Zott and Amit, 2007, 2010), and ends with innovation at the basis of the entrepreneurial process that reveals itself in the shape of entrepreneurial opportunities (Sarasvathy, 2001; Alvarez and Barney, 2007, 2013; Suddaby et al., 2015; Wood, 2016; Braver and Danneels, 2018; Foss and Klein, 2018; Alvarez and Barney, 2019; Rastkhiz et al., 2019). Therefore the elements at the basis of entrepreneurship trajectories are achievable/achieved performance, business model, and entrepreneurial opportunities.

At this stage, it is appropriate to recall the results obtained from the reviews conducted in the previous chapters and to properly frame them. The main challenge is to find the right distance from which to assess a broader view of entrepreneurship trajectories. Needless to say, by zooming out some details become blurred;

Entrepreneurship Trajectories. DOI: https://doi.org/10.1016/B978-0-12-818650-3.00005-2

however, at the same time, larger chunks become clearer. Put simply, there is a risk of missing some theoretical aspects from dedicated reviews (these are the details that blur). However, since there is the expectation to disclose entrepreneurship trajectories (these are the larger chunks that become clearer), it is worth facing this risk and trying to formalize and catalog entrepreneurship trajectories.

Despite some criticalities (Denrell et al., 2014; Coad et al., 2016) and the common reference to the "up or out dynamic" (Haltiwanger et al., 2013; Decker et al., 2014), both theoretical and empirical studies that focus on performance reach the conclusion that entrepreneurial firms can grow, develop, survive, or fail.

All four of these concepts need to be carefully specified. Growth (or even high-growth) is the superior performance that true startups, which are new and innovative by definition, expect to achieve. Development is a positive concept because it represents an improvement of the startups' relationships with the external environment. Survival is about persisting on the market. Failure confirms its negative meaning because it is synonymous of bankruptcy and insolvency and is in opposition to voluntary closure (i.e., entrepreneurial firms are pushed out of the market). The specification of the concepts of growth, development, survival, or failure is necessary for the assessment of the definition of performance of entrepreneurial firms and for starting to draw entrepreneurial trajectories correctly.

In order to make the possible entrepreneurial performances more easily intelligible, they are represented in Fig. 5.1.

Despite the numerous definitions of a business model (Baden-Fuller and Morgan, 2010; Chesbrough, 2010; Zott et al., 2010, 2011; DaSilva and Trkman, 2014) and several factors that can affect their set up—such as the industry (Demil and Lecocq, 2010; Teece, 2010; Baden-Fuller and Haefliger, 2013; DaSilva, 2018) or the age of firms (Fiet and Patel, 2008; McGrath, 2010; Sosna et al., 2010; Teece, 2010, 2018; Saebi et al., 2017)—scholars mostly agree about the importance of

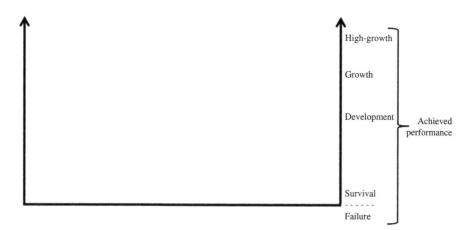

Figure 5.1 Drawing entrepreneurship trajectories: entrepreneurial performances.
Source: Personal elaboration.

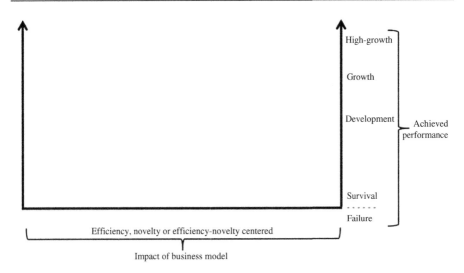

Figure 5.2 Drawing entrepreneurship trajectories: business models.
Source: Personal elaboration.

experimenting with a business model (Chesbrough, 2010; McGrath, 2010) when investigating the possible performances that firms can achieve.

In particular, in reference to entrepreneurial firms, Zott and Amit (2007) focus their attention on two concepts that can be at the basis of setting up a business model—novelty and efficiency. The above-cited scholars specify that business models focused on novelty and efficiency are neither mutually exclusive nor uncontaminated (efficiency design elements can refer to novelty-related issues and vice versa). Thus, in reference to entrepreneurial firms, it is appropriate to consider business models designed around novelty, efficiency, or both at the same time. Fig. 5.2 aims to clarify how business models can affect entrepreneurship trajectories.

According to Zott and Amit (2010), "the overall objective of a focal firm's business model is to exploit a business opportunity by creating value for parties involved" (p. 217). This statement discloses what may lie at the basis of business models by driving attention toward entrepreneurial opportunities.

From a dedicated literature review, it is shown that three types of entrepreneurial opportunities exist. They are neoclassical, Austrian, and contemporary. While the neoclassical and Austrian opportunities exist on their own, the contemporary ones need to be created. Accordingly, the role of entrepreneurs is minimal in neoclassical opportunities, assumes some relevance in Austrian opportunities, and reaches its peak in contemporary opportunities that cannot exist by themselves. Neoclassical opportunities are recognized as a result of systematic research (Shaver and Scott, 1991); Austrian opportunities are derived from an act of discovery (Kaish and Gilad, 1991; Kirzner, 1997); and contemporary opportunities are created and so they come to existence because of serendipity (Buenstorf, 2007). The classification of entrepreneurial opportunities, according to their origins, is shown in Fig. 5.3.

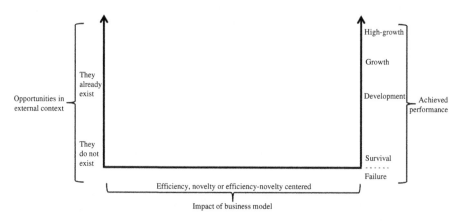

Figure 5.3 Drawing entrepreneurship trajectories: entrepreneurial opportunities.
Source: Personal elaboration.

At this stage, after recalling the performances that can be achieved, the business models that can be defined and implemented, and the types of opportunities that entrepreneurs can identify, it is possible to get enough latitude for action. Put simply, it is possible to get all three aspects closer in order to formalize and catalog entrepreneurship trajectories.

The primary issue that arises when trying to draw entrepreneurship trajectories is related to the approach (specifically, forward or backward) that needs to be used. Theoretically, since the beginning of this volume, a backward approach has been used. The analysis began with entrepreneurial performance, moved to the business model, and then focused on entrepreneurial opportunities. Such an approach is very useful for identifying the components of entrepreneurship trajectory.

However, in order to draw an entrepreneurship trajectory, the above approach does not seem appropriate anymore. Scholars who assume that entrepreneurship is a process or a journey (Eckhardt and Shane, 2003; Shane, 2003; Companys and McMullen, 2007; McMullen et al., 2007; Eckhardt and Ciuchta, 2008; Foss and Foss, 2008; Cha and Bae, 2010; McMullen and Dimov, 2013; Davidsson, 2016) share the idea that entrepreneurship is a cumulative process.

Diambeidou et al. (2007), who recall one of the most prominent scholars interested in the growth of firms—Penrose (1959)—clearly underline that entrepreneurial processes are the results of cumulative interactions between "interconnected causes, outcomes and further feedback effects" (Diambeidou et al., 2007, p. 6). Entrepreneurial processes take place stage after stage (OECD, 2010) and reveal themselves in accordance with a model or a pattern that—as proposed by Khun (1962) in reference to a scientific paradigm—focuses on a problem and defines a procedure and task for solving that problem. This view of entrepreneurship is based on a sequential decision-making approach (McMullen and Dimov, 2013; McMullen, 2015) that, time after time, drives toward the identification of problems and solutions. Thus a forward approach is necessary to formalize and catalog entrepreneurship trajectories.

In light of what was said above, the approach able to draw entrepreneurship trajectories cannot proceed in reverse but needs to move forward. In order to formalize entrepreneurship trajectories, it is appropriate to start with entrepreneurial opportunities, move on to the business model,[1] and then reach entrepreneurial performance.

5.2   Flat trajectory

From the review of entrepreneurial opportunities, three types of opportunities are revealed. The first type that was analyzed is the neoclassical one. Without recalling all the characteristics of this opportunity type, it is sufficient to remember the predominance of external reality over individual qualities—entrepreneurial opportunities already exist on their own and entrepreneurs only have to recognize them. Neoclassical entrepreneurs, in fact, are just a means that can introduce innovations into the economic field (this is the Schumpeterian view). The process of recognition of neoclassical opportunities seems to be objective and, above all, to happen without relevant participation of entrepreneurs (Shaver and Scott, 1991; Sarason et al., 2006; Smith et al., 2009), who are very involved in the competition for resources instead, as they must be able to obtain them.

This main task that neoclassical entrepreneurs need to carry out affects their choice of the business model to implement. As already pointed out, entrepreneurs can choose between three alternatives in reference to entrepreneurial firms. The business model can be centered on efficiency, novelty, or both at the same time. Efficiency-centered business models focus on cost-reducing transactions and activities in order to improve economic efficiency. Novelty-centered business models focus on new activities and new ways of linking and managing them. Efficiency- and novelty-centered business models aim to exploit novelty by leveraging efficiency or, vice versa, aim to exploit efficiency by leveraging novelty.

Entrepreneurs who recognized neoclassical opportunities do not seem interested in the theme of novelty. By definition, in fact, they are interested in the theme of efficiency (*equilibrium* on the market). They aim to reduce transaction costs through simplified or repetitive transactions with the same stakeholders (Williamson 1975, 1983; Meyer et al., 1992). Hence, the choice of a business model to implement depends on the nature of the entrepreneurial opportunity underlying it.

At this stage, it is appropriate to wonder about the performance that entrepreneurs exploiting neoclassical opportunities and implementing an efficiency-centered business model can achieve. In reference to the short-term, it is not reasonable to expect that these entrepreneurs can achieve growth, because they aim to implement and manage simplified or repetitive transactions with the same stakeholders.

---

[1] Recently, Di Muro and Turner (2018) have labeled this approach as project perspective. In particular, the scholars have investigated the pursuit of entrepreneurial opportunities through business model transformation.

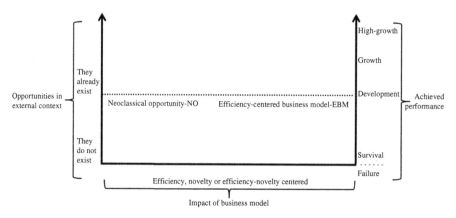

Figure 5.4 Flat trajectory.
Source: Personal elaboration.

Accordingly, the performance that these entrepreneurs aim to achieve consists of either survival (i.e., persisting on the market) or development (i.e., an improvement of the startups' relationships with the external environment) of entrepreneurial firms. In the long run, the development of firms seems to be the best result that entrepreneurial firms exploiting neoclassical opportunities and implementing an efficiency-centered business model should aspire to.

The first case analyzed herein deals with neoclassical opportunities (already existing on their own) that drive entrepreneurs to define and set up an efficiency-centered business model (aiming for transaction costs reduction) and to achieve a performance that varies between survival and development (managing relations with stakeholders in a proper way is the most important task to achieve).

The sequence—neoclassical opportunity/efficiency-centered business model/survival or development of firms—draws an entrepreneurship trajectory that can be labeled as flat (see Fig. 5.4).

5.3   Incremental trajectory

The second type of opportunity that has been analyzed is the Austrian one. According to the Austrian approach, entrepreneurial opportunities are derived from the external reality, but only some individuals who have specific qualities—for example, Kirzner's alertness (1973)—can discover them. Similar to the neoclassical opportunities, the Austrian ones already exist. However, unlike the neoclassical opportunities, the Austrian opportunities are discovered due to the individual features that are typical of entrepreneurs only. Thus the Austrian approach assumes that opportunities exist but need to be discovered. As previously noted,[2] this approach looks at the process in which individuals and reality interact. In particular, since the early stages of the entrepreneurial process, entrepreneurs following this approach compete for strategies that would enable them to discover opportunities.

This strategic competition between aspiring entrepreneurs who are aiming to discover opportunities affects the choice of the business model as well. After discovering Austrian opportunities, entrepreneurs are torn between two different and yet, at the same time, complementary approaches. On the one hand, since Austrian opportunities already exist on their own, entrepreneurs can aim for efficiency in their exploitation (just as it is supposed for the neoclassical approach). On the other hand, since entrepreneurs compete for strategies that would enable them to discover opportunities, they could also compete for strategies that would enable them to exploit these opportunities through the business model.

It has already been pointed out, in reference to entrepreneurial firms, that the business model can be centered on efficiency, novelty, or both at the same time. With scarce reservation, it is reasonable to suppose that entrepreneurs exploiting Austrian opportunities are interested in business models centered on efficiency and novelty at the same time (Zott and Amit, 2007; Zott and Huy, 2007). These entrepreneurs can aim to exploit novelty and to leverage efficiency, or they can aim to exploit efficiency and to leverage novelty. The concepts of efficiency and novelty can nurture each other. They can be mixed because they are neither mutually exclusive nor uncontaminated (efficiency design elements can refer to novelty-related issues and vice versa).

Thus, what is the performance that an efficiency- and novelty-centered business model can have? Starting from the assumption at the basis of the Austrian approach, according to which entrepreneurial opportunities already exist but entrepreneurs need to leverage individual qualities to discover them, the firms based on Austrian opportunities can aspire toward development (efficiency can improve the startups' relationships with their stakeholders) or even growth (novelty can lead to superior performances).

The second case analyzed herein deals with Austrian opportunities (already existing on their own but individuals are expected to possess certain characteristics in order to discover them) that lead entrepreneurs to define and set up an efficiency- and novelty-centered business model (aiming for transaction costs reduction and exploitation of novelty) and to achieve a performance that varies between development and growth.

The sequence—Austrian opportunity/efficiency- and novelty-centered business model/development or growth of firms—draws an entrepreneurship trajectory that can be labeled as incremental (see Fig. 5.5).

---

[2] See paragraph 4.3.

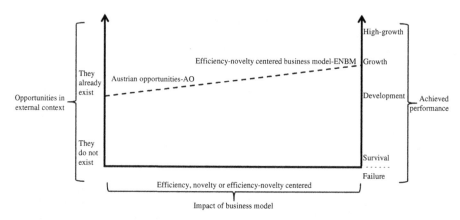

Figure 5.5 Incremental trajectory.
Source: Personal elaboration.

5.4 Adventurous trajectory

The third type of opportunity that has been analyzed is the contemporary one. This approach criticizes the neoclassical and the Austrian ones and underlines the relevance of individuals over external reality. Here, it is individual action that creates opportunities *ex nihilo* and, consequently, gives birth to entrepreneurship phenomena. Moreover, according to this approach, individuals compete strategically in order to create value. Opportunities do not exist on their own—thus it is up to individuals to create value.

How do entrepreneurs create value in reference to contemporary opportunities? They need to choose the most appropriate business model. Again, the business model for startups (Zott and Amit, 2007; Zott and Huy, 2007) can be centered on efficiency, novelty, or both at the same time. Since entrepreneurs create contemporary opportunities, which, by definition, embody the concept of newness, then the choice to implement a novelty-centered business model seems understandable and—actually—rather obvious. Furthermore, by definition, business models designed around novelty exploit the concept of newness in many different ways. They can include new ways of understanding an entrepreneurial opportunity, of designing and managing economic transactions, of linking external parties, of referring to the external market—by new products or services (Björkdahl and Holmén, 2013).

Starting with the idea that contemporary opportunities do not exist but that entrepreneurs create them and then moving attention toward the business model that can be novelty-centered in order to exploit the novelty of contemporary opportunities, it seems reasonable to assume that the higher the degree of business model novelty is, the higher the performance that entrepreneurs can achieve would be. If customers, suppliers, and stakeholders recognize the novelty (which, in management terms, stands for innovativeness) at the basis of an entrepreneurial opportunity and of a business model, then they can be locked-in, preventing them from easily switching

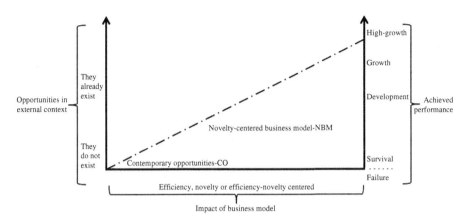

Figure 5.6 Adventurous trajectory.
Source: Personal elaboration.

to another firm. Accordingly, it is rational to suppose that entrepreneurs aim to achieve growth or even high-growth—that is, a superior performance—because of the novelty characterizing this trajectory.

The sequence—contemporary opportunity/novelty-centered business model/ growth or high-growth of firms—draws an entrepreneurship trajectory that can be labeled as adventurous (see Fig. 5.6).

5.5 Entrepreneurship trajectories

The three types of entrepreneurial opportunities discussed in dedicated literature (Sarasvathy et al., 2005; Alvarez and Barney, 2007; Buenstorf, 2007; Zahra, 2008; Smith et al., 2009; Martin and Wilson, 2016), the different types of business models that are typical of startups (Amit and Zott, 2001; Zott and Amit, 2007, 2010), and the performances that startups can achieve (Birley and Westhead, 1990; Murphy et al., 1996; Delmar et al., 2003; OECD, 2008; Braunerhjelm, 2010; Henrekson and Johansson, 2010) provide a conceptual toolkit that enables entrepreneurs to draw entrepreneurship trajectories and scholars to formalize and catalog them.

From the theoretical analysis, three entrepreneurial trajectories have been outlined: (1) a flat trajectory that has the sequence: neoclassical opportunity/efficiency-centered business model/survival or development of firms; (2) an incremental trajectory that has the sequence: Austrian opportunity/efficiency- and novelty-centered business model/development or growth of firms; and (3) an adventurous trajectory that has the sequence: contemporary opportunity/novelty-centered business model/growth or high-growth of firms. These three entrepreneurship trajectories are shown in Table 5.1.

The trajectories proposed above are the result of a sequential, incremental approach to entrepreneurship processes that begins with the type of opportunity, passes through the business model, and reaches a performance (see Fig. 5.7).

Table 5.1 Entrepreneurship trajectories.

Types of entrepreneurship trajectories	Elements characterizing them
Flat	Neoclassical opportunity; Efficiency-centered business model; Survival or development of firms.
Incremental	Austrian opportunity; Efficiency- and novelty-centered business model; Development or growth of firms.
Adventurous	Contemporary opportunity; Novelty-centered business model; Growth or high-growth of firms.

Source: Personal elaboration.

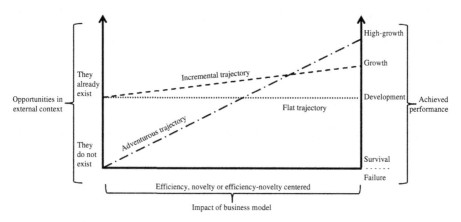

Figure 5.7 Entrepreneurship trajectories.
Source: Personal elaboration.

At this stage, two reflections come to mind.

First, from a theoretical point of view, none of the proposed trajectories (flat, incremental, or adventurous) overlaps with another. Since they begin with different opportunity types, are included in business models centered on different themes, and aim to achieve different performances, they develop along different trajectories that—according to the theoretical analysis carried out above—cannot be mixed or confused.

At this point, it is appropriate to think about extreme cases (neoclassical and contemporary opportunities) to validate the above assumption.

If entrepreneurs recognize a neoclassical opportunity (which does not require individual capabilities to be discovered because it already exists on its own) and if they are only involved in a competition for resources (i.e., efficiency) in order to exploit it, then it is difficult to hypothesize that a business model can be centered on novelty and that the expected performance can be growth or even high-growth.

Similarly, if entrepreneurs create a contemporary opportunity (that does not exist on its own) and if they compete strategically in order to create value, then it is difficult to hypothesize that a business model can be centered on efficiency and that the expected performance can be survival or development.

The above reflections recall a very important aspect that, in entrepreneurship studies, is well-known and largely accepted—the concept of path-dependence. According to David (1985) and Arthur (1988), previous events can affect the subsequent choices of individuals. It is a mechanism that reduces the alternatives to evaluate and choose from (North, 1990). The concept of path-dependence was first proposed in reference to natural sciences, then transposed to social sciences (Arrow, 1994), and, eventually, referred to entrepreneurship studies as well (Liebowitz and Margolis, 1995; David, 1997, 2000).

In particular, Liebowitz and Margolis (1995) identify three levels of path-dependence in reference to entrepreneurship: the first level refers to cases that identify a path leading to the best results; the second level refers to cases that identify a path that does not lead to the best results because some information is missing; and the third level refers to cases that identify a path leading to unsatisfying results. In the last case, entrepreneurs are driven to evaluate new alternatives and, if necessary, to modify their choices and the path previously addressed.

The second reflection is linked to what was just said about the possibility to modify the path or trajectory previously addressed. The analysis carried out, in fact, considers only positive situations that, despite the different trajectories addressed, lead to survival, development, growth, or high-growth. Of course, market experiences remind us that all entrepreneurial trajectories are exposed to the risk of failure. Accordingly, entrepreneurial trajectories might not follow the path hypothesized by entrepreneurs and lead to failure as well (Fig. 5.8).

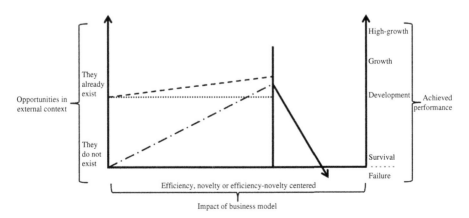

Figure 5.8 Entrepreneurship trajectories and failure risk.
Source: Personal elaboration.

In case of failure, entrepreneurs cannot easily modify only the trajectory to address (because of the path-dependence described above). If possible, they are expected to work on the entrepreneurial opportunity again in order to focus attention on other aspects of the same entrepreneurial opportunity and to exploit them on the market. This, in turn, might allow entrepreneurs to evaluate new business models to set up (through experimentation of different business models) and different performances to achieve.

From the above reflections, it can be concluded that entrepreneurship trajectories differ from one another but share two main aspects at the same time—the role of path-dependence and the risk of failure. Of course, and this is a very important aspect to note, if entrepreneurs modify the entrepreneurial opportunity to exploit, the business model to set up, and the performance to achieve, then it is reasonable to assume that they are going to address a new, different entrepreneurship trajectory.

References

Alvarez, S.A., Barney, J., 2007. Discovery and creation: alternative theories of entrepreneurial action. Strat. Entrepr. J. 1 (1−2), 11−26.

Alvarez, S.A., Barney, J.B., 2013. Epistemology, opportunities, and entrepreneurship: comments on Venkataraman et al. (2012) and Shane (2012). Acad. Manage Rev. 38 (1), 154−157.

Alvarez, S.A., Barney, J.B., 2019. Has the concept of opportunities been fruitful in the field of entrepreneurship? Acad. Manage Perspect. . Available from: https://doi.org/10.5465/amp.2018.0014.

Amit, R., Zott, C., 2001. Value creation in e-business. Strategic Manage J. 22 (6−7), 493−520.

Arrow, K.J., 1994. Methodological individualism and social knowledge. Am. Econ. Rev. 84 (2), 1−9.

Arthur, W.B., 1988. Self-reinforcing mechanisms in economics. In: Anderson, P.W., Arrow, K.J., Pines, D. (Eds.), The Economy as an Evolving Complex System. Addison-Wesley, Readings, MA.

Audretsch, D.B., Kuratko, D.F., Link, A.N., 2015. Making sense of the elusive paradigm of entrepreneurship. Small Bus. Econ. 45 (4), 703−712.

Baden-Fuller, C., Haefliger, S., 2013. Business models and technological innovation. Long Range Plann. 46 (6), 419−426.

Baden-Fuller, C., Morgan, M.S., 2010. Business models as models. Long Range Plann. 43 (2−3), 156−171.

Birley, S., Westhead, P., 1990. Growth and performance contrasts between 'types' of small firms. Strategic Manage J. 11 (7), 535−557.

Björkdahl, J., Holmén, M., 2013. Business model innovation: the challenges ahead. Int. J. Prod. Dev. 18 (3/4), 213−225.

Braunerhjelm, P., 2010. Entrepreneurship, innovation and economic growth: interdependencies, irregularities and regularities. In: Audretsch, D.B., Flack, O., Heblich, S., Lederer, A. (Eds.), Handbook of Research on Innovation and Entrepreneurship. Edward Elgar, Cheltenham, UK, pp. 161−213.

Braver, L., Danneels, E., 2018. Propensities return us to the discovery-creation debate about entrepreneurial opportunities. Acad. Manage Rev. 43 (4), 812−815.

Buenstorf, G., 2007. Creation and pursuit of entrepreneurial opportunities: an evolutionary perspective. Small Bus. Econ. 28 (4), 323−337.

Cha, M.S., Bae, Z.T., 2010. The entrepreneurial journey: from entrepreneurial intent to opportunity realization. J. High Technol. Manag. Res. 21 (1), 31−42.

Chesbrough, H., 2010. Business model innovation: opportunities and barriers. Long Range Plann. 43 (2−3), 354−363.

Coad, A., Segarra, A., Teruel, M., 2016. Innovation and firm growth: does firm age play a role? Res. Policy 45 (2), 387−400.

Companys, Y.E., McMullen, J.S., 2007. Strategic entrepreneurs at work: the nature, discovery, and exploitation of entrepreneurial opportunities. Small Bus. Econ. 28 (4), 301−322.

DaSilva, C.M., 2018. Understanding business model innovation from a practitioner perspective. J. Bus. Models 6 (2), 19−24.

DaSilva, C.M., Trkman, P., 2014. Business model: what it is and what it is not. Long Range Plann. 47 (6), 379−389.

David, P.A., 1985. Clio and the economics of QWERTY. Am. Econ. Rev. 75 (2), 332−337.

David, P.A., 1997. Path dependence and the quest for historical economics: one more chorus of the ballad of QWERTY. University of Oxford Discussion Papers in Economic and Social History, n. 20.

David, P.A., 2000. Path-dependence, its critics and the quest for "historical economics". In: Garrouste, P., Ioannides, S. (Eds.), Evolution and Path Dependence in Economic Ideas: Past and Present. Edward Elgar Publishing, Cheltenham, UK.

Davidsson, P., 2015. Entrepreneurial opportunities and the entrepreneurship nexus: a re-conceptualization. J. Bus. Venturing. 30 (5), 674−695.

Davidsson, P., 2016. The field of entrepreneurship research: some significant developments. In: Bögenhold, D., Bonnet, J., Dejardin, M., Garcia Pérez de Lema, D. (Eds.), Contemporary Entrepreneurship. Springer, Cham, pp. 17−28.

Decker, R., Haltiwanger, J., Jarmin, R., Miranda, J., 2014. The role of entrepreneurship in US job creation and economic dynamism. J. Econ. Perspect. 28 (3), 3−24.

Delmar, F., Davidsson, P., Gartner, W.B., 2003. Arriving at the high-growth firm. J. Bus. Ventur. 18 (2), 189−216.

Demil, B., Lecocq, X., 2010. Business model evolution: in search of dynamic consistency. Long Range Plann. 43 (2−3), 227−246.

Denrell, J., Fang, C., Liu, C., 2014. Perspective: chance explanations in the management sciences. Organ. Sci. 26 (3), 923−940.

Di Muro, P., Turner, J.R., 2018. Entrepreneurial opportunity pursuit through business model transformation: a project perspective. Int. J. Proj. Manag. 36, 968−979.

Diambeidou, M.B., François, D., Gailly, B., Verleysen, M., Wertz, V. (2007). An empirical taxonomy of start-up firms growth trajectories. Working paper 07/09 at Louvain School of Management.

Eckhardt, J.T., Ciuchta, M.P., 2008. Selected variation: the population-level implications of multistage selection in entrepreneurship. Strat. Entrepr. J. 2 (3), 209−224.

Eckhardt, J.T., Shane, S., 2003. The individual-opportunity nexus. In: Acs, Z.J., Audretsch, D.B. (Eds.), Handbook of Entrepreneurship Research: A Interdisciplinary Survey and Introduction. Kluwer Academic Publishers, UK.

Eckhardt, J.T., Shane, S.A., 2013. Response to the commentaries: the individual-opportunity (IO) nexus integrates objective and subjective aspects of entrepreneurship. Acad. Manage. Rev. 38 (1), 160−163.

Fiet, J.O., Patel, P.C., 2008. Forgiving business models for new ventures. Entrepr.: Theory Pract. 32 (4), 749−761.

Foss, K., Foss, N.J., 2008. Understanding opportunity discovery and sustainable advantage: the role of transaction costs and property rights. Strat. Entrepr. J. 2 (3), 191−207.

Foss, N.J., Klein, P., 2018. Entrepreneurial opportunities: who needs them? Acad. Manag. Perspect. . Available from: https://doi.org/10.5465/amp.2017.0181.

Haltiwanger, J., Jarmin, R.S., Miranda, J., 2013. Who creates jobs? Small versus large versus young. Rev. Econ. Stat. 95 (2), 347−361.

Henrekson, M., Johansson, D., 2010. Gazelles as job creators: a survey and interpretation of the evidence. Small Bus. Econ. 35 (2), 227−244.

Johannisson, B., 2008. Bengt Johannisson's Prize Lecture: towards a practice theory of entre-preneuring, International Award for Entrepreneurship and Small Business Research, pp. 1−12.

Johannisson, B., 2011. Towards a practice theory of entrepreneuring. Small Bus. Econ. 36 (2), 135−150.

Kaish, S., Gilad, B., 1991. Characteristic of opportunities search of entrepreneurs versus executives: sources, interests and general alertness. J. Bus. Venturing. 6 (1), 45−61.

Khun, T., 1962. The Structure of Scientific Revolution. Chicago University Press, Chicago, IL.

Kirzner, I.M., 1973. Competition and Entrepreneurship. The University of Chicago Press, Chicago and London.

Kirzner, I.M., 1997. Entrepreneurial discovery and the competitive market process: an Austrian approach. J. Econ. Lit. 35 (1), 60−85.

Kuckertz, A., Prochotta, A., 2018. What's hot in entrepreneurship research 2018? Hohenheim Entrepr. Res. Brief 4, 1−7.

Kuratko, D.F., Morris, M.H., 2018. Examining the future trajectory of entrepreneurship. J. Small Bus. Manag. 56 (1), 11−23.

Liebowitz, S.J., Margolis, S.E., 1995. Path dependence, lock-in, and history. J. Law Econ. Org. 11 (1), 205−226.

Martin, L., Wilson, N., 2016. Opportunity, discovery and creativity: a critical realist perspec-tive. Int. Small Bus. J. 34 (3), 261−275.

McGrath, R.G., 2010. Business models: a discovery driven approach. Long Range Plann. 43 (2−3), 247−261.

McMullen, J.S., 2015. Entrepreneurial judgment as empathic accuracy: a sequential decision-making approach to entrepreneurial action. J. Inst. Econ. 11 (3), 651−681.

McMullen, J.S., Dimov, D., 2013. Time and the entrepreneurial journey: the problems and promise of studying entrepreneurship as a process. J. Manag. Stud. 50, 1481−1512.

McMullen, J.S., Plummer, L.A., Acs, Z.J., 2007. What is an entrepreneurial opportunity? Small Bus. Econ. 28 (4), 273−283.

Meyer, M., Milgrom, P., Roberts, J., 1992. Organizational prospects, influence costs, and ownership changes. J. Econ. Manag. Strat. 1 (1), 9−35.

Murphy, G.B., Trailer, J.W., Hill, R.C., 1996. Measuring performance in entrepreneurship research. J. Bus. Res. 36 (1), 15−23.

North, D.C., 1990. Institutions, Institutional Change and Economic Performance. Cambridge University Press, Cambridge.

OECD, 2008. A Framework for Addressing and Measuring Entrepreneurship. OECD Statistics Working Paper. OECD Publishing, Paris. STD/DOC(2008)2.

OECD, 2010. High-growth enterprises: what governments can do to make a difference. OECD Studies on SMEs and Entrepreneurship. OECD Publishing, Paris. Available from: https://doi.org/10.1787/9789264048782-en.

Penrose, E., 1959. The Theory of the Growth of the Firm. Basil Blackwell and Mott, Oxford.

Rastkhiz, A.S.E., Dehkordi, M., Farsi, J.Y., Azar, A., 2019. A new approach to evaluating entrepreneurial opportunities. J. Small Bus. Enterpr. Devel. 26 (1), 67−84.

Saebi, T., Lien, L., Foss, N.J., 2017. What drives business model adaptation? The impact of opportunities, threats and strategic orientation. Long Range Plann. 50 (5), 567−581.

Sarason, Y., Dean, T., Dillard, J.F., 2006. Entrepreneurship as the nexus of individual and opportunity: a structuration view. J. Bus. Venturing. 21 (3), 286−305.

Sarasvathy, S.D., 2001. Causation and effectuation: toward a theoretical shift from economic inevitability to entrepreneurial contingency. Acad. Manag. Rev. 26 (2), 243−264.

Sarasvathy, S.D., Dew, N., Velamuri, S.R., Venkataraman, S., 2005. Three views of entrepreneurial opportunity. In: Acs, Z.J., Audretsch, D.B. (Eds.), Handbook of Entrepreneurship Research: An Interdisciplinary Survey and Introduction. Springer, New York, NY.

Shane, S., 2003. A General Theory of Entrepreneurship. The Individual-Opportunity Nexus. Edward Elgar Publishing, Cheltenham, UK.

Shaver, K.G., Scott, L.R., 1991. Person, process, and choice: the psychology of new venture creation. Entrepr.: Theory Pract. 16 (2), 23−46.

Smith, B.R., Matthews, C.H., Schenkel, M.T., 2009. Differences in entrepreneurial opportunities: the role of tacitness and codification in opportunity identification. J. Small Bus. Manag. 47 (1), 38−57.

Sosna, M., Trevinyo-Rodríguez, R.N., Velamuri, S.R., 2010. Business model innovation through trial-and-error learning: the Naturhouse case. Long Range Plann. 43 (2−3), 383−407.

Suddaby, R., Bruton, G.D., Si, S.X., 2015. Entrepreneurship through a qualitative lens: insights on the construction and/or discovery of entrepreneurial opportunity. J. Bus. Venturing. 30 (1), 1−10.

Teece, D.J., 2010. Business models, business strategy and innovation. Long Range Plann. 43 (2−3), 172−194.

Teece, D.J., 2018. Business models and dynamic capabilities. Long Range Plann. 51 (1), 40−49.

Welter, F., Baker, T., Audretsch, D.B., Gartner, W.B., 2017. Everyday entrepreneurship: a call for entrepreneurship research to embrace entrepreneurial diversity. Entrepr.: Theory Pract. 41 (3), 311−321.

Williamson, O.E., 1975. Markets and Hierarchies: Analysis and Antitrust Implication − A Study in the Economics of Internal Organizations. Free Press, MacMillan, New York, NY.

Williamson, O.E., 1983. Credible commitments: using hostage to support axchange. Am. Econ. Rev. 73 (4), 519−540.

Wood, M.S., 2016. Misgiving about dismantling the opportunity construct. J. Bus. Ventur. Insights 7, 21−25.

Zahra, S.A., 2008. The virtuous cycle of discovery and creation of entrepreneurial opportunities. Strat. Entrepr. J. 2 (3), 243−257.

Zott, C., Amit, R., 2007. Business model design and the performance of entrepreneurial firms. Organ. Sci. 18 (2), 181−199.

Zott, C., Amit, R., 2010. Business model design: an activity system perspective. Long Range Plann. 43 (2−3), 216−226.

Zott, C., Amit, R., Massa, L., 2010. The business model: theoretical roots, recent developments, and future research. IESE Bus. Sch. − Univ. Navarra 1−43.

Zott, C., Amit, R., Massa, L., 2011. The business model: recent developments and future research. J. Manag. 37 (4), 1019−1042.

Zott, C., Huy, Q., 2007. Symbolic emphasizing: how entrepreneurs use symbolism to acquire resources. Adm. Sci. Q. 52 (1), 70−105.

Selected cases

6

6.1 The choice of the research method

The main aim of this chapter does not concern the generalization of a phenomenon and the consequent building of a new theory. On the contrary, the following lines just aim to verify if some entrepreneurs—consciously or even unconsciously—draw and follow entrepreneurship trajectories when launching and managing their startups.

In order to get to the generalization of a phenomenon and the building of a new theory, in fact, both theoretical and empirical perspectives—nurturing each other—need to be considered. According to Kuhn (1970) it is possible to get to a new theory through incremental empirical testing and additional extensions. Generalized phenomena and consequent new theories depend on past literature plus empirical observations or experience. Even if this volume seems to address this path, it is too premature to aspire to identify a generalized phenomenon and to build a new theory. The probable generalization of the phenomenon and the building of a new theory are further steps that are not considered herein.

Instead, in order to achieve the main aim of this chapter (again, it is to verify if some entrepreneurs—consciously or even unconsciously—draw and follow entrepreneurship trajectories when launching and managing their startup) attention is focused on empirical observations. They are useful to corroborate or deny the addressing of entrepreneurship trajectories emerged from the review of entrepreneurial literature.

After clarifying the aim pursued, the problem to solve consists in determining which is the best method in order to get empirical observations. It is generally accepted that the choice between quantitative or qualitative research methods strictly depends on the topic of research.[1] Far from being engaged in the debate about research methods, it can be useful to proceed by analyzing strengths and weaknesses of both the methods.

The strength of quantitative methods is that they aim to produce a set of generalizations (Procter, 1993). These are based on available data that are used to investigate the relationship between variables (two or more). For example, they can be useful to establish whether a correlation between factors determining entrepreneurship and final results of entrepreneurship itself (i.e., firm performance) exists or

---

[1] As noticed by Silverman (2001), quantitative methods are useful to discover how people want to vote; qualitative methods, instead, are favored when inquiring people's life histories or everyday behavior. See also Corbetta (1999).

Entrepreneurship Trajectories. DOI: https://doi.org/10.1016/B978-0-12-818650-3.00006-4

not. However, this is not the aim of the present work. Entrepreneurship trajectories, in fact, deal with the process starting with the identification of an entrepreneurial opportunity, moves toward the choice of the most suitable business model to set up and ends with the achievement of a performance. There is no correlation to be tested.

As a weakness of quantitative methods, it is possible to consider that researchers define, count, and analyze data by using procedures arbitrarily or unknowingly (Silverman, 1975). This way of researching seems to be focused on the final results more than on the first part of a research when hypotheses need to be tested. As noticed by Glaser and Strauss (1967), in fact, a statistical approach can fail to help generating hypotheses from data and can prevent developing further researches. Specific procedures and connected results cannot be sacrificed in favor of measurable results. Entrepreneurship trajectories still need to develop a broader set of hypotheses that can spontaneously emerge from empirical research.

Attention now can be moved toward qualitative methods. Their strength derives from the assumption that some areas of social reality cannot be measured (Hammersley and Atkinson, 1983; Gubrium, 1988). In some cases, in fact, the influence of internal or external factors cannot be measured or counted exactly. Qualitative methods help to overcome this difficulty and to explore nonmeasurable factors. As already said, entrepreneurship trajectories are based on entrepreneurial opportunities to identify, on business models to set up and on performance to achieve. In fact, entrepreneurial opportunities and business models are nonmeasurable factors (differently performance to achieve is a measurable factor) and so qualitative methods seem to be more suitable for the present research.

Eventually, the weakness of qualitative methods depends on reliability and validity of research. The former deals with the critical choice to categorize all the possible cases (it depends on the researcher and so it is a highly personal decision). The latter concerns the impossibility to test rival cases. Researchers are not going to evaluate them if they do not emerge from final results.[2] Since entrepreneurship trajectories are new, their categorization and validity (e.g., through rival hypotheses) still need to be guaranteed and so qualitative methods seem more suitable.

Strengths and weaknesses of both quantitative and qualitative methods are summarized in Table 6.1.

According to the above analysis, qualitative methods are chosen to inquiry entrepreneurship trajectories since they seem to fit more with the purpose of the present research. In this vein, it seems appropriate to cite Strauss and Corbin (1998, p. 11) arguing: "there are many valid reasons for doing qualitative research." Beyond personal attitude, a relevant criterion of choice depends on the origin of the research problem. Specifically, entrepreneurship trajectories are a qualitative rather than a quantitative phenomenon.

At this stage, it is appropriate to choose the specific research method to be used. In reference to entrepreneurship studies, after the seminal proposal by Eisenhardt

---

[2] In quantitative methods the test of contrary cases can happen more often despite it can happen arbitrarily or unknowingly.

Table 6.1 Strengths and weaknesses of quantitative and qualitative methods.

	Strengths	Weaknesses
Quantitative methods	They aim to investigate relationships (e.g., the correlation) between variables	Researchers define, count, and analyze data by using procedures arbitrarily or unknowingly in order to investigate relationships between variables
Qualitative methods	They are useful to measure internal or external factors; cannot be measured or counted exactly	Reliability and validity of research

Source: Personal elaboration.

(1989), many scholars[3] leverage the methodology of case study since it allows a deep investigation of cases through which phenomena reveal themselves (Clarysse and Moray, 2004; Park, 2005; Mair and Marti, 2009; Sosna et al., 2010; Datta and Gailey, 2012; Henry and Foss, 2015; Anderson et al., 2019; Stirzaker et al., 2019). Accordingly, this methodology is adopted also for the present study.

6.2 The data collection system: semistructured interviews

Three entrepreneurs have been involved in the present research through semistructured interviews (Box 6.1). The main feature of semistructured interviews consists in having a framework to refer to (in this case the entrepreneurship trajectories and—more precisely—the identification of entrepreneurial opportunities, the setup of business models and the achieved performance) but, at the same time, the amount of questions is not preestablished. Given some tracks, in fact, the interviewer can add other questions if they arise as the interview goes.[4]

---

[3] Despite the by and large use of this methodology, scholars debate about the number of cases to be considered. According to Eisenhardt (1989, p. 545) "while there is no ideal number of cases, a number between four and ten cases usually works well." Some scholars have supported this view and so they have proposed generalization of phenomena by referring to eight cases (Harris and Sutton, 1986; Gersik, 1988), to six cases (Burgelman, 1983) or even to four cases (Dalton, 1959). Other scholars do not share this view. Dyer and Wilkins (1991), for example, consider this proposal as paradoxical since—from their point of view—Eisenhardt's proposal is on the half way between a single case study and a hypothesis-testing research. Yin (1981, 1984) supports the case study approach but underlines that addition of new cases needs to be stopped if meaningful new data cannot be derived from incremental cases.

[4] This is the difference with structured interviews that include a predetermined list of question the interviewer has to ask. The main risk connected with structured interviews is that "what the researcher thinks is a domain is not a domain for the informants" (Weller and Romney, 1988, p. 12). If there is no agreement on the domain of research, the subjects involved have to look for a sense of the interview itself. For a general overview of interviews see Kvale and Brinkmann (2009).

Box 6.1 Semistructured interview

Questions about entrepreneurial opportunities

1. Could you please describe the entrepreneurial opportunity at the basis of your startup?
2. Do you think that the entrepreneurial opportunity at the basis of your startup mainly derives from the economic/social context you are in or from your personal capabilities (such as skills, competences, education, and network...)? Could you please explain why?
   Questions about business model
3. Could you please describe the business model you adopted for your startup?
4. Do you think that the business model adopted for your startup tends more toward novelty, efficiency or both? Could you please explain why?
   Questions about performance
5. Which were the results in terms of performance (survival, development, or growth) that the firm expected before launching your startup?
6. Which are the results in terms of performance (survival, development, or growth) that the firms achieved after launching your startup?

In order to be sure that the questions were easy to understand and strictly connected to the topic of research, a pilot interview was conducted with another entrepreneur, not included in the final sample. The results got from the pilot interview showed that the questions, without any reference to entrepreneurship trajectories, drove the entrepreneurs to respond and to develop their answers with specific details, dedicated comments, and personal reflections. This was the expected aim of semistructured interviews.

As for operative aspects, the questions were sent via email to some entrepreneurs and were personally asked to others (in this last case entrepreneurs have been interviewed for 1 up to 1½ hours). Some of the interviewed agreed to tape recording, the remaining asked for hand-written notes.

Once debriefed the whole interviews (personally asked or received via email), phone calls have been conducted to clarify the general assumption of each interview. Eventually, all the interviews have been transcribed. This way of proceeding is due to two main reasons. The first is related to the nature of semistructured interviews that need to be checked. Semistructured interviews are highly characterized by the risk of addressing attention (and so responses) toward other topics of research and—in turn—missing the main one. The second is due to the used framework. The components of entrepreneurship trajectories (entrepreneurial opportunity, business model, and firm performance) require being very precise when describing a personal approach to such a wider field of research.[5] In this vein, several data

---

[5] As noticed by Carroll and Mosakowski (1987), the static research design is one of the most serious limits in entrepreneurial studies. According to this, the interviews have tried to rebuild the whole process in order to catch the dynamics followed by entrepreneurs.

Table 6.2 Selected cases for semistructured interviews.

Selected firm	Industry	Respondent	Role in the firm
Lascò ltd	Innovative services for companies	Gianluca Abbruzzese	Entrepreneur
Ludus Magnus Studio llc	Hobby/game industry	Vincenzo Piscitelli	One of the cofounders
Xonda Derm ltd	Pharmaceutical industry	Veronica Raimondo	Founder

sources (Alnaim, 2015) were used such as press releases or reports and websites. Data and information gathered from the interviews were compared with archival data and observations to crosscheck their consistency and validity.

6.3 Selected cases

Selected firms are operative in different industries such as innovative services for companies, hobby/game industry, and pharmaceutical industry. The firms have been working onto markets for some years so that it is possible to rebuild their performances. In particular, the firms included in the present study, the respondents to the semistructured interviews, and their role in the firms are shown in Table 6.2.

6.4 Lascò ltd

Lascò ltd is a corporate innovation company for the development of innovative projects, products, and solutions within companies. The entrepreneur who was interviewed, Gianluca Abbruzzese, is not the initial proponent of this project (who is still in the firm). However, he took over in 2016 (at the very beginning of the entrepreneurial process) and he managed all the most important passages[6] of Lascò (from the definition of the entrepreneurial opportunity that is now exploited on the market to the setup of the business model). He has brought the company to its current state. Up to now, Lascò is focused on:

- Innovative solutions (ready-to-go): That help companies to grow by designing digital transformation paths in your company or creating new experiences for your customers;
- Customized projects: These help to improve the customer's experience, develop a platform, a POC (proof of concept), or integrate multiple solutions, and create a new digital

---

[6] According to Yin (1981, 1984) and to Huber and Power (1985), respondents can be chosen according to different criteria. Tenure in the company and/or direct involved in reference to the investigated phenomenon are two examples. Accordingly, even if Gianluca Abbruzzese is not the proponent of the idea, he is a knowledgeable informant who can provide relevant information because of his involvement and experience in the firm.

strategy. They range from the analysis of customer needs to the design of more suitable technologies and applications to make their company project sustainable;
- Training: Together with partners they plan training experiences aimed at spreading digital skills and managing innovation in companies. Workshops with dedicated communities (such as the Startup Grind community) are organized to inspire and connect partners;
- Corporate innovation: The firm offers coaching activities and innovative tools to structure, grow, and easily tackle innovation paths, challenges related to change and create an innovation ecosystem around organizations;
- Growth strategies: Lascò designs and develops digital marketing strategies whose sole objective is growth. Based on the objectives, the firm chooses the right channels to grow, develops the client business, and designs useful content to gain new customers and increase interest in the client brand; and
- Innovation culture: Doubts, ideas for reflection, and possibilities offered by the new technologies are analyzed together with partners, within an editorial project Philosophy of innovation and in every meeting branded Startup Grind.

The mission of Lascò is: "We guide companies, people, and organizations in paths of innovation and digital transformation. A lean, smart, agile approach to create small innovation ecosystems within or around companies."

In order to clarify its offer to the market, Lascò has published a *manifesto* that sums up its vision of innovation (Table 6.3).

In particular, in order to carry out established achievements, Lascò has organized some innovation teams (start-up or project-based teams or teams involved in workshops and coaching activities) that support their partners through four distinct phases:

1. Discover: The aim of this phase is to find out opportunities together. Lascò defines the characteristics to develop around our partner organizations the sprint of corporate innovation;
2. Design: Thanks to design thinking, the costumer's needs, problems, and challenges are the starting point for every project;

Table 6.3 The *manifesto* of Lascò.

The content of the Manifesto of Lascò
Innovation seen through our eyes
Knowledge is not based on opinions or simple intuitions. It should be tested and validated in constant interaction with the market. A lean, smart, and agile approach to create small innovation ecosystems within or around companies
Every strategy must be flexible, open to change, and adapt to contexts and ecosystems that arise around people
Knowing customers is a continuous, profound search that goes from listening to constant observation by focusing on their real needs
Innovation is a habit that is acquired in small steps, that is, a continuous improvement
Marketing must generate experiences and quality relationships
Aut inveniam viam aut faciam (I shall either find a way or make one)

Source: Personal elaboration.

3. Develop: Lascò believes in agile design, lean, and continuous development. Each of our projects is broken up into small parts so that every action, structure, process is validated first in the market and then developed in its following steps; and

4. Measure: Every action, idea, strategy is continuously monitored and verified. The information, to be understood both as market responses (customer feedback) and additional requests, become part of the production cycle of future developments.

Nowadays, the innovative projects, products, and solutions that Lascò offers to companies are:

- Enzymes: It is the Lascò program for corporate innovation projects. Tools, Business Design instruments, techniques, and frameworks to bring the company paths and sprint of innovation;
- Philosophy of Innovation: An editorial project (magazine and book) aiming to explore issues and processes of innovation management from people's perspective;
- Blockdaimon: A blockchain-based solution to make safe, transparent, and immutable all the steps of a supply chain;
- Foodnandopoli: With the "block methodology" Lascò has created paths of personalized training. Associating a series of elementary bricks constituted by common skills (soft and hard) required by the professions, Lascò offers complementary modules (blocks) directly built with partner companies, based on their formats and specific needs and skills they require;
- Autoincloud: A complete and innovative management system. From the small car showroom to the big company with lots of car parks. It is simple and intuitive SaaS software, designed around needs, sales, and management processes analyzed in car showrooms and new and used car dealerships;
- Sevenda: Business Intelligence Platform for data Analysis, Report, Extract, and Display in tabular and graphic form; and
- RAC Genius: An innovative tool for diagnosis and performance of air conditioning and refrigeration systems.

At this stage, because of exhaustiveness of the firm profile, it is interesting to analyze the entrepreneurial opportunity that was identified, the business model that was set up and the performance achieved. In this case, information was collected through a written questionnaire (see Box 6.1) sent to the entrepreneur, Gianluca Abbruzzese. After the interview, the results emerging from the questionnaire were clarified and verified through some phone calls. Eventually, the interview was transcribed.

As for the entrepreneurial opportunity at the basis of Lascò, the entrepreneur declares that from the first tests that were carried out (interviews, field observations in over 25 dealerships and showrooms), they had the chance to observe how the introduction of digital services inside company processes was still an enormous problem to be faced, with the consequent loss of relevant information and impossibility to create valuable customer journeys.

From the market researches that were carried out, they discovered that in Italy there was an entire ecosystem made up of small and medium-sized companies (dealerships and car showrooms) that still today manage information and processes in a very elementary way. About 65% still manage the car fleet only with excel sheets or other simple solutions and out of these about 55% have basic or very low profile digital communication channels. Most of the competitors and large Enterprise Resource Planning software (ERPs) in the sector are concentrated only on the high level, leaving out any possibility of contact with the medium−low target (due to costs and difficulties linked to the introduction of technology into the company). Having identified a particular need, they launched the challenge with the innovation team. They structured several interviews within companies, analyzing the needs of managers, dealers, and retailers and they transferred these needs into a first solution: a modular software, easy to use, with a quick and intuitive interface, in order to compensate as much as possible the difficulties the company faced in relation to the acquisition of a new technology and the related processes.

In particular, in reference to the origin of the entrepreneurial opportunity, the entrepreneur argues that it was born from a series of intuitions (partly referable to the initial proponent of the business idea) and was verified step by step through the analysis of experiences, direct comparisons and interviews carried out within companies. As noted by the entrepreneur:

> *This first knowledge base let us gather key information that were helpful as basis for the development of the first prototypes used to carry out further tests in order to validate our solution and more: through a cycle of building, experimenting and measuring of results, we managed to standardize the features of the software around the entire ecosystem that revolves around the target company and its stakeholders.*

According to the entrepreneur, this methodology brought enormous advantages: first of all, it allowed them to create solutions that, designed around the real needs of our customers, were valuable for them; second, it brought savings in development costs since, through an AGILE methodology, they first developed the fundamental parts, those that offered them the possibility to immediately test the real palatability of the product, but at the same time, with a certain permeability of the product itself, they managed to create interfaces the technology has an impact on that are as simple as possible for the professional figures involved. At the same time, this continuous comparison with other companies made the product-market fit phase much more solid, allowing them to test both the channels to acquire our customers and how to communicate the price and the technical characteristics for the three final solutions offered to the market.

The business model adopted by Lascò is based on a freemium type (since they offer a basic product solution with a limited use) and on two versions for a fee, basic and professional. The free version is used to generate leads (to acquire people contacts) and, after experimenting and activating the solution, it invites them to upgrade to one of for a fee version. The professional version is on a monthly subscription basis. In order to maintain a high level of customer loyalty, a series of upgrades with new tools and advanced features are carried out every 3 months.

In order to be competitive on the market, they continuously test the business model (by constantly monitoring parameters such as potential new needs, potential changes, new competitors). The objective is to confirm to real and potential customers that they can always solve real problems and for this reason they look for constant feedbacks on how they can improve it. They verify the channels and the strategy of support, price, marketing, distribution, and maintenance costs.

In response to the question about the logic at the basis of the business model, the entrepreneur argues that it is efficiency/novelty centered. In this vein, the entrepreneur argues:

> *First, we worked around the idea of connecting dealers and retailers, in order to offer a solution that would allow the creation of a sales ecosystem around the company at relatively low costs (without additional costs for the company for each activated account). Since the solution is in SAAS we have very low marginal costs. Companies that have a significant amount of dealers have seen a huge possibility in this functionality. Then, we also worked in terms of efficiency and we managed to lower the acquisition costs of the new technology for the company.*

In order to lower the acquisition costs and achieve efficiency, two main features were of great relevance: the ability to deliver a human-centered solution that allowed users of the platform to more easily understand functionality and processes; the modularity of the functions allowed even small companies to acquire the solutions at a price that is convenient for them, by activating only the functions that are necessary according to the company size.

The complicated process driving to the identification of the entrepreneurial opportunity and to the setup of the business model has taken place also in reference to the definition of firm performance.

At first, in fact, tested the solution proposed to the market was proposed to 20 dealerships. The test considered the acquisition of the basic solution for a price of 99 Euros. Out of 20, only three of them decided to adopt the solution. The entrepreneur and his team realized that the product adoption was facing a barrier related to its price. This is the reason why they released a freemium solution with the possibility to expand the solution with paid modules thanks to an internal marketplace. As a matter of fact, even after this experiment, they achieved unsatisfying growth parameters.

In order to better understand the phenomenon, they introduced a product presentation with a remote demo. The result was that conversing with customers during the presentation proved to be a winning strategy. Not only they could solve the doubts, the perceived difficulties and the fears related to the acquisition of an unknown product, but above all, the team of Lascò had the chance, during the calls, to tell customers other dealers' positive experiences with the product, to underline how the solutions solved similar problems in other showrooms: this made customers more projected to activate the solution. At the end of the test, the entrepreneur activated a small video academy that explains all the features of the solution through short videos or a direct chat as further support to contrast the fear of change.

After testing the above hypothesis, Lascò began the expansion phase (aiming to growth). The firm activated a strategy aiming to achieve potential customers through online funnel marketing. In reference to achieved performance, the entrepreneur declares:

> *Thanks to the introduction of marketing automation we obtained almost 70% of freemiun activations, 50% of which activate a paid module. The churn rate for users who have activated a paid solution is less than 5% with an average lifetime value per customer (5-year reference period) of around € 5,050.80.*

The entrepreneurial opportunity that was identified by Lascò ltd, the business model that was set up and the performance achieved are summarized in Table 6.4.

Table 6.4 The entrepreneurship trajectory drawn by Lascò.

Characteristic of the firm	Classification of the characteristics
From market researches, Lascò discovered that In Italy there is an ecosystem of small and medium-sized companies that still manages information and processes in a very elementary way. This means there is a gap in the market. Lascò and its innovation team accepted a noticeable challenge: to analyze the needs of potential customers and to propose them new solutions	The entrepreneurial opportunity at the basis of Lascò ltd can be catalogued as Austrian
Lascò worked on the offering of a solution that would allow the creation of a sales ecosystem around the small-medium companies identified as potential customers (something new for them) at relatively low costs	The business model at the basis of Lascò ltd is novelty-centered since it aims to offer something new (i.e., a modular software) to new potential customers (i.e., small-medium companies identified). At the same time, the business model is also efficiency-centered since customers are sensitive to price
After some tests, Lascò started its expansion phase aiming to growth. The firm activated a strategy aiming to achieve potential customers through online funnel marketing. The main goals were the amount of activations and the average lifetime value per customer. Both of them are satisfying	The performance of Lascò ltd aims to growth
The sequence Austrian opportunity (recognized in the market)/efficiency-and novelty-centered business model/growth of firm drives to the identification of an entrepreneurship trajectory that can be labeled as incremental	

Source: Personal elaboration.

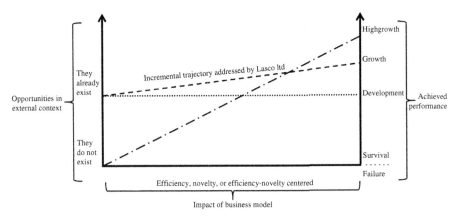

Figure 6.1 The entrepreneurship trajectory addressed by Lascò ltd.
Source: Personal elaboration.

In reference to the classification of entrepreneurship trajectories presented in Chapter 5, it results that the sequence Austrian opportunity (recognized in the market)/efficiency-and novelty-centered business model/growth of firm drives to the identification of an entrepreneurship trajectory that can be labeled as incremental (Fig. 6.1).

6.5   Ludus Magnus Studio llc

Ludus Magnus Studio llc is an Indie hobby game company born in Riverside, California, in 2014. In 2016, the company gained its international reputation as creator of table games based on innovative ideas, modern mechanics, and high-quality materials when its first successful Kickstarter Project, that is, *Nova Aetas*, was launched. Nowadays, the activities carried out deal with design, production, and commercialization of board games, cards, miniatures, and role-playing games (RPG). In particular, the firm is currently focused on:

- 3D Sculpt: The 3D designers at Ludus Magnus studio have several years of experience in the 3D sculpts of every kind and in different scales. Over the years, the firm produced different miniatures, from smalls (Spriggan) to large models (Golem). The team is able to bring a 2D concept to life, transforming it into a highly detailed three-dimensional computer model. Furthermore, the company offers its experience to print and product n large scale of 3D models;
- Game Design: Ludus Magnus Studio offers consulting and assistance in developing game projects, thanks to the collaboration with several Game Designers. The team of experts is able to assess the degree of feasibility, providing a detailed overview of development strategies and related production and launch costs;
- Concept Art Design: Ludus Magnus Studio offers the opportunity to benefit from the services of our talented artists for the development of complete illustrations. The team consists of designers able to work on different genres, from photorealism to manga. They

support the development of new games from the conceptualization of the characters, to the practical declination of all the components of the game; and
- Board games: Ludus Magnus Studio has launched several board games onto market such as Nova Aetas in 2016, Sine Tempore in 2017, Black Rose Wars in 2018, and Dungeonology in 2019.

The several activities on which Ludus Magnus Studio is mainly focused are due to the different backgrounds of the four friends involved in this startup. They all shared the same passion for the board games, but their diversified but complementary skills, their practical experience and—at the same time—their creativity attitudes are the ingredients of their success. Andrea Colletti is founder, lead game designer, and art director. After completing his studies at the school of comics in Rome, he worked for 4 years at Games Workshop Italia as manager of the events area and as member of the team responsible for organizing Italian Games day. In recent years he has spent all his time on the development of *Nova Aetas*, the first game produced by Ludus Magnus Studio. Vincenzo Piscitelli is founder, owner, and responsible for marketing, administration and production, and finance areas. He is an ICT security engineer. He has been involved in the management of ICT infrastructures for the public administration and he has many experiences in the development of web platforms and network systems. In Ludus Magnus Studio he manages the postkickstarter processes, from e-commerce to production, to product shipment, in addition to administration and digital marketing. He is passionate about multiuser dungeon (MUD), about RPG, web programming, and new technologies. Fernando Armentano is owner and lead 3D sculpting. He is a sculptor and he aims to combine its attention to detail with the engineering skills required for printing in polyvinyl chloride (PVC) models. Following his first experience in Game Workshop Italia, he collaborated with various companies in the field of miniature production. Luca Bernardini is founder, owner, game designer, and responsible for customer care. He is an archeologist and, together with Andrea, he started the development process. In Ludus Magnus Studio he deals with Game Design and is responsible for evaluating the development of external projects. Moreover, he is focused on the development and coordination of the setting in which the scenarios of the games produced by Ludus Magnus Studio take place.

Even if the story of Ludus Magnus Studio is mostly linked to crowd-funding campaigns, one of the founders—Vincenzo Piscitelli—has tried to rebuild and analyze the entrepreneurial opportunity at the basis of this start-up, its business model, and the performance achievable/achieved.

As for the entrepreneurial opportunity at the basis of Ludus Magnus Studio llc, the founders were aware of the importance of the value proposition to the market. Even if, on the one hand, they knew that the development of new technologies has radically changed the approach to consumers (today it is more direct than it was in the past), on the other hand they know what is not changed on the market: the need to turn an idea or an innovation in a business project. In particular, as emerged from the interview, founders cannot launch a mere idea. They have to run different preliminary activities to identify project features and evaluate its feasibility.

The process adopted in reference to crowd-funding campaigns can be assumed at the basis of the whole entrepreneurial project. It is important to plan everything through a gradual process starting from the clarification of the idea and the achievable goals, moving toward market and competition analysis, passing on to the evaluation of the underlying financial and economic aspects and ending with a clear definition of the primary and secondary objectives to be achieved. The Ludus Magnus Studio Team has a practical and dynamic approach to the market. This process of learning by doing and observing has clearly helped the team gain a greater awareness and critical sense respect to the idea to develop, a wider capacity to plan and define project driver, in order to immediately build a direct relationship with the public, reducing the chances of failure.

As for the business model, Ludus Magnus Studio Team is aware that it is the ability to attract consumers potentially interested to buy the product that exponentially increases success probability. If consumers are not active and involved in the firm projects, then it is highly improbable that they will spontaneously support the project and—in turn—that will make it successful. The business model is mainly centered on advertising and communication campaigns finalized to catch, built, and engage consumers really interested in the firm offering. By taking inspiration from crowd-funding campaigns, Ludus Magnus Studio Team decide to test products' appeal directly on the market in order to disclose the products' potential to satisfy the potential customers' needs. To improve the credibility degree of the initiative it is important to present the product to experts, bloggers, and influencers in order to obtain an independent review. This review is both useful to improve the product fit with potential customers' needs and to increase the reliability of the proposal. Even if the way value is created is always new—it changes time after time according to the characteristics of the firm products—all the activities are carefully planned and launched on time.

The last part of the interview has been focused on the performance to achieve. Ludus Magnus Studio team has always had a strong orientation toward growth (or even high-growth). This is rather clear from the characteristics of the entrepreneurial opportunity to pursue—always based on new ideas that did not exist before—and from the way the business model is set up—involving potential customers in order to be able to fully satisfy their needs. In particular, consumer analysis—through monitoring —is a constant task to run for the team and it discloses its strong orientation toward growth. A strategic monitoring allows evaluating promptly how consumers react to the firm communication strategies. Monitoring also allows controlling the performance in terms of pledge level, updates, and community behavior. Ludus Magnus Studio team has acted in particular on three levers to keep the flow of contributions constant and successfully reach the successful performances: (1) grasp community (to keep high attention on the firm); (2) brand loyalty (to build a consolidated customer portfolio); and (3) lookalike forever (investments in advertising to expand the audience).

At this stage, information provided by Vincenzo Piscitelli, one of the founders of Ludus Magnus Studio llc in reference to the identification of entrepreneurial opportunity, to the business model to set up and to the performance expected/ achieved can be classified in order to verify if the firm has adopted one of the entrepreneurship trajectories proposed before (flat, incremental, or adventurous).

The entrepreneurial opportunity at the basis of Ludus Magnus Studio llc seems to be contemporary. It is rooted in the different backgrounds of the founders and it does not derive from external context. Actually, the high competition that the firm has to face would discourage any kind of involvement rather than disclosing an entrepreneurial opportunity. The business model setup by the founders results centered on novelty rather than on efficiency. The choice is due to the fact that Ludus Magnus Studio works in a specific industry (related to board games, cards, miniatures, and RPG) where customers need to be involved in order to acquire products/services and create value. Eventually, as for expected performance, growth is the only alternative that founders could expect. New products/services to offer and customers' involvement is at the basis of significant growth expectations.

The entrepreneurial opportunity that was identified by Ludus Magnus Studio llc, the business model that was set up, and the performance achieved are summarized in Table 6.5.

Table 6.5 The entrepreneurship trajectory drawn by Ludus Magnus Studio llc.

Characteristic of the firm	Classification of the characteristics
The Ludus Magnus Studio Team has a practical and dynamic approach to the market. This process of learning by doing and observing has clearly helped the team gain a greater awareness and critical sense respect to the idea to develop, an wider capacity to plan and define project driver, in order to immediately build a direct relationship with the public, reducing the chances of failure	The entrepreneurial opportunity at the basis of Ludus Magnus Studio llc can be catalogued as contemporary
The business model is mainly centered on advertising and communication campaigns finalized to catch, built, and engage consumers really interested in the firm offering. The way value is created is always new—it changes time after time according to the characteristics of the firm products	The business model at the basis of Ludus Magnus Studio llc is novelty-centered since founders aim to involve customers in different ways in order to create value
Consumer analysis—through monitoring —is a constant task to run for the team and it discloses its strong orientation toward growth	The performance ranges between growth and high-growth
The sequence contemporary opportunity (created by the founders)/novelty-centered business model/growth of the firm drives to the identification of an entrepreneurship trajectory that can be labeled as adventurous	

Source: Personal elaboration.

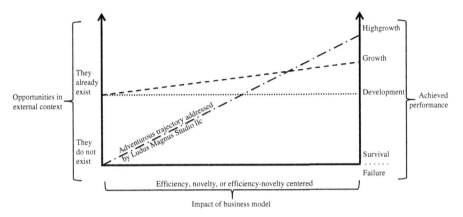

Figure 6.2 The entrepreneurship trajectory addressed by Ludus Magnus Studio llc.
Source: Personal elaboration.

The sequence contemporary opportunity (created by the founders)/novelty-centered business model/growth of the firm drives to the identification of an entrepreneurship trajectory that can be labeled as adventurous (Fig. 6.2).

6.6 Xonda Derm ltd

Xonda Derm ltd is an Italian firm, launched in 2010. Xonda Derm offers its proper and efficient 100% "made in Italy" dermatological and dermocosmetic products on the pharmaceutical and parapharmaceutical market suitable especially for sensitive, allergic, and reactive skins.

All the products are characterized by hypoallergenic formula and submitted to specific tests that guarantee high tolerance on the skin. Xonda Derm products are nickel tested and do not have mineral oils, parabens, perfumes, sodium sulfate, and gluten. Thanks to their characteristic, Xonda Derm products are perfect for baby skin, for specific treatments and, generally, for clients who want to take care of their skins.

The continuous attention to the specific requests—presented by dermatologists, pediatricians, gynecologists, and ophthalmologists through pharmaceutical representatives—allows the firm developing always more efficient solutions for the entire family.

In 2019, the firm is on the market with specific products such as:

1. Zinc oxide cream: Formulated with active ingredients which soothe and soften, creating a protective coating that helps prevent and calm skin irritations and abrasions caused by external elements;
2. Cleansing makeup remover (for face and eyes): Ensures a delicate and deep cleansing of the face and eye contour. It removes water-resistant makeup; it soothes and refreshes the skin, taking away any feeling of irritation left by makeup removal;

3. Face cream (for sensitive and delicate skin): It is a delicate equalizing cream that soothes and moisturizes, indicated for all skin conditions caused by external agents. Assists in the restoration of the hydrolipidic film to prevent and calm redness and itchiness;
4. Face and body cleanser (for sensitive and dry skin): It is a foaming cleansing gel for daily facial and body care. It respects the skin's natural PH, leaving it soft and perfectly clean;
5. Delicate intimate wash (soothing and protective): It is an intimate wash with a delicate action. Chamomile extract and panthenol soothe and refresh while marine collagen prevents dehydration and leaves a sensation of comfort and well-being; and
6. Delicate shampoo: This shampoo is formulated with vegetable-based surfactants and enriched with caffeine and orange juice extract. It delicately cleanses the scalp and hair respecting their natural balance. Indicated as a complementary dermocosmetic product in the treatment of fragile hair and in hair loss prevention and in the case of fragile hair. Ideal for frequent use.

Xonda Derm ltd sells all the above products in a selection of the best pharmacies and drugstores stocking personal care products.

From the short version of the firm profile (provided by the founder, Veronica Raimondo), it is clear the way the firm entered the market: a strategy of differentiation that enhances the characteristics of the products through a selective distributive channel.

Rather than providing any comment to the firm profile, it is more appropriate to investigate the choices concerning the entrepreneurial opportunity that was identified, the business model that was set up and the performance achieved. In this case, a direct interview, lasting more than 1 hour, was carried out. The questions asked to the founder, Veronica Raimondo, are the ones included in Box 6.1. After the interview, the general assumptions emerging from the interview were clarified and verified through some phone calls. Eventually, the interview was transcribed.

In reference to the entrepreneurial opportunity lying at the basis of Xonda Derm ltd, the founder, Veronica Raimondo, argues that the firm is born from the idea of creating a line of dermocosmetic products that can help dermatological therapies and respect the skin. The entrepreneurial opportunity behind the startup comes from the need to produce specific products for sensitive, delicate, allergic, and reactive skin. All the products are characterized by a hypoallergenic formula and subjected to specific tests that guarantee high tolerability on the skin. Xonda Derm products are nickel-tested and contain no mineral oils, parabens, perfumes, sodium sulfate, and gluten. Thanks to their characteristics, Xonda Derm products are perfect for baby's skin, for specific treatments and, in general, for customers who want to take care of their skin. The founder declares:

> The entrepreneurial opportunity at the basis of Xonda Derm derives from the
> social context, as more and more people are subject to allergies.

As for the business model, the founder states that Xonda Derm ltd operates in the domestic market (the Italian one) and sales are made through the pharmacy channel. Selected pharmacies and drugstores stocking personal care products can buy Xonda Derm products directly from the firm (thanks to the presence of sales representatives) or through wholesalers. The wholesalers order the products directly from Xonda Derm warehouse after the request of the pharmacies and drugstores that in turn get requests from end consumers. End consumers buy the products on medical advice.

In reference to the business model, the founder declares that Xonda Derm business model is focused on the role of wholesalers that provide scientific information only to specialist doctors and on the way the firm satisfies the requests of end consumers that pass through pharmacies and drugstores and then through wholesalers. In reference to this point, the founder states:

> This is the only kind of business model that I could set up for the Xonda Derm after studying the market and the competitors.

In particular, the founder underlines that her personal abilities in creating a network of informants and commercial sponsors of the product line have been determinant for Xonda Derm.

In reference to the performance, the founder did not provide detailed information. However, she argues that before the launch of the startup all the founders expected to survive for 4 years and grow up from the fifth year onward. Achieved results have delayed 1 year. The firm started growing up only after the sixth year. Of course, by considering the dynamics of pharmaceutical markets in Italy, all the founders are more than satisfied with achieved results.

At this stage, information provided by the founder of Xonda Derm ltd in reference to the entrepreneurial opportunity that was identified, to the business model that was set up and to the performance expected/achieved can be classified in order to verify if the firm has adopted one of the entrepreneurship trajectories proposed before (flat, incremental, or adventurous).

The entrepreneurial opportunity at the basis of Xonda Derm ltd derives from the social context, as more and more people are subject to allergies. Since it is the result of a stimulus coming from the external context, the entrepreneurial opportunity at the basis of Xonda Derm ltd can be catalogued as neoclassical.

The business model is focused on the role of wholesalers that provide scientific information to specialist doctors and on the way the firm satisfies the requests of end consumers that pass through pharmacies and drugstores and then wholesalers. As a matter of fact, the business model is more oriented toward efficiency (the distribution of products is upon request of end consumers) rather than novelty (wholesalers provide scientific information only to specialist doctors who suggest the use of Xonda Derm products). This means that Xonda Derm set up an efficiency-centered business model.

The performance expected before the launch of Xonda Derm was survival and then growth.

The entrepreneurial opportunity that was identified by Xonda Derm, the business model that was set up and the performance achieved are summarized in Table 6.6.

The sequence neoclassical opportunity (recognized in the market)/efficiency-centered business model/survival or growth of the firm drives to the identification of an entrepreneurship trajectory that can be labeled as flat (Fig. 6.3).

Table 6.6 The entrepreneurship trajectory drawn by Xonda Derm ltd.

Characteristic of the firm	Classification of the characteristics
The entrepreneurial opportunity derives from the social context, as more and more people are subject to allergies, and from the entrepreneurial abilities in creating a network of informants and commercial sponsors of the product line	The entrepreneurial opportunity at the basis of Xonda Derm ltd can be catalogued as neoclassical
The business model is focused on the role of wholesalers that provide scientific information to specialist doctors and on the way the firm satisfies the requests of end consumers that pass through pharmacies and drugstores and then wholesalers	The business model at the basis of Xonda Derm ltd is efficiency-centered since distribution of products is upon request of end consumers
The performance expected before the launch of the start-up was survival and then growth. Growth was achieved 1 year later than expected	The performance ranges between survival and growth

The sequence neoclassical opportunity (recognized in the market)/efficiency-centered business model/survival or growth of the firm drives to the identification of an entrepreneurship trajectory that can be labeled as flat

Source: Personal elaboration.

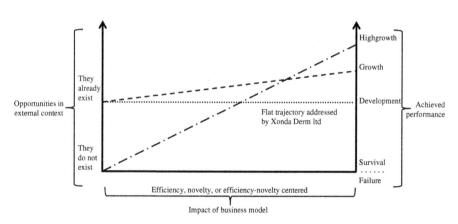

Figure 6.3 The entrepreneurship trajectory addressed by Xonda Derm ltd.
Source: Personal elaboration.

6.7 Comments on the cases

In reference to the above cases, a very interesting comment derives first. It deals with the industries the selected firms are in. As already said, Lascò ltd offers innovative services for companies, Ludus Magnus Studio llc is operative in the hobby/game industry while Xonda Derm ltd is in the pharmaceutical industry.

From the above analysis, it results that Xonda Derm ltd follows a flat trajectory; Lascò ltd follows an incremental trajectory, and Ludus Magnus Studio llc follows an adventurous trajectory. Even if this result can be due to the specific cases selected, it is possible that—with due reservation—this result can be partly ascribed to changes intervening onto markets and concerning the ongoing of specific industries.

Even if the pharmaceutical industry is considered innovative, noticeable investments are necessary to produce and sell products. This can reduce the inclination toward risk of startups (new and innovative firms) operating in this industry. On the contrary, innovative services and hobbies/games are intangible and—maybe—for this reason founders/entrepreneurs in this industry are more inclined to draw and follow incremental or even adventurous trajectories. Of course, this is just a hypothesis (not pertaining to the main aim of the volume) and more research is needed in order to verify this.

However, what matters here the most is that the cases of Lascò ltd, Ludus Magnus Studio llc, and Xonda Derm ltd have been useful to verify that entrepreneurs—consciously or even unconsciously—draw and follow entrepreneurship trajectories when launching and managing their startups.

The analysis of each case study has proven that there is a kind of path dependence. Founders/entrepreneurs follow this when they identify the entrepreneurial opportunity at the basis of their startup, set up the business model, and foresee the performance to achieve.

References

Alnaim, F., 2015. The case study method: critical reflection. Global J. Human-Soc. Sci. 15, 29–32.

Anderson, B.S., Wennberg, K., McMullen, J.S., 2019. Enhancing quantitative theory-testing entrepreneurship research. J. Bus. Ventur . Available from: https://doi.org/10.1016/j.jbusvent.2019.02.001.

Burgelman, R.A., 1983. A process of internal corporate venturing in the diversified major firms. Adm. Sci. Q. 28, 223–244.

Carroll, G.R., Mosakowski, E., 1987. The career dynamics of self-employment. Adm. Sci. Q. 32 (4), 570–589.

Clarysse, B., Moray, N., 2004. A process study of entrepreneurial team formation: the case of a research-based spin-off. J. Bus. Ventur 19 (1), 55–79.

Corbetta, P., 1999. Metodologia e Tecnica della Ricerca Sociale. Il Mulino, Bologna, IT.

Dalton, M., 1959. Men Who Manage. Wiley, New York.

Datta, P.B., Gailey, R., 2012. Empowering women through social entrepreneurship: case study of a women's cooperative in India. Entrepr. Theory Pract. 36 (3), 569–587.

Dyer, W.G., Wilkins, A.L., 1991. Better stories, not better constructs, to generate better theory: a rejoinder to Eisenhardt. Acad. Manag. Rev. 16 (3), 613–619.

Eisenhardt, K.M., 1989. Building theories from case study research. Acad. Manag. Rev. 14 (4), 532−550.

Gersik, C., 1988. Time and transition in work teams: toward a new model of group development. Acad. Manag. Rev. 31 (1), 9−41.

Glaser, B.G., Strauss, A.L., 1967. The Discovery of Grounded Theory. Aldine Publishing Co., Chicago, IL.

Gubrium, J.F., 1988. Analyzing Field Reality.. Sage Publications, London, UK.

Hammersley, M., Atkinson, P., 1983. Ethnography: Principle in Practice.. Tavistock Publications, London and New York.

Harris, S., Sutton, R., 1986. Functions of parting ceremonies in dying organizations. Acad. Manag. J. 29 (1), 5−30.

Henry, C., Foss, L., 2015. Case sensitive? A review of the literature on the use of case method in entrepreneurship research. Int. J. Entrepr. Behav. Res. 21 (3), 389−409.

Huber, G.P., Power, D.J., 1985. Retrospective reports of strategic-level managers: guidelines for increasing their accuracy. Strat. Manag. J. 6, 171−180.

Kuhn, T., 1970. The Structure of Scientific Revolution, second ed. University of Chicago Press, Chicago, IL.

Kvale, S., Brinkmann, S., 2009. Interviews, Learning the Craft of Qualitative Research Interviewing, second ed. Sage Publications.

Mair, J., Marti, I., 2009. Entrepreneurship in and around institutional voids: a case study from Bangladesh. J. Bus. Ventur 24 (5), 419−435.

Park, J.S., 2005. Opportunity recognition and product innovation in entrepreneurial hi-tech start-ups: a new perspective and supporting case study. Technovation 25 (7), 739−752.

Procter, M., 1993. Analyzing other researchers' data. In: Gilbert, N. (Ed.), Researching Social Life.. Sage Publications, London, UK.

Silverman, D., 1975. Accounts of organizations: organizational structures and the accounting process. In: McKinlay, J. (Ed.), Processing People, Cases in Organizational Behavior. Holt, Rinehart, Winston, London, UK.

Silverman, D., 2001. Interpreting Qualitative Data: Methods for Analyzing Talk, Text and Interaction, second ed. Sage Publications, London, UK.

Sosna, M., Trevinyo-Rodríguez, R.N., Velamuri, S.R., 2010. Business model innovation through trial-and-error learning: the Naturhouse case. Long Range Plan. 43 (2−3), 383−407.

Stirzaker, R., Galloway, L., Potter, L., 2019. Business, aging, and socioemotional selectivity: a qualitative study of gray entrepreneurship. J. Small Bus. Manag. . Available from: https://doi.org/10.1111/jsbm.12516.

Strauss, A., Corbin, J., 1998. Basics of qualitative research. Techniques and Procedures for Developing Grounded Theory.. Sage Publications, London, UK.

Weller, S.C., Romney, A.K., 1988. Systematic Data Collection.. Sage Publications, London, UK.

Yin, R., 1981. The case study crisis: some answers. Adm. Sci. Q. 26 (1), 58−65.

Yin, R., 1984. Case Study Research.. Sage Publications, Beverly Hills, CA.

Conclusion

7

In order to provide a conceptual toolkit that enables entrepreneurs to draw entrepreneurship trajectories and scholars to formalize and catalog them, this research study started with a review of the main research themes addressed by scholars in entrepreneurship literature. Obviously, it is neither possible nor even useful to compare the main research themes in order to assess which is the most or least relevant one. The literature review, in fact, is useful for disclosing the *leitmotiv* of entrepreneurship, that is, what underpins all the above themes of research and bonds them.

As already mentioned, the *leitmotiv* of entrepreneurship begins with the role of innovation that (in the shape of entrepreneurial opportunities) lies at the basis of entrepreneurship and ends with the impact of entrepreneurship (which is measured by comparing achievable and achieved performances).

By embracing the idea that entrepreneurial opportunities and achieved performances can be the boundaries of entrepreneurial phenomena, then the right approach to their study seems to consist of considering entrepreneurship as a practice, an organizational process, or a journey.

Entrepreneurs—putting into practice a process and experiencing a journey—are expected to be interested in the trajectory to address. By definition, a trajectory is the path followed when an individual or an object moves from one place to another. It is the result of the intertwining of unexpected events with purposeful decisions.

As such, it requires a system of assumptions, choices, and changes that are related to unexpected events—coming from the environment or due to the dynamics of the market itself—and to purposeful decisions that entrepreneurs make when they plan the strategy to implement. In this vein, the volume has investigated and rebuilt what really happens after that an entrepreneurial opportunity is identified (recognized, discovered, or created) and up until an expected performance is achieved.

At first, a backward approach has been used to derive the elements at the basis of entrepreneurial trajectories that are: entrepreneurial performance, business model, and entrepreneurial opportunities. In reference to the performance, both a theoretical and a pragmatic approach remind us that entrepreneurial firms can grow, develop, survive, or fail. As for the business model, it can be designed around novelty, efficiency, or both. Eventually, three types of entrepreneurial opportunities exist. They are neoclassical, Austrian, and contemporary.

In order to draw an entrepreneurship trajectory, the backward approach is not appropriate. By sharing the idea that entrepreneurship is a cumulative process, in

Entrepreneurship Trajectories. DOI: https://doi.org/10.1016/B978-0-12-818650-3.00007-6

fact, a forward approach is needed. This approach has revealed three entrepreneurship trajectories:

1. flat trajectories based on the sequence neoclassical opportunity/efficiency-centered business model/survival or development of firms;
2. incremental trajectories based on the sequence Austrian opportunity/efficiency- and novelty-centered business model/development or growth of firms; and
3. adventurous trajectories based on the sequence contemporary opportunity/novelty-centered business model/growth or high growth of firms.

Entrepreneurship trajectories differ from one other, but they share two main aspects at the same time: the role of path dependence and the risk of failure.

After providing a conceptual toolkit that enables entrepreneurs to draw entrepreneurship trajectories and scholars to formalize and catalog them, three cases have been used to verify if entrepreneurs—consciously or even unconsciously—draw and follow entrepreneurship trajectories when launching and managing their startups. From the analysis of selected cases, it derives that founders/entrepreneurs follow any of entrepreneurship trajectory formalized before when they identify the entrepreneurial opportunity at the basis of their startup, set up the business model, and foresee the performance to achieve.

At this stage, some concluding remarks need to be underlined.

First, the above proposal gives birth to three entrepreneurial trajectories that—needless to say—are not definitive (neither in the number nor in the concept). The present is just a theoretical proposal that starts with entrepreneurial opportunities and develops according to an incremental approach. The entrepreneurial trajectories proposed herein can be criticized, discussed, and modified and—of course—other entrepreneurial trajectories can be proposed.

Second, some topics of research (typical of entrepreneurship and management studies) are not considered herein. The entry and market strategies, the competitive advantage, the revenue model, and so on are not included in the present analysis. As a matter of fact, the above topics are partly—or even totally—included in the concepts of entrepreneurial opportunities, business model, and performance or they overlap with them so they are not totally ignored in the present analysis. However, furthers research could make a clear reference to this topic as well.

Third, it is implicitly assumed that entrepreneurs evaluate the opportunities they identify and—accordingly—define an appropriate business model in order to achieve a certain performance. As a matter of fact it can happen that entrepreneurs make some assumptions about the nature of the opportunity to exploit, the kind of business model to set up and the performance to achieve but—in fact—these assumptions can be not related to one another. If so, entrepreneurial trajectories can be not representative of what consciously happens, but they can describe a whole process that is put into practice unconsciously.

In conclusion, several studies are evoked herein to add something to the present work that is not in a position to offer a complete and exhaustive analysis of entrepreneurship trajectories but—with due reservation—may open up a hopefully intriguing research path that deserves further development.

Index

Printed in the United States
By Bookmasters